The White Cat's Revenge

as Plotted from the Dragon King's Lap

Volume 4

Author: Kureha
Illustrator: Yamigo

Joshua
Chelsie's grandson and a spy for the Nation of the Dragon King. On top of being able to handle pretty much any task thrown at him, he's sociable and can make friends easily with almost anyone.

Ewan
Finn's young brother and subordinate. He is absolutely obsessed with Finn and will go on a rampage at the drop of a hat if it's about his brother, but he doesn't seem like a bad kid.

Heat (Heat-sama)
The supreme-level spirit of fire, currently using a demi-human's body. He's self-centered and a ladies' man, but he's very brusque with Ruri for some reason.

Jade
The young and wise ruler of the Nation of the Dragon King. Takes Ruri, a Beloved, into his care. In contrast to his cool and suave demeanor, he has a soft spot for all things cute and cuddly. He dotes on Ruri not only when she's in cat form, but when she's in human form as well.

Celestine

The Nation of the Beast King's Beloved. A bird demi-human with an unrequited love for Jade. She is prideful but well-mannered.

Ruri Morikawa

A girl summoned to an alternate world after getting wrapped up in her childhood "friend's" nonsense. She is a Beloved, a person whose mana is especially attractive to spirits. By putting on a special bracelet, she can transform into a white cat. Jade seems to have feelings for her, but she remains oblivious.

Character Introductions

THE WHITE CAT'S REVENGE AS PLOTTED FROM THE DRAGON KING'S LAP:
VOLUME 4

by: KUREHA
Illustrations by Yamigo
Translated by David Evelyn
Edited by Suzanne Seals
Layout by Jennifer Elgabrowny
English Print Cover by Kai Kyou

First published in Japan in 2017 by Frontier Works Inc.
Publication rights for this English edition arranged through Frontier Works Inc., Tokyo
English translation © 2021 J-Novel Club LLC

Find more books like this one at www.j-novel.club!

Managing Director: Samuel Pinansky
Light Novel Line Manager: Chi Tran
Managing Editor: Jan Mitsuko Cash
Managing Translator: Kristi Fernandez
QA Manager: Hannah N. Carter
Marketing Manager: Stephanie Hii
Project Manager: Nikki Lapshinoff

ISBN: 978-1-7183-1998-1
Printed in Korea
First Printing: July 2022
10 9 8 7 6 5 4 3 2 1

Contents

Contents

Prologue

In a room in the partially destroyed first sector of the Nation of the Dragon King's royal castle, the Dragon King, the Beast King, and their respective nation's Beloveds all sat across from one another, partaking in a meal. The majority of their conversation was occupied by the incident from the other day.

"Sorry that you were wrapped up in this," said the Dragon King.

"That was quite the ordeal, I'd say," replied the Beast King.

"Yes, I never would have expected something like that to happen within the castle walls."

Since someone was targeting Beloveds in other nations, Jade had predicted that the Nation of the Dragon King would be next, but he hadn't expected it to turn into such a massive situation. Everyone had been on the lookout, but still Ruri was kidnapped right from under them. She was willing to brush the matter off, but Jade and the spirits were extremely torn up about it—especially Kotaro. Both he and Jade seemed to be beating themselves up over it. Also, ever since the incident was resolved, the spirits clung to Ruri's side and wouldn't leave. As for Kotaro, he kept up his duty as a faithful guard dog, not leaving the area near Ruri's feet for anything.

"Ruri, are you okay? I heard you were dropped into the ocean," asked Arman in concern, apparently having heard the story of Ruri's ordeal.

"I'm fine. I'm sorry for making you worry."

Although the incidents caused by the fake Reapers and the followers of the Church of God's Light had come to a close, the leader of the Church of God's Light, the mastermind, hadn't been apprehended as of yet. They had interrogated Noah, the perpetrator, but he seemed to be just a fall man. He wouldn't divulge a single detail about their organization's whereabouts.

"Using a kid for their plan is revolting," Arman commented.

Ruri was in complete agreement and nodded her head vehemently. Noah had complied with this plot, believing in an offer to revive his deceased parents. Ruri could feel nothing but anger toward the act of deceiving a young child to use them as a pawn.

"As much as I would love to apprehend the mastermind, we unfortunately lack information. We don't even know if the Church of God's Light's base is in the Nation of the Dragon King," Jade explained.

"Considering they've been causing trouble in the Nation of the Beast King and Cerulanda too, they might've come from another land… They might even be in the Nation of the Beast King for all we know," Arman added.

"Yes, which is why I ask you to be alert. Ruri will be heading your way, after all."

With Sector One in disrepair, the castle was going through reconstruction. Not only that, but since a raider had been able to penetrate their defenses, the overall security of Sector One was being overhauled as well. Because of that, security was currently lax with the many people coming in and out. With the memory of Ruri's assault fresh in his mind, Jade wanted to avoid leaving her someplace poorly guarded, so Ruri was set to go to the Nation of the Beast King per his suggestion—granted, Celestine was the one who had proposed the idea in the first place. While Ruri could have just as easily taken refuge at Chelsie's house, that idea lost out to the allure of the Nation of the Beast King's hot springs.

"I appreciate it in advance," Ruri said, bowing her head to both Arman and Celestine in gratitude for being her caretakers while she visited.

"Just leave it to us. Still, you sure about letting your oh-so-precious jewel go like this?" Arman said with a smarmy grin. He glanced at the necklace on Ruri's neck, the one with the glass bead encasing Jade's scale.

Ruri was the only one who was oblivious to what Arman was implying, but she *did* notice that the look in Celestine's eyes became slightly more intense upon him saying that.

"It's only until the castle is repaired. Once it's done, I'll come straight over to pick her up," Jade said, slowly bringing the food on his fork up to Ruri's mouth. This was common behavior from Jade when the two of them were dining alone, but they weren't alone now—Arman and Celestine were around. Jade seemed completely unaffected and acted like normal. Arman also seemed to pay it no mind as he continued his meal, but Celestine shot a death glare Ruri's way. Ruri found it harder and harder to open her mouth because of it.

"What's the matter, Ruri?" Jade asked.

Ruri still hadn't cleared up the confusion about her not being Jade's mate, and this was only going to further complicate matters. She wasn't entirely sure if Jade realized that or not. But seeing as she wasn't going to dissuade him from feeding her, she reluctantly opened her mouth and proceeded with the slightly awkward meal.

 Dragon's Blood

Ruri walked through the hallway of Sector One. It was crumbling apart, a shell of its former beauty. Piles of rubble littered the floor, and the blue sky above peered through the remains of the ceiling.

Ruri felt downcast and guilty over what she had done. Every pillar that stood in the castle was decorated with exquisite engravings, much as you would expect from where the mighty Dragon King dwelled—except now they all stood cracked and bent. The expensive-looking paintings that hung on the wall and the flower vases that adorned the halls were all mercilessly ripped and cracked, strewn on the floor. It looked like a tornado had passed through the area.

Ruri shuddered at the thought of what the total cost of the damage was. She thought about giving some of the valuables in her pocket space to Euclase to be used for the cost of reconstruction later on. She had an abundance of paintings, flower vases, and furniture in there, all of which were probably gathered by the First Dragon King and Lydia. The sheer amount she had meant she would never use them all. Instead of wasting away, she figured that the items could be used in place of the damaged goods, if Euclase didn't mind. Her pocket space held all sorts of items of varying quality—from run-down to regal—so they were perfectly usable so long as they didn't clash with the aesthetic of the castle.

Reconstruction of Sector One would begin after Ruri departed for the Nation of the Beast King. She was set to leave tomorrow, so she needed to prepare. She walked to her own room and opened her closet. Her large belongings were stored inside of her pocket space, but she kept the smaller items and clothes she used on a daily basis in her room instead.

She took all those things and started throwing them one after another into her pocket space. Fortunately, nothing around Ruri's room was destroyed, meaning the interior remained pristine, but since there would be a stream of traffic coming in and out in order to heighten security, it was better to leave as little in the room as possible. She had planned on taking her personal belongings with her to the Nation of the Beast King anyway.

"I guess this'll do," Ruri said as she packed the last of her things.

She then left Sector One and headed toward Jade's temporary office in Sector Two, where Jade and the main aides of his court were currently gathered.

"Jade-sama, I've collected my things from my room."

"I see. Then I'll call in the peddlers so you can go with Joshua and pick out whatever you need. You'll need to make preparations for your trip to the Nation of the Beast King. Also, Joshua will be accompanying you. After all, it's better that you have someone close by your side, wouldn't you say?"

"Oh, Joshua is coming too?" Ruri asked.

Ruri would have the spirits, but she feared the thought of going to an unknown land with someone she wasn't close with. Hearing that it'd be a familiar face was a relief. Also, since the Nations of the Beast King and Dragon King had completely different cultures and customs, it was reassuring to have Joshua, a well-traveled and worldly intelligence operative, accompanying her on the journey.

"Also," Jade continued as he presented Ruri with a small glass bottle filled with red liquid, "take this with you as well."

"What is this? It's about as red as blood," Ruri commented as she held up and shook the bottle, stirring the thick, red liquid.

"As you surmised, it's my blood," Jade affirmed in a nonchalant manner.

However, Ruri jumped in surprise, almost dropping the bottle. "Your blood?! Wh-Wh-Wh-Why did you give me this?!"

Jade cracked an awkward smile. "Just calm yourself, Ruri. To be precise, it's medicine made from my blood."

"It's…medicine? Okay, but this is still your blood, is it not?"

"Indeed it is. You are aware of the extraordinary resilience we dragonkin possess, aren't you?"

"I am," Ruri said, remembering their monstrous resilience—like brushing off stabs to the stomach or healing a normally fatal wound in a matter of days. Even when the fake Reapers came upon Ewan and stabbed him with that sword, he was moving around like normal. Even now, he was walking around as if nothing ever happened. None of the troops held back when they trained because there was no fear of them dying from "minor" injuries, so the training grounds were a literal bloodbath on a daily basis. However, since no other race was capable of keeping up with that level of training, the training grounds were separated for dragonkin and non-dragonkin.

"Dragonkin blood rejuvenates cells and has strong restorative abilities. Our blood makes our bodies powerful and extraordinarily resilient," explained Jade.

"So, if you were to drink it or place it on a wound, would it heal injuries like a dragonkin?"

"Not taken as is, no. Dragonkin blood is far too strong for other races. This liquid is processed so that non-dragonkin can use it. If you use this medicine, it'll immediately heal any wound—big or small. I want you to take it just on the off chance something happens. After all, I won't be able to come along."

"Oh wow. I didn't know something like this existed. I appreciate this very much."

The news of it being blood initially gave her a slight scare, but now that she knew it was medicine made from dragon blood like you'd see in a video game, Ruri marveled, (*Ooh, very fantasy-like.*)

"Handle that stuff with care, now," Joshua added, joining the conversation. "I'd suggest not busting out that stuff in public, Ruri. The method for processing dragon's blood medicine is a secret only known to dragonkin; they don't sell that medicine at markets. It's a rare item, and since it cures any injury, there's tons of nations and people in power licking their chops at the prospect of getting their hands on it. If word got out that you had it, there'd be no shortage of people lining up and begging you for it."

"Huh? Are you serious?"

"Serious as serious can be. That's why I'm warning you not to spill the beans about having it."

Foreseeing the problems that came with the medicine, Ruri prayed that she never had to use it and then placed it into her pocket space.

"Just ask Joshua for instructions if you need them," Jade said.

"Right," Ruri replied.

"Welp, shall we go?" Joshua suggested. They needed to go to the peddlers' location in order to prepare for tomorrow's trip.

Ruri nodded and was about to reply to Joshua, but then Ewan, who was also in the room, stepped in front of Jade. "Um, Your Majesty!"

"What is it?"

"Would you allow me to accompany Ruri to the Nation of the Beast King as well?"

"I wouldn't mind, but are you sure? Finn won't be going."

"Yes, I am well aware, Sire."

Nobody who heard Ewan's request could believe their ears. Ewan, brother complex extraordinaire who was constantly attached to Finn by the hip, was requesting to go somewhere *away* from Finn? Unbelievable. It might just *snow* tomorrow if this was any indication.

"Ewan, you're asking to go *away* from Finn-san? Do you have a fever? Or is there a reason you need to go to the Nation of the Beast King?" Ruri asked.

Ewan fidgeted, his cheeks blushing.

"What's with the reaction?" Honestly put, it was unsettling to her.

Whether Ewan picked that up from the look in Ruri's eyes or not, he yelled at her in response as if he were covering up something. "Th-There's no hidden reason. I just want to go!" he said, turning back to Jade and taking a deep bow. "So, I implore you, Your Majesty!"

"Well, if you insist on going, then I don't mind, but are you really sure? You won't be able to come back until the castle is fixed. Which also means you won't be able to see Finn until then," Jade reminded him.

Ewan nodded firmly in reply. "Yes, I am fine with that."

Since he was so set on going, Jade couldn't very well refuse him. He allowed Ewan to accompany Ruri on her trip.

With their discussion over, Ruri, alongside Joshua and the hastily added Ewan, headed to the room where the peddlers were awaiting them.

"By the way, what are we supposed to be buying?" Ruri asked.

"We might camp outdoors along the way, so we need stuff for that. Also, the Nation of the Beast King is hot, so we need some lighter clothes. Granted, they probably have stuff prepared over there, but…"

"Is there some issue with their clothes?"

"You've met the Beloved of the Nation of the Beast King, right? That outfit is the norm over there. If they've got any clothes prepared, they're most likely gonna be *pretty* similar."

Ruri imagined the outfit that Celestine, the Beloved of the Nation of the Beast King, regularly wore. It was pretty much a dancing girl's outfit. The skirt was made out of thin, wispy material that was almost completely transparent, and her low-cut crop top exposed her midriff. It was a scanty outfit that could only be worn if you were absolutely confident in your figure. Celestine, for example, had a great figure, so she filled the clothes out nicely. Ruri, on the other hand...

"Yeah, I don't think I could wear that," Ruri said, opposing the outfit out of embarrassment.

"Yup, I figured. That's why we're gonna buy some clothes. Also, we need some food."

"They'll have food over there, won't they?" Ruri asked.

"Well, they *do*, but it's *pretty* darn spicy," said Joshua.

Ewan nodded profusely and furrowed his brow. "It's not like it tastes bad, but their spices really hit you, so it'd be really rough to eat that every day. Humans aren't accustomed to it, and since Ruri's not used to it, we should probably get some stomach medicine for her too."

"You're right. Eating habits over there are altogether different from here, so we better get a hefty stock of medicine and rations."

Ruri was fine with spicy foods to a certain point, but *every day* seemed rough. Following Ewan's suggestion, they decided to go to the infirmary later on to pick up some stomach medicine.

"Oh, right. We'll have to go to the city to buy food. What are we going to do?" Ruri asked.

The matter with the Church of God's Light was yet to be resolved, and there was always the threat of them attacking again, which meant going into town was dangerous. It was so dangerous that they instead called the traveling peddlers to the castle for preparations for the trip. Ruri couldn't go into town to buy food.

"We're having them whip up a bunch of food in the castle kitchen right now. Aside from Ewan and me, a few soldiers will be coming along to act as bodyguards, so they're making enough for them too. I'd wager that the kitchen is a madhouse right now."

Since fixing the castle was going to take more than just one or two weeks, they would need that much food in reserve. Of course, they would be eating the food provided to them while abroad, but they would likely want an occasional bite of something familiar, seeing as it was going to be a long stay. The food wouldn't spoil if they kept it in Ruri's pocket space either, so the more the better. Ruri just had to make sure to tell Lydia not to eat any of it without permission.

"If there's anything you'd want to eat over there, you should go make a request."

"Right. Well, I would like something sweet." A daily dose of sweet indulgence was necessary. Ruri wasn't familiar with their cuisine, meaning she was equally clueless about what their sweets had to offer, but considering their hot climate, she wanted some cold treats.

First the peddlers, then the infirmary, and finally the kitchen as Ruri plotted those next few destinations in her mind, the three of them reached the room where the peddlers were set up.

The peddlers were probably informed in advance of their destination because most of the clothes they had prepared were light and bore some very Nation of the Dragon King-esque designs. While Ruri really wanted to get Euclase's opinion on what apparel to buy, Euclase was busy with the aftermath of the last set of incidents. That being the case, Ruri relied on Rin and the peddlers' own advice to make her selection. Then, she picked out all the essentials by listening to Joshua since he was used to traveling to various lands as an intelligence operative.

Ruri was in for a long trip, but she figured the people of the Nation of the Beast King would provide her with a warm and hospitable welcome once she arrived, so they would most likely also provide her with essentials for her stay in their royal castle. Therefore, she only needed clothes, since she wasn't confident in the selection at her destination, and items that might be useful along the way to the nation. The accompanying soldiers were going to prepare the heavy equipment like camping tents, so Ruri actually didn't have to pick much out.

Once she was done with everything, she placed it all into her pocket space. Then, following Joshua and Ewan's advice, she made a trip to both the infirmary and the kitchen to pick up the remaining goods. With her preparations for the next day set, she decided to go to sleep early.

After Ruri left his office, a stern-faced Jade gripped the report of the past incident as Euclase gave him news on a certain event.

"We've searched the castle, but we haven't been able to locate him, Your Majesty."

"And you're saying they're not still pinned under the rubble?" Jade asked.

"We've searched using the spirits, but there's nothing under the rubble."

"I see…"

A heavy silence fell over the room.

After the last incident, a dragonkin soldier went missing. According to the other accounts, that soldier was feeling sick due to food poisoning and was resting in the infirmary. Then, when he went to use the toilet, he disappeared off the face of the map. Jade considered that he just so happened to be around when Sector One was destroyed and was still pinned underneath the ensuing rubble, but Euclase denied that possibility. Of course, it was possible that he simply went back home, but he apparently didn't do that either. No one knew where this soldier suddenly went off to.

"He couldn't possibly be a traitor, could he…?" murmured Agate, whose voice echoed clearly in the silent office. This soldier *had* disappeared as soon as the case was closed. No one wanted to believe that a dragonkin would have taken part in this plot, but there was plenty of room for doubt.

Euclase, however, calmly refuted those concerns. "We can't jump to conclusions just yet. According to that child's story, another member of the Church of God's Light was planning something behind the scenes. There's a chance our soldier became embroiled in it, though."

"Yes, but, I can't imagine a dragonkin being subdued so easily," Agate replied.

"Many of the soldiers around then were feeling sick from their food poisoning, so the possibility isn't off the table."

The effects of the poisoning varied from dragonkin to dragonkin, but those with bad symptoms felt languid and couldn't wake from bed for several hours. That soldier apparently had enough energy to go to the bathroom, but who knew what would happen if someone had ambushed them while they were still sick.

"You mentioned that the Church of God's Light was doing something behind the scenes, but do you know what that was exactly?" Jade asked.

"We aren't sure yet," Euclase said with a shake of their head. "The child has calmed down now, and he's complying to our interrogation, but it's clear he was a mere pawn to be disposed of at any time. Seems they only told him what he needed to know. However, there haven't been any odd disturbances in the castle or in town. The only noticeable oddity is the lone disappearance of our soldier."

"Have you informed Joshua and Ewan of that?"

"Yes. I've informed them to be vigilant on their journey since we haven't uncovered their motives yet."

"Good. In that case, keep investigating the matter." After a short pause, Jade sighed disappointedly and whispered, "I wish I could go along too…"

All of his aides gave him an awkward smile.

"You know that you cannot, Your Majesty. You have *much* work to do. If you were to leave the kingdom now, it would be a disaster," Claus said, putting Jade down lightly.

"I am well aware of that," Jade replied with a small glare, "but the thought of being apart from Ruri for who knows how long puts me in a dour mood."

"In that case, you would have been better sending her off to my mother's house rather than the Nation of the Beast King. You could have gone to see her whenever you wanted."

"It wasn't really my choice to make. I wanted to do just as you suggested, but Celestine insisted." Ruri had to be relocated from the castle for renovations, so Jade had suggested going to the Nation of the Beast King and sightseeing, but the one to initially propose the idea was Celestine. The reason for such was clear.

"I assume she wants to examine Ruri's intimacy with Your Majesty, yes?" Euclase said.

"Celestine is not a fool like the Beloved from Cerulanda. She wouldn't pick a fight with another Beloved, so it'll be fine," Jade assured. Though while she wouldn't try to bump heads with Ruri, Jade could see Celestine eyeing her as a means of observation. He was worried about what her plan was.

"What is the big idea here anyway, Your Majesty?" Euclase asked, drawing near Jade with squinted eyes.

"Big idea behind what?"

"That trinket around Ruri's neck. That is a dragonheart, is it not? You're not in a romantic relationship with her yet, right? How could you give her such an important thing if you're not? Not only that, but Ruri doesn't seem to comprehend the meaning behind it in the first place."

"It's a good luck charm. It'll help me know wherever Ruri might be. And it will ward off any men that might approach her while I'm not around."

Euclase and Claus both looked utterly bemused, having already predicted that being the reason. Normally, one wouldn't just freely give away something that they only had access to once in their entire lives. Euclase and the other vassals of Jade's court were terrified about the thought of Ruri entering into a relationship with another man despite having Jade's dragonheart.

That being said, you probably couldn't find a single demi-human willing to court Ruri while she was wearing that necklace even if you tried. It made Euclase feel a tad sorry for her. Ruri's luck had run out now that a dragon had eyes for her, so Euclase secretly prayed that she didn't fall in love with another man. If she were to fall for another, then the strongest dragon among all dragonkin would go berserk. Not even all the dragonkin in the land would be able to stop him. Sector One of the castle wouldn't be the only place in ruins.

"If she's wearing that around Celestine, then her assumptions about Ruri are going to become even stronger. She will undoubtedly notice the dragonheart," Claus said in an exasperated tone.

Jade sighed deeply and said, "I just hope Celestine takes her rampage somewhere I can't see it."

"Ruri is a Beloved, so I doubt that she'll be too harsh. Also, I believe those two get along quite well."

"I sure hope so." Jade recalled a few examples of Celestine swatting away any women who'd come near him in the past, so he couldn't help but feel a little worried.

2 Signs of Romance

The skies were clear and the weather was fair, the perfect conditions for travel. As the sun shone overhead, the wide terrace of the castle was packed with people ready to go forth to the Nation of the Beast King and those ready to bid those people farewell.

They would be traveling to the Nation of the Beast King by air. Many who came from the Nation of the Beast King were winged beast people. Anybody who lacked wings and couldn't fly had to ride on the soldiers coming from the Nation of the Dragon King. Flying by way of magic was also an option, but a long flight to somewhere as far as the Nation of the Beast King could drain one's mana and send them crashing down before they could reach the end, so no one dared to try that method. Ruri had enough mana to ensure that wasn't a problem, but she planned on riding on Kotaro's back all the way.

"Ruri, are you all ready?" asked Jade as he approached her. He was there to see her off. Finn and Claus were behind him, most likely having come to see both Ewan and Joshua respectively.

"Yes, I'm good to go at any time," Ruri replied.

"Make sure to take care of yourself," Jade advised.

"I'll be fine. I have the spirits, Joshua, and Ewan with me," Ruri responded cheerfully.

That didn't help wipe the worry from Jade's expression, however, as his face practically screamed that he wanted to accompany Ruri if he could.

"I've already asked Arman to handle things, so if something happens with Celestine, go to him."

"What happens?"

"Um, well, you know? Something."

Ruri scratched her head at Jade's vague wording. She couldn't help but be equal parts curious and concerned about what Jade was implying.

That was when Celestine arrived. "My, you needn't worry, Master Jade. I will be responsible for Lady Ruri and show her the utmost hospitality during her stay," she said with an elegant smile.

Jade looked at her with a rather sour expression. "Celestine, I implore you, I *beseech* you not to go out of line," he said, giving a heavily emphasized warning.

Celestine looked somewhat surprised. "Why, I'm not going to take and eat her. However, I will say that compromising on many long years of affection is not an easy task, Sire."

Seeing the tinge of sorrow on her face, Jade found himself at a loss for words. His brow turned upward apologetically, and he said, "If that will satisfy you, Celestine, I hope you have a nice, long chat with Ruri."

"Yes, I shall."

Watching Celestine and Jade's exchange, Ruri felt her heart drop into her stomach. She wondered if she was going to be bullied in the Nation of the Beast King.

Possibly displeased with the extremely nervous look in Ruri's eyes, Celestine asked Jade, "But...you wouldn't mind if I'm a little mean, now would you?"

"Huh?" Ruri replied, confused.

"Well..." Jade started, "only if it's in moderation."

"What?! Why are you giving her *permission*, Jade-sama?!" Ruri asked, shocked that he would sign off on something like that considering that *she* would be the one getting bullied.

"It's fine. Celestine wouldn't do anything insidious to a Beloved...I think." Jade didn't seem confident enough to state this with certainty.

"You *think*?!"

"Tee hee hee. I simply jest," Celestine said with a giggle.

However, from Ruri's perspective, Celestine's uninviting eyes seemed to paint a different picture—something that Ruri wished was just a figment of her imagination. She was starting to think her trip to the Nation of the Beast King was a bad idea.

"Um, I think you might be mistaken, so I assure you Jade-sama and I are..."

"Your Majesty, preparations are in order!"

Ruri was attempting to clear up the confusion about her being Jade's mate while she had the chance, but Ewan and Joshua, who had finished scrambling to make their final travel preparations, interrupted her to give a status report.

"Very well," replied Jade.

Once Ewan's eyes fell upon Celestine, standing by Jade's side, his face turned red and he hurried to move his sights elsewhere—while still looking at her out of the corner of his eye. It was a reaction that not only Ruri noticed with curiosity but Claus and Finn as well. Even Jade could feel something was amiss, but he decided to introduce the two to Celestine for the time being instead.

"Celestine, this is Ewan and Joshua. They'll be accompanying Ruri to the Nation of the Beast King. I assume Joshua needs no explanation. However, Ewan is Finn's younger brother."

"Hello, it has been quite some time," she greeted Joshua, apparently having a degree of familiarity with him. She then turned to face Ewan, presumably for the first time, and smiled sweetly. "This is not our first meeting. I don't believe we exchanged words, but we have met before, have we not?"

She was talking about the time Azelda barged into Sector One of the castle. It was basically Finn's job to accompany Jade as a bodyguard during his trips abroad. While Ewan went to other nations, his path would never intersect with Celestine. And though she had visited the Nation of the Dragon King in the past, despite being in the military, Ewan performed a lot of clerical work, meaning he wouldn't be assigned to bodyguard duty for royal guests. Because of that, he would never meet face-to-face with Celestine. As a result, while this was technically their second meeting, it was the first time they actually exchanged words. However…

"Y-Y-Y-Yes! My name is Ewan. Very pleased to make your acquaintance!" Ewan stammered, blushing and tremendously flustered.

"Come now, don't be so tense. I'm sure this will be the first of many chances we have to chat, so I'm pleased to meet you."

"Y-Y-Y-Y-Yes, the pleasure is all mine!" Ewan said as he glanced at Celestine. He looked hot and bothered—like a boy in love.

Ruri looked at Joshua, and she could tell from his expression that they both had the same idea, which caused them both to grin devilishly.

"I never thought I would see the day. Look at Ewan, the little card…" Ruri said.

"Well, now I know what I'm looking forward to on this trip. Maybe I should keep an observation diary," Joshua commented.

"Finn-san, Ewan might just be out of his brother complex phase," Ruri said, thinking that Finn would be happy that his clingy younger brother was starting to stand on his own. Finn, however, looked like he had mixed feelings, and Claus, standing by his side, seemed the same. "You're not pleased?"

"Err, well, I wouldn't say I'm not pleased, but the target of his affection being the Beloved of the Nation of the Beast King makes things a little, err…"

"Is there a problem with that?"

"She has always been smitten with His Majesty. She still is, in fact. I can only imagine him being rejected even if he tried."

"Oh, good point," Ruri replied.

"And that isn't all," Claus remarked from beside Finn. "Ewan is incapable of seeing spirits. And because of that, his devotion in the spirits is low in comparison to others. I cannot imagine someone like him being an apt fit for a Beloved born to the most devout spirit-religious tribe in a nation already as devout as the Beast King's domain. Also, she is a Beloved of that very nation. Even if she were to become his mate, she most likely couldn't come here. That would mean that Ewan would have to go to her. But do you think Ewan, of all people, would part ways with Finn to go there?"

Ruri agreed with that quandary. If Ewan went to the Nation of the Beast King, he would rarely get to see Finn anymore. It was hard to imagine someone with a brother complex like his being able to endure that.

"But Ewan is a dragonkin like us. Of course he'll prioritize a mate more than his brother, no matter how much he adores him," Joshua added. Among dragonkin, finding a mate reigned supreme. Joshua looked at Claus and Finn, both remaining silent, and started to lose a bit of his assuredness. "Hmm, but this *is* Ewan we're talking about…"

Ewan's devotion to Finn was unmatched, so both Finn and Claus had similar doubts.

"Well, I wouldn't think that he would ignore finding a mate, being a dragonkin, but…" Finn trailed off.

"But he does come across as the type to forgo finding a mate completely if it meant staying with you, yes?" Claus said, finishing the thought.

Ruri added, "This is going to end up being an issue whether Celestine-san is who he's after or not, right? If he'd rather cling to his brother than a mate, any future wife of his is going to have a tough time. It could lead to divorce if he's not careful."

Divorce for dragonkin, a race known for loving their mate for life, was unheard of, but given Ewan's track record, he was on pace to be the very first case—a true milestone. Ewan's future seemed to be a cause of concern for Finn as he racked his brain over it.

"Well, nothing is set in stone just yet, so I don't think you need to brood over it too much, Finn-san," Ruri assured.

"A-Aye, you're right. He isn't in a romantic relationship with the Nation of the Beast King's Beloved just yet."

"Yup, yup. Besides, this might be his chance to quit being so dependent on you, Finn," Joshua said with a teasing smile, seeming to enjoy the current state of affairs.

Claus shot a quick, dismissive stare at Joshua for being so flippant about the situation before turning back to Finn with a consoling look. "Well, this is the first time that Ewan proposed to leave Finn by going to the Nation of the Beast King. I would say that he has grown somewhat. All we can do for the time being is watch and wait, wouldn't you agree?"

"Yes, a fair point," Finn agreed.

"We'll observe Ewan's behavior and report in from time to time. Won't we, Ruri?"

"Yes, leave it to us, Finn-san! We will help Ewan realize his love while we're at it!"

"Um, no, I'd appreciate it if you didn't intervene," Finn said, quickly stopping Ruri, who was raring to play cupid.

"Aww, really?" Ruri said in disappointment.

"If you were to get involved, I feel things would just get complicated," Claus said, knowing that disaster awaited if this developed into a national dilemma. Joshua and Finn nodded in agreement.

"Keep an eye on him in secret. We're just gonna observe him and run in to stop him if he goes out of control," Joshua said.

"Yessir. Sure thing…" Ruri said with a pouty expression, dissatisfied.

Jade then interjected, "Ruri, it's about time to go."

"M'kay. Let's go, Joshua."

"Right-o. All right, I'm off, dad," Joshua said, giving a short wave goodbye to Claus.

"Make certain that you protect Ruri," Claus replied.

"Yeah, thanks for the reminder," Joshua quipped.

Ewan came running over to Finn. "Brother, I'll be going now."

"Right, do your best out there," Finn replied, rustling Ewan's hair.

It made Ewan so happy you could almost see an imaginary tail wagging from his rear end. After their exchange was done, he joined the rest of the departing party.

Finally, Ruri gave Jade her send-off. "Okay, I'll be off too, Jade-sama."

As if not wanting her to go, Jade instinctively gave her a hug. "I'll make sure to repair the castle as fast as possible, so just be patient."

"I'll bring you back a souvenir, okay?"

"Yes, I look forward to it."

Ruri then stepped away from Jade and made her way to Joshua and the others.

As the farewell party prepared to leave, Joshua and the other dragonkin bound for the Nation of the Beast King started to transform into their dragon forms one after another. Ruri's field of view was instantly taken up by the gigantic dragons encasing the area around her.

Once she placed Chi on Kotaro and Rin on her shoulder, Ruri straddled Kotaro's back. "All ready," she said.

"Move out!" signaled Arman, riding a carriage being pulled by several winged beastmen. This prompted all the members of the departing party to file in line to take to the skies.

Ruri waved to Jade and the others standing on the terrace below as she traveled onward toward the Nation of the Beast King.

Journey

A few hours had passed since Ruri and the others departed from the castle, and their journey had been smooth sailing for the most part. Ruri rode on Kotaro while Arman and Celestine rode aboard the carriage pulled by winged beastmen. The other soldiers flew in a protective circle around the three high-profile individuals.

In terms of speed, Kotaro was the fastest, followed by the dragonkin and then the demi-humans of the Nation of the Beast King. Everyone else matched their pace to the winged beastmen.

While the dragonkin were flying comfortably, the winged beastmen were struggling to keep up. But even so, Kotaro started to feel their party was going *too* slow. He decided to use his powers to conjure up the winds and speed up the stragglers. Now with a gracious tailwind assisting all of them, their speed increased and the beastmen were able to fly a little more comfortably by relying more on the wind than their manpower. Arman and the others were thrilled they were flying at a faster pace than when they first left.

As soft and fluffy as Kotaro's back was, hours on end in the same position was starting to do a number on Ruri's derriere. They had taken a few short breaks along the way, but with hunger starting to set in, Ruri wanted to take a legitimate break.

Just as she thought that, Arman called out, "I know it's a little early, but we're setting up camp around here, so take us down!"

Ruri was relieved to hear those words as they descended upon an area with a tiny lake. Apparently, Arman and his party had taken a break here when they initially came to the Nation of the Dragon King. They quickly proceeded with the prep work, as if following a set process.

Ruri jumped off of Kotaro's back and proceeded to stretch with a satisfied grunt. Once she had warmed up her stagnant and stiffened muscles, she said, "Joshua, I'll help. What should I do?"

"Oh, thanks. I'd appreciate it. Well…on second thought, you should probably just kick back and take it easy."

"Why?"

"Well, 'cause, look at that," Joshua said, pointing. There, as everyone else around them ran around trying to set up camp, Arman and Celestine relaxed in a hastily constructed rest area.

"I mean, it's only natural that a Beloved be treated on the same level as a king. We normally wouldn't let them do this kind of menial labor."

"Hmm. Well, they do their own thing. Celestine-san is probably used to being waited on hand and foot since she's lived that lifestyle her entire life, but I can't really sit by and kick up my feet while everyone else is working," Ruri said, stating her true opinions on the matter.

Joshua simply chuckled. "You should probably act a little more like a Beloved should, Ruri. Every nation's Beloved is used to being cared for from a young age. They normally don't have that sense of selflessness."

"I can't really help it, though. People only started referring to me as a Beloved since I came to this world. Also, no one in the castle treats me in the same courteous way they treated Celestine-san. Okay, actually, I think they did treat me pretty politely at first, but it kind of got more and more sloppy over time. Then again, I'd hate it if they started standing on ceremony *now*, this late into things."

"Well, you were a cat at first. Besides, dragonkin tend not to ham it up even toward someone like His Majesty."

"Well, you may have a point," Ruri conceded. The Dragon King reigned as the supreme being in the kingdom, but the other dragonkin interacted with Jade in a rather friendly manner. Of course, there was a certain level of courtesy to their speech and manners, but there were times when dragonkin would hail him down in the hallways and chat things up with him. Jade never got angry in response. In fact, he would often actively engage in conversation and include himself in the circle, so dragonkin probably valued camaraderie over social status.

Naturally, that camaraderie only applied between dragonkin. Other races weren't nearly as friendly. In fact, other races were always awestruck by the Dragon King, and even if they wanted to speak to him, they would be too tense to hold an amicable conversation.

That apparently wasn't the case for humans. Most of them possessed little to no mana, and their senses were inferior to demi-humans, so they neither noticed the immense mana nor the instinct-triggering awe that dragonkin exuded. That was why there were so many human officials in the nation's ranks. The reason why there were so few in the military went without saying, but it was obviously because they couldn't hold a candle to dragonkin or any other demi-humans in terms of magical and physical prowess. Also, perhaps as a result of their lack of fear, a great number of dragonkin picked humans for their mates as well.

Basically, to put a long story short, dragonkin acted friendly with Jade, so they acted that way with Ruri as well. Granted, since Ruri only traversed the upper floors of the castle, which were mostly composed of dragonkin, if she happened upon a member of a different race, they would likely stand on ceremony for her.

"Well, all of that aside, I should help anyway."

"I get ya, but just imagine what they'd think. 'Look at those dragonkin, making their Beloved work like that.'"

"Our business is ours, and theirs is theirs. If Jade-sama were here, I'm positive he'd tell me to do as I please. Or rather, he'd be taking initiative and moving around."

"Well, you got a point. His Majesty could just order us around, but he's an awfully active ruler, all things considered." That much was clear from the fact that he would travel around the royal capital in secret.

"If Jade were here" seemed to be the line that sealed the deal as Joshua reluctantly gave Ruri a task. "Gather some dry branches and build a bonfire for us, then."

"All righty!" Ruri said, triumphantly starting her newly assigned work.

As she carried out her task, the people of the Nation of the Beast King came up to her saying, "No, let us," and, "You shouldn't, Lady Beloved." They couldn't believe that the dragonkin were letting her perform menial labor. Ruri simply ignored them.

As Ruri lightheartedly lifted sticks into a bundle, Kotaro and the other spirits started to lend a hand—except for Chi, who was enjoying his time chasing butterflies nearby.

"*Ruri~ We've brought you some~*" said one spirit.

"*Whole big stack!*" said another.

Thanks to the spirits' overwhelming enthusiasm to help, Ruri collected what seemed to be a little *too* much wood. Nevertheless, she piled the branches up and started a flame. By the time the fire was lit, Joshua and the others had already finished setting up camp, and they called her for a midday meal.

Arman and Celestine sat atop a tapestry laid out over the grass, Arman with his legs crossed and Celestine with her legs cordially off to the side. In front of them both was a hearty assortment of dishes. Urged by Joshua, Ruri sat by Arman and Celestine's side, forming a circle around the food. This, however, was the only area with dishes laid out. There wasn't nearly enough for everyone. Joshua and the others weren't sitting either; they instead stood diligently and watched from a distance.

"What about you, Joshua? And the others?" asked Ruri.

"We'll eat later," he replied.

Ruri had been sure that they'd all eat together, but it seemed it would only be the three of them dining for now. The others started to serve those seated or completed other tasks.

Ruri felt awkward sitting around eating while a massive group of people watched, but Arman and Celestine seemed unfazed by any of this.

"Do you not eat your meals with everyone?" she asked.

"In the Nation of the Beast King, outside of feasts, the king and his vassals don't share in meals together. Those in higher positions like Celestine and myself eat first, and then everyone else eats afterward," Arman explained.

The Nation of the Beast King apparently had a more distinct class division than the Nation of the Dragon King. That was the impression Ruri gained just by looking at how the people from the Nation of the Beast King interacted with Arman and Celestine. They were courteous and respectful—to an outrageous degree, in fact. Even discounting their speech, nothing about the way they interacted with Arman and Celestine drew even the slightest parallel to the friendliness Jade and the dragonkin shared in the Nation of the Dragon King.

"In the Nation of the Dragon King, I get the impression that things are a lot more lax. You have social statuses put in place, but everyone casually interacts with the King. That, however, is where our two nations clearly differ. There are boundaries we don't cross, and we're careful about how we interact. Even more so toward Beloveds. You helping out the soldiers earlier would be inconceivable in our nation. No one within eyeshot would allow it."

"Hmm, that seems a little too constricting," Ruri said, thinking that sort of treatment would be a tad too unbearable for herself. Her eyes trailed over to Celestine.

"I was essentially born in this sort of environment, so I don't feel it's constricting at all."

"Oh, I see." Since Celestine had been exposed to this treatment since childhood, she was probably accustomed to it. However, Ruri was unable to wrap her head around it, and it showed in her perplexed expression.

Arman saw this and let out a lighthearted laugh. "Doesn't meet your standards, I take it. You're the type to work right along with the soldiers. Taking that into consideration, it's a good thing you're affiliated with the Nation of the Dragon King, isn't it? The dragonkin are pretty lax about all that. Probably their strong sense of camaraderie to blame. Honestly speaking, I think other nations are similar to the Nation of the Beast King. Royalty, Beloveds, nobles, commoners—they're all very distinctly separated into social classes."

"I see," said Ruri. "I thought that the people of the Nation of the Dragon King would be overprotective just because I'm a Beloved, but I think they give me much more free rein than the people of the Nation of the Beast King would." They at least allowed her to work outside the castle walls for a time, an act that probably wouldn't be allowed in the Nation of the Beast King. It was something that she finally realized after seeing how the people of the Nation of the Beast King treated Celestine.

"*Hey, hey. Let's dig in already,*" Chi said, shaking Ruri's lap with his front legs. He was impatient for the meal to start.

"You're eating too, Chi?" Ruri asked.

"*Sure am! I'm in the mood to eat something.*"

"Right, well, let's get to it, then," Arman said, initiating the meal. The Nation of the Beast King's men acted as servers and promptly handed out plates.

With plates in hand, Ruri started to divvy up what Chi wanted to eat as Arman and Celestine began their meals.

"*I want that, and that, and, ooh, some of that.*"

"Okay, okay. How about you, Kotaro, Rin?" Ruri asked, turning to Kotaro lying comfortably on the tapestry and Rin lying atop his head. However, both of them shook their heads.

Ruri placed Chi's plate down in front of him and he happily started to chow down. Watching Chi eat in delight, Ruri started eating herself.

Even though it was the middle of the day, Arman was sipping from a cup filled with what appeared to be alcohol. His eyes fell upon Joshua, who was standing off from the tapestry.

"Joshua, you can come join us to eat, if you'd like."

"I'll pass. I'm technically here to guard Ruri."

Ruri overheard their conversation and stopped what she was doing. "Wait, why is Joshua fine to join us?" Ruri questioned. Arman had just said that he didn't share meals with vassals.

"Oh, what? She doesn't know?" Arman asked, his question directed more toward Joshua—as if actually asking, "Didn't you tell her?"

"Now that you mention it, I don't think she does," Joshua said.

Ruri glanced between Joshua and Arman. "Huh? What? What?"

"Joshua's dad and I are half brothers on our mom's side, meaning Joshua is my nephew and I'm his uncle," Arman explained.

Ruri's eyes shot wide open. "Wait, *huh*? What do you mean?"

"Just like you heard, dad and the Beast King are brothers. Dad is the previous Beast King's son."

"By 'dad' you mean Claus-san, right?" Ruri asked for clarity.

"Yep, yep."

"Huh? But you and Claus-san are dragonkin."

"Interracial children take after the stronger race's blood. Basically, between a lion and a dragon side, the dragon side had stronger genes."

Ewan was a good example of this since he was born from a human and dragonkin. His mother was human, but Ewan wasn't; he was a dragonkin.

"Dad and I carry the blood of the previous Beast King, but since we're dragonkin, we can't inherit the Nation of the Beast King's throne. We're just simple dragonkin, born and raised in the Nation of the Dragon King."

"Huh, I didn't know."

Chelsie gave birth to Claus, meaning that Chelsie's former mate was—the previous Beast King. Ruri was shocked that Chelsie, the old lady living a quiet life in the woods, had a mate so *grandiose*. However, that was when a question came to mind.

"But, wait, Beast Kings usually have multiple wives, don't they? Meanwhile, dragonkin only stick to one. Are you saying Chelsie-san was okay with that?"

"Nah, she apparently was totally *not* okay with it. That's why her and the previous Beast King were never wed. Yeah, Granny couldn't marry a guy with a bunch of wives. But since she wanted children with the person she loved, she brute-forced her way in and basically said, 'Fork over your genes, bud.'"

"Wow, so Chelsie-san…is the aggressive type," Ruri commented, thinking it very *in character* for Chelsie, to put it lightly.

"And that's how she ended up giving birth to three sons. Granny sure is one tough lady."

"And that's the last she heard from the former Beast King?" Ruri asked.

"The former king said something about going on an adventure one day," Arman replied with a bitter expression. "He just left the throne and went off to who-knows-where. He didn't even care how much hell I went through succeeding the throne after him."

From the way Arman clenched his fist, Ruri could feel his embittered feelings.

"He used that as his chance to separate from his wives, but he apparently paid visits to Lady Chelsie's place, though infrequently."

"And we're talking *really* infrequently," Joshua tacked on.

His presence really was as limited as Joshua said, seeing as Ruri never met him in the two whole years she lived at Chelsie's house.

"Who even knows where he could be now?" Arman said, shrugging his shoulders.

He seemed like a pretty wild and impulsive person. "Sounds like he would get along with Grandpa," Ruri said, a mental image of her own grandfather in her mind.

The Bracelet

After Ruri, Arman, and Celestine had finished eating, Joshua and the others finally started their own meals. However, since Ruri's group enjoyed a leisurely spot of post-meal tea, the servers remained and alternated going to eat.

Chi seemed satisfied after eating his hearty meal; he was lying down and kicking back on Kotaro, using him as a makeshift bed. Ruri thought that sleeping after eating was a surefire way to get fat, but he was probably fine since he was a spirit inhabiting a rodent's body.

Once everyone had settled, Ruri asked, "So, the Nation of the Beast King has hot springs, right?"

"We sure do. Do you like hot springs?" Arman asked.

"Like them? I *love* them!" Ruri emphatically responded.

"The baths in the castle draw hot water from the underground springs, so you can enjoy them to your heart's content morning, noon, or night. A dip in the springs is great, but wait until you try a naturally heated sand bath."

Sparkles formed in Ruri's eyes. "I'm so jealous! The Nation of the Dragon King doesn't even have *baths*, much less hot springs, so I'm dying to try them!" Her anticipation was growing all the more higher since bathing wasn't a concept in the Nation of the Dragon King.

"Ah, I see. Yeah, the Nation of the Dragon King *does* use magic to handle everything."

"That's right. Using magic to clean is convenient and easy, but I need to soak in some hot water to take the fatigue away!" Ruri explained fervently.

Arman nodded in agreement. "Yes, I would bet."

Since it wasn't in the Nation of the Dragon King's culture to bathe in warm water, any explanation she gave about the wonders of bathing went in one ear and out the other. Back when she lived with Chelsie, in order to get permission to build a bathhouse in the woods, she tried to explain the benefits of soaking in hot water, but Chelsie simply replied with a halfhearted, "Do whatever you want."

Chelsie couldn't quite understand Ruri's fervor since she used magic to get the job done. That was why Ruri was so thrilled that Arman was agreeing with her.

"Still, if you love baths that much, why not just build one in the Nation of the Dragon King?" Arman asked.

"I would, but do hot springs flow in the Nation of the Dragon King?"

"You have the supreme-level spirits of both earth and water there, so wouldn't you be able to pull water from deep underground if you employed their help? The Spirit of Earth should easily be able to unearth a hot spring if asked by a Beloved. After all, the capital of the Nation of the Beast King was originally an arid wasteland, but the Beloved at the time implored the spirits and shaped it into an oasis."

"Oh wow, you're saying that's possible?" Ruri tried asking the spirits to be sure. "Hey, Rin, Chi? Can you make hot springs in the Nation of the Dragon King?"

Chi was half asleep, but he apparently had been listening to the conversation. "*Yeah, sure can~*" he replied in a sleepy, listless tone.

"*Sure can!*" Rin replied, pumping her tiny wing-like arms in confidence.

"*But you want the spring for hot water, right?*" Chi asked. "*I can pull out the water vein, but it would just be cold water, so you need to warm it up with natural geothermal heat. You'll need a fire spirit's help.*"

"A fire spirit, huh? It doesn't necessarily have to be the *supreme* spirit, right?"

"*Well, I won't say it's impossible, but a spirit of equal level would have an easier time using their powers in conjunction with ours.*"

"Oh, I see. But I assume that a supreme-level spirit isn't going to just give me their help."

"*For you, he just might. He's a real flirt.*"

"A flirt? What kind of spirit is this?"

"*The kind that's been chasing tail and hitting on women since forever now.*"

"Oh my, sounds like he'd get along swimmingly with Master Arman," Celestine murmured.

"Hey now…" Arman said with a bitter expression.

"Well, even if I tried to employ his help, I wouldn't know where he is anyway," Ruri stated.

"*Last I heard, he was in the Nation of the Spirit King to visit the Spirit of Trees,*" Rin replied. "*Well, that was about a millennium ago, but still…*"

"Do other spirits know where each other are?"

"*I could search if I wanted to. Should I?*" Rin asked.

Ruri considered it but shook her head. "No, you don't have to. The other fire spirits can do it too, right? I'll just ask them to do it. Can I ask you guys to do that?"

The spirits floating around her all gave motivated responses.

"Sure!"

"Yeah, leave it t'us!"

"We'll do our best for you, Ruri!"

"I'd like to see the sights of the royal capital once I get to the Nation of the Beast King, but will I be allowed?" Ruri asked, remembering that she said she would buy Jade a souvenir. She wanted to see the sights around town, but the issue with the Church of God's Light was yet to be completely resolved. Considering that Celestine was assaulted in the Nation of the Beast King, Ruri was hesitant to just go waltzing around town. After all, it was possible that cohorts of the Church of God's Light were still around.

Arman pondered over Ruri's question for a moment. "Right, let's see... Well, I would give you permission right away if the matter with the Church of God's Light was wrapped up, but... we still don't even know where their base is. We can't rule out the possibility that they might attack in our nation either."

"So, it is still too chancy after all..." Ruri murmured, slumping her shoulders. She was disappointed that her first time in a foreign nation would be so restricted.

During this conversation, Ewan had swapped places with Joshua so he could eat. "How is the security of the castle? I assume they infiltrated your castle the same way they infiltrated the Nation of the Dragon King's walls. We gained testimony from the raiders themselves that they transformed into rats. We don't know how many of those magic bracelets exist, but there still might be more out there," Ewan explained, bringing the situation to Arman's attention.

"Right after we learned of their infiltration method, I had the castle interior combed, but, honestly speaking, defending the castle against extremely small beings is sort of an uphill battle. And we don't have the time either."

A small room was one thing, but a place as expansive as a castle was a whole different story. Even the act of combing the entire castle for blind spots took time. Add even further countermeasures to the mix and it wasn't going to be something completed overnight. It would be easier just to demolish the castle and rebuild it from scratch, like the partially destroyed castle back in the Nation of the Dragon King. It might have saved them time as well.

"I don't plan on leaving your side for even a second while in the Nation of the Beast King, and I'll have a barrier around you at all times. Even if any raiders do show up, they won't be abducting or hurting you like last time, so fear not," Kotaro said. He sounded rather frustrated by the fact that the fake Reapers managed to get to her before.

Ever since Ruri was rescued, Kotaro hadn't left her side. He even went with her in the bedroom and Jade's office, places he normally stayed away from, out of concern. Ruri knew that she'd made Kotaro worry, so she didn't refuse him from following her, but it was actually making her worried for Kotaro. After all, being so high-strung all the time had to be a tiring experience. However, it was doubtful that Kotaro would listen even if she tried to convince him otherwise—at least, not until the situation with the Church of God's Light was completely resolved.

"Say, Kotaro? Do you think you could place that barrier onto Celestine-san as well until the Church of God's Light stuff is taken care of?" So long as Beloveds were being targeted, Celestine was also in danger.

"Yes, I could."

"Then I'd appreciate it if you did."

Kotaro nodded, and a soft wind blew around Celestine, forming an invisible barrier around her.

Surprised, Arman bowed his head to Ruri. "Appreciated."

"Yes, thank you very much," Celestine said in gratitude.

"You're in just as much danger as I am, after all. Please, don't worry about it. The more pressing issue here is that bracelet that turns people into rats. If they didn't have that, they'd neither have a way to break into the castle nor a means to assassinate a Beloved."

Ruri pulled out two bracelets from her pocket space. One of them was the bracelet she used to turn into a cat, and the other was a bracelet she got off the fake Reapers. The more you looked at the two bracelets, the harder it was to tell them apart.

"That's the bracelet that turns you into a rat, huh?" Arman asked.

"Yes, this is the one," Ruri replied, handing the item over to him.

He turned it around in his hands and even put it on his arm to check, but since it had expended its number of usages, it had turned into just another bracelet.

After Arman was done with his check, he turned his attention to the other bracelet she was holding. "And that one?"

"This is the bracelet I own that turns you into a cat. It originally belonged to the First Dragon King, though. You've noticed that it's pretty similar to that bracelet, yes?" They looked almost identical, but performance-wise, Ruri's bracelet was far better. Since it didn't have a usage limit, she used it practically all the time.

"Give us a demonstration," Arman demanded, looking somewhat excited. Since he never saw the raiders actually transform, he was probably interested in seeing how it worked.

Left with no choice, Ruri placed the bracelet on her wrist and instantly transformed into a white cat.

Arman was absolutely delighted with what he saw. "Ooh! You really *did* turn into a cat!"

"*May I turn back now?*"

"No, wait, come over here for a second," Arman said, scooping Ruri up into his arms. He proceeded to fuss over her, petting her kitty head and touching the plump undersides of her paws. He was having a blast with the fact that she was a cat. "Who would have thought humans could become beasts like demi-humans. And *anyone* can become one? That is mighty interesting, to say the least."

"You're messing up my hair~"

"What a fine coat of hair it is."

Ruri's soft, shiny fur was probably thanks in part to Jade's frequent brushing. He used a variety of specialized brushes to carefully groom her. Jade's love for the soft and cuddly ran deep.

Ruri knew that Arman wanted to keep touching her fluffy and well-groomed coat, but his touch showed *zero* restraint. The dragonkin, especially Jade, would pet her gently and somewhat timidly out of consideration for her, but Arman's big, thick hands were mercilessly kneading the surface of her body. After he finished petting her and let her go, Ruri felt worn out. She turned back into human form before he had a chance to touch her again.

"Perhaps we might be able to figure something out if we were to find out where the bracelets were made," Ruri suggested.

She had meant to ask Lydia about the bracelets, but she forgot with everything else going on. However, that was when she caught a glimpse of Chi. Chi also had a spirit contract with the First Dragon King, meaning he might have information about the bracelet.

"Hey, Chi, do you know anything about these bracelets?"

"No clue about the rat one, but I know about the one you've got. Weidt got that from a witch."

"A witch?"

"*Yeah. They don't use spirit magic; they use their own brand of sorcery. A lot prefer to conduct research on magic, and that leads to a whole bunch of magic tools being brought into the world. That bracelet is one of them.*"

Ruri looked down at the bracelets as she listened to Chi's explanation. "So, if the cat bracelet was made by a witch, then does that also go for this rat one?"

"It's possible," Arman declared.

"Meaning the Church of God's Light might be linked to a witch as well, right?" Celestine added.

"In that case, we're in for a lot of trouble," Ewan said. "There's also a chance they've got magic tools aside from the rat bracelet. After all, it seems witches are adept at making them."

Arman furrowed his brow as he listened. Then he muttered, "I should probably tell Jade about this as well, just to be safe." It would have been faster to have the spirits tell him instead, but with their rather childlike speech, there was a chance they would flub some of the nuance. Instead, he decided to write Jade a letter once they reached the kingdom.

5 Arrival in the Nation of the Beast King

Near the royal capital of the Nation of the Beast King existed a volcanic mountain called Mt. Ulawoon. The hot springs that flowed because of the volcano's tidings contributed to a large part of the Nation the Beast King's tourism industry and became paramount to its existence. But that wasn't the half of it. Since locations like volcanoes produced immense natural power, they were comfortable places for spirits to inhabit, so spirits naturally flocked to it.

For the spirit-religious Nation of the Beast King, Mt. Ulawoon was managed by the kingdom as sacred ground; no one was allowed to enter without permission. However, deep in the mountain walked one man. He had long, crimson hair and gold-colored eyes.

The man furrowed his determined and neatly-trimmed brows, stopping in his tracks. His eyes fell upon a manner of being that appeared humanoid but was devoid of any trace of humanity—a mangled shell of its former self.

"Unghhh, aaaaaargh…"

"How disgusting…" the man said as he glanced at the inhuman life-form and turned around. That was when the inhuman life-form let out an unearthly bellow and pounced at the man's back.

It seemed that the creature would land its strike, but almost as soon as it jumped, it was doused in fire. Erupting into a ball of flames, it was less than a blink of an eye before the ashen remains of the creature lay motionless on the ground. Without so much as a glance back at the thing, the man walked on.

"This place is getting a lot of unwanted activity as well. Maybe it's about time to go. Still, I can't just leave this mess as is…"

The man looked off into the distance—toward the Nation of the Beast King's capital.

"The castle it is, then…"

Ruri's party was currently flying through a seemingly endless desert wasteland. They had entered the boundaries of the Nation of the Beast King some time ago, and once they did, the land started to get dry. Once they got closer to the royal capital, the land became more and more arid. It was a world of difference from the Nation of the Dragon King, which was abounding with greenery and rich in bountiful soil.

Since the Nation of the Beast King was a veritable desert, the nation itself wasn't very self-sufficient. They regularly imported their food supplies from the Nation of the Dragon King. In exchange, they exported rural crafts and minerals back.

As they flew overhead, looking over the desolate earth, a gigantic oasis came into view right in the middle of the desert.

"Wow, it's amazing!" Ruri exclaimed.

A huge palace sat right in the middle of the oasis, and an entire town lay around it. White smoke-like clouds billowed up all over, but it wasn't smoke from fires; it was steam. A scent evocative of hot springs wafted through the air.

The phrase "land of hot springs" flashed in Ruri's mind, and her excitement shot through the roof.

"Hot springs! Hot spri~ngs♪" Ruri said in a gleeful, singsong tone as the party descended upon the royal castle's garden.

Unlike the Nation of the Dragon King's European-styled castle structure, the Nation of the Beast King's construction mimicked an Indian palace. There was even a giant fountain in the garden.

Once they landed, Joshua and the other dragonkin morphed back into their human forms.

"Woo boy, finally made it," Joshua said, twirling around his arms to relieve the fatigue.

He said "finally," but thanks to Kotaro's wind powers, they made it to the kingdom shockingly early. They had originally scheduled the trip to take an entire day.

A short distance away, Arman was talking to his vassals who had assembled for their king's return.

"Is everything ready?" he asked.

"Indeed, Sire. Per your instructions, we have made preparations to welcome the honorable Beloved from the Nation of the Dragon King."

"Ruri, come here," Arman called.

All eyes fell upon Ruri as she walked over, and it made her feel *incredibly* uncomfortable. They weren't staring at her out of spite or malice, though. It was just the opposite—they were all looking at her with worship and adoration.

"This is the Beloved of the Nation of the Dragon King, Ruri."

"Hi, nice to meet you all," Ruri greeted with a slight nod of her head.

The people before her all dropped to their knees and bowed so deep that it looked like their foreheads would scrape the ground. "It is but our honor to make your acquaintance. We shall dedicate all our efforts into ensuring you remain as comfortable as can be," one of them greeted her.

"P-Pleased to meet you too..." Ruri stammered, feeling a little weirded out. She'd never received such extremely courteous treatment before. She looked over to Joshua and Ewan as a cry for help, but they simply met her gaze with awkward smirks. There was no way out for her.

As they all lifted their heads, one of them stared at Kotaro, who was standing behind Ruri, in wonderment. "Might I ask, Your Majesty, that white beast over there seems to be the sacred beast of the Nation of the Spirit King, but what brings it here of all places?"

"That's not the Nation of the Spirit King's sacred beast. It's the supreme-level spirit of the winds inhabiting its body. We are also joined by the supreme-level spirits of earth and water as well. You are to treat them with respect just as the Beloved."

Chi lifted up his front paw and greeted them. "*Yo!*"

They all looked at Chi, Kotaro, and Rin one after another with swelling excitement.

"Goodness, spirits with physical bodies...and supreme-level spirits on top of that. To think we'd be so blessed by good fortune—living to see the day in which we are graced by such noble presences. We shall provide you with the utmost hospitality the Nation of the Beast King has to offer." The vassals bowed deeply, their bows filled with such reverence that any of them seemed likely to break down in tears at any moment.

This display started to make Ruri a trifle worried for the rest of her stay. She was told that the nation was incredibly spirit-religious, but their love for the spirits seemed far more than what she bargained for.

"I understand your elation," started Arman, "but just how long do you intend to make the Beloved stand around? Show her to her quarters."

The people trembling in joy at the prospect of meeting the supreme-level spirits came back to their senses upon hearing Arman's command.

"Ah, a thousand apologies. You must be quite tired from your long journey. Allow us to show you to your quarters right away," said the vassal. He clapped his hands and summoned several women. They were clad in a completely different manner than anyone in the Nation of the Dragon King. They sported dresses less exposing than Celestine's outfit and more akin to indigenous garb than textbook garments. They proceeded to show Ruri to where she would be staying.

As Ruri walked around and looked at her new surroundings, they came to a halt in front of a door.

"This will be your quarters, Lady Beloved," the woman said. She explained that the room, which was in the back of the castle, was the safest and most well-secured area in the entire place. Perhaps it was the incomplete resolution of the Church of God's Light incident playing a part, but Ruri felt an odd sense of tension crackling through the air—or maybe it was just her imagination.

The woman slowly opened the door and showed her inside.

The scenery that popped out at Ruri as soon as she entered the room made her want to turn tail and run away. The room was large and expansive—hard to believe it was meant for just one person. An Arabian motif ran throughout the entire room, including its sophisticated, custom-made furniture and goods. It was apparent that this room was made for high-class guests of royalty.

However, that wasn't the problem. Lined up in a row within the room were several women, both knees on the floor in prostration.

The women heard Ruri open the door and all greeted her in unison. "Hello and welcome, Lady Beloved!"

That perfectly coordinated greeting scared the daylights out of Ruri. She felt a mix of confusion over their actions and fear of not knowing what was happening.

"U-Um, who are these people...?"

"These people will be taking care of you during your stay in our kingdom, Lady Beloved. Our humblest apologies for there being so few in number. We attempted to choose only those who we could proudly present to your esteemed presence, but this is all we could gather... However, they are all capable of suiting your needs. They shall not inconvenience you in any way, shape, or form, so please rest at ease," the woman explained.

She was apologetic over the *small number* of girls, but there seemed to be at least twenty present. This many people acting as caretakers was far from *small*—it was huge.

"Oh, don't give it any worry. I'm your guest here, so one or two people will be plenty," Ruri said. She was actually baffled. What was she supposed to do with *twenty* caretakers?

"What are you saying, milady? This is paltry service when we have almost *fifty* caretakers assigned to our nation's Beloved."

"F-Fifty..." Ruri stammered, unable to contain her shock. She had maids acting as caretakers for her back at the Nation of the Dragon King, but only two or three who alternated shifts. Considering that she was perfectly capable of taking care of her own needs, the most she needed others to handle was cleaning her room and setting the table. She felt no sort of inconvenience at that.

Jade, being king, had a little more staff attending to his needs, but even then it was only about ten servants. Yet she was quoted *fifty*. It was an obscene number. What in the world would she even be *doing* to require that many people? Most of the servants would be left bored with nothing to do.

"Please, do not feel reserved; utilize our services however you please. We are all honored to serve you for what short time you shall be staying in our humble kingdom, Lady Beloved," said one of the servants.

The women all lifted their heads, looking at Ruri with glittering sparkles in their eyes. The mixture of reverence and adoration in their expressions proved that the woman's words were as honest as honest could be.

The difference in treatment between this nation and the Nation of the Dragon King was so extreme that it simply left Ruri feeling shocked and uneasy.

6 The Second Day

On the morning of Ruri's second day in the Nation of the Beast King, she was awoken by the presence of several other people in the room with her. She looked around to see a group of women standing by her bedside. It wasn't clear how long they'd been there, but they all stood in silence, simply staring at her. Ruri couldn't help but flinch.

Startled wide awake in an instant, Ruri jumped up in surprise. "Wh-What's going on?!" she screamed.

Also in the room were the many caretakers assigned to her. They were filed in behind the women standing by her bedside, eagerly awaiting Ruri to awake.

"Good morning, Lady Beloved," said one of them with a sweet smile.

As if in adherence to that, all the other servants said in unison, "Good morning, Lady Beloved."

Ruri felt a headache coming on despite the early hour. That was when one of the girls presented her with a pail of water. Ruri looked up at her in bewilderment, unsure of what to do with the bucket thrust in front of her.

"This is hot water from the springs of the Nation of the Beast King, milady. Please, use this to wash your face. It will surely make your skin smooth and soft."

The words "skin," "smooth," and "soft" instantly blew away the pain in Ruri's head. Normally, she would clean her face and teeth with Purification magic, but in the Nation of the Beast King, they usually used the hot springs to wash their face in lieu of magic. Upon closer inspection, Ruri could see that the skin of all the girls in her room seemed rather immaculate. The idea of it being a result of the spring water sent her hopes sky-high. If she wanted silky smooth results, then the hot spring water was her best bet.

As soon as she washed her face with the water from the pail, another woman handed her a towel to dry herself with. Once that was finished, the women immediately started to strip her of her sleepwear. Ruri's eyes widened in surprise, but before she could object, they'd unclothed her and started dressing her in new apparel.

At first they were going to put her in something more revealing like Celestine's outfit, the typical local attire, but she stood firm against it, opting to wear the simple, short-sleeved dress she brought with her from the Nation of the Dragon King. However, the ladies even assisted her into *that*.

After dressing her, they combed her hair for her—the caretakers were truly pulling out all the stops. It started to make Ruri feel like some sort of pampered princess. Granted, since she was a Beloved, the royal treatment was probably only natural. After all, Celestine apparently had a slew of attendants assigned to her. However, since Ruri wasn't used to being treated in this manner, she felt *hugely* embarrassed.

Since her experience with other Beloveds was limited, Ruri didn't know if this or the Nation of the Dragon King's way was standard practice for Beloveds. She tried to recall how Cerulanda's former Beloved, Azelda, had been received, but Ruri had only really met her when she went to stop her rampages back at the castle. Considering she had no idea what kind of life Azelda led, she couldn't use her as a frame of reference.

"Your breakfast is ready, milady," said the attendant.

In the corner of the room, dishes were lined up on top of a beautiful, intricately designed tapestry. Unlike the tables and chairs used in the Nation of the Dragon King, the Nation of the Beast King's style was to eat sitting atop a tapestry laid out on the floor. Ruri was raised in a land where it was tradition to sit on the floor on their knees, so she had no aversion to eating in this manner. But as she sat as instructed, she could feel the strong difference between this nation's culture and that of the Nation of the Dragon King.

They must have brought the food in while Ruri was getting ready because it was still piping hot. The assortment and the amount present was big enough to feed everyone in her room, much less Ruri herself, and she wondered if the others would eat too. But once she saw no one aside from Kotaro, Rin, and Chi was sitting with her, it confirmed that all this food was meant for her alone. Then again, perhaps they figured that Kotaro and the others would be joining her. In fact, Chi was raring to eat. Nevertheless, this was still a little *too much* food. Even with Ruri and Chi both digging into the meal, there was still a lot left over.

Also, just like Joshua mentioned, the spice-laden dishes were a bit too rich for breakfast. This could cause issues if it was going to be a daily occurrence. Ruri proceeded to eat, but she picked out the lighter foods and avoided the heavier ones.

As Ruri sat full and satisfied, taking a post-meal breather, one of the attendants offered her a suggestion. "Lady Beloved, I was informed that you were greatly interested in our nation's hot springs. Would you care to take a visit?"

"Absolutely!" Ruri replied instantly. This was her initial goal, after all. It wasn't long before she headed toward what was considered the biggest and most luxurious hot spring in the castle, reserved exclusively for royalty.

There were a multitude of bathhouses in the castle—ones for royalty, ones for the queens, and ones for the castle workers. The bathhouses for royalty and the queens were especially ample in variety, each with different interiors. Since the bathhouses for royalty were open to Beloveds as well, Ruri gladly took the chance to utilize one of them.

Considering that Ruri also had her caretaking attendants and her guard detail—Joshua, Ewan, and the dragonkin soldiers—the walk to the bathhouse wound up being quite the mass migration. Once there, Joshua and the other men stopped and held at the entrance since they couldn't follow her inside. But the problem lied with Kotaro and the others. Rin always spoke in a feminine manner, so it was probably safe to assume that she was female. Maybe it was also safe to assume that Kotaro and Chi were male since they spoke pretty manly. However, there were always cases like Euclase.

Ruri was at an extreme loss, but she decided to ask them anyway. "Hey, so, what about all of you? Are you coming with? Staying out here?"

"I'm going with you, Ruri," Kotaro replied.

"Of course we're going with you," Rin added.

"I wanna take a dip in the springs," Chi said.

All three were eager to follow her.

"I don't mind if you all come along, but what are you guys? Male? Female?" If they answered with male, then, as much as it would pain her, she would have to make them wait outside with Joshua and the rest.

Chi replied, *"We ain't either."*

Ruri cocked her head at the vague response, but Rin came fluttering in. *"Spirits don't have the concept of sex or gender. We're technically neither male nor female, so you don't need to worry."*

"Oh, I see," Ruri said, satisfied with that answer. She proceeded to bring Kotaro, Rin, and Chi inside with her.

The bathhouse was rife with the evocative aroma only hot springs could provide. The bath itself was massive and seemed to be great for a nice, long soak. Ruri slowly dipped her toe into the water to check the temperature. Finding it just right, she dipped herself in up to her elbows.

"Aaah, this feels wonderful~"

The spirits then followed her into the bath. Kotaro and Rin were first, followed by Chi—who rambunctiously dove into the water with a loud splash. They all seemed delighted.

"Lady Beloved, how does the temperature fare?"

"It's perfect. No complaints here. It's heavenly~"

"I'm relieved it's to your liking, milady."

It'd been so long since Ruri had taken a bath in a hot spring that she forgot how great it felt. The sense of relief and comfort from soaking in the hot water was indescribable. The people of the Nation of the Dragon King were *definitely* missing out. It made her want to build a hot spring there so she could share this splendor with them. She was positive they would all get hooked once they experienced it firsthand.

Ruri's hot spring fever was starting to climb higher and higher. "I want this in the Nation of the Dragon King *toooo*! I'm building one once I get back."

"*Hear, hear!*" chanted Rin and Chi, both comprehending how great hot springs could be after soaking in one. Kotaro didn't seem opposed to it either. Judging from how he was smiling, his body submerged up to his neck, it seemed the hot spring suited his fancy. They were all enjoying it in their own way. Kotaro and Rin silently soaked while Chi swam all over the place like it was his own personal pool.

By the time Ruri's body warmed up, one of her caretakers addressed her. "Lady Beloved, preparations are set if you wouldn't mind stepping out of the bath."

Ruri had noticed the women bustling around for a while now, but it appeared that whatever they were preparing was ready. Staying in the bath for too long was bound to make her light-headed anyway, so she stepped out of the water as instructed. That was when she saw the cot the women had laid out for her.

"Would you mind lying down here?" one of them asked. Ruri followed instructions and sprawled facedown on the cot.

"Now then, pardon me as I proceed," the caretaker said as she applied a thick, sweet-smelling oil onto Ruri's body and started a massage. Her technique was so good you'd suspect she was a professional masseuse. Ruri felt like she was in some high-class spa as the oil's delightful scent relaxed her tense body.

"This feels so extravagant..."

As Ruri lay on the cot, absorbed in sheer bliss, Chi came trotting up, brimming with curiosity. "*Hey, hey! I wanna try that too!*"

"Oh, would you? Step up here, please."

As soon as Chi lay down, the woman lathered him in the same oil as Ruri and proceeded to massage his capybara body.

"*Ooh!*" he exclaimed from the pleasure.

"I'm so glad we're taking this trip," Ruri said. This was an invaluable treat that she couldn't experience in the Nation of the Dragon King, and it was one that she wished to spread there as well. Massages might already exist, but if anything, she wanted this kind of high-class spa. Euclase would probably know about beauty treatments like that. She decided to ask when she got back.

As such, Ruri closed her eyes in delight, with hopes that Euclase would help her build a hot spring of her very own.

The Misunderstanding

After her bath and beauty treatment, which greatly satisfied her mind and body, Ruri returned to her room with a glut of people trailing behind her. Chi headed out with the other spirits to go explore the castle, but Kotaro and Rin stayed by her side.

As she strolled down the hallway, she saw several women walking over from the opposite side. Two of the women clearly led the pack. They were dressed in extremely revealing clothes and decked out in lavish jewelry. Several other women followed behind them, one of which seemed to be carrying a pail of some kind.

Ruri wasn't paying them much mind, but the two ladies in front glared at her for a second. Ruri's eyes sprang open in confusion, but since she wasn't familiar with either woman, she let it drop. However, out of the corner of her eye, she saw the woman with the pail hand it over to one of the lavishly dressed women.

As she went to pass by the group, one of the women quickly stuck out her leg. "Whoa!" Ruri exclaimed, the action happening too fast for her to dodge. She tripped and lurched forward. Convinced she was going to fall, she braced for the imminent pain of hitting the floor, but Kotaro's winds softly dropped her to the ground instead.

Ruri's relief was short-lived, however, as a massive amount of water came pouring down on her from overhead. It wasn't just any water either—it was dirty water that emanated an intensely foul odor. Fortunately, Kotaro's barrier was still in place around her, assuring that not even one drop touched Ruri's body. Even so, an assaulting odor wafted through the air as the dirty water formed puddles around her.

The woman discarded the now empty pail where she stood. It hit the ground with a set of hollow clunks that echoed through the hallway.

Ruri was dumbfounded by what just happened. That was when she heard the woman's shrill laugh from overhead.

"Oh dear, pardon me. It seems my hand slipped." The woman sneered spitefully at Ruri from above, denoting that this was not a mere accident but an intentional act of ill will. "Still, lying there in such a pathetic stupor suits you quite well."

"*Excuse me*? Who are you?" Ruri asked, glaring up at them.

"Oh, how scary," the woman replied in a contrived manner.

The woman's attitude was doing an excellent job of pushing Ruri's buttons. This was the first time she'd met any of them, so there was absolutely no reason for them to treat her this way.

"What's the big idea out of nowhere?" she asked.

"We're simply teaching the newcomer to learn her place on the pecking order," replied the woman. "You must come from a rather exalted family in the Nation of the Dragon King to become the king's bride, but don't get too ahead of yourself. Your family's status doesn't mean a thing here. What's important is how capable you are of winning His Majesty's affection."

The other woman added, "If you think that someone as *scrawny* as yourself could ever serve by His Majesty's side, then you are sorely mistaken. His Majesty prefers more *voluptuous* bodies like ours."

"Uh, what?" Ruri hadn't the foggiest idea what she meant. She assumed that "His Majesty" referred to the Beast King, but she couldn't figure out what his preferences had to do with herself. Also, it was surprising to see them accost a Beloved, especially since the people of the Nation of the Beast King were supposed to be oh-so-devoted to the spirits.

Ruri's attendants standing behind her all went pale, paralyzed from witnessing the situation. Joshua and the other dragonkin also remained frozen, too afraid from Kotaro and Rin's display of anger to act without prudence. Ruri was unscathed thanks to Kotaro's assistance, but the mere act of trying to inflict harm on Ruri was enough to earn Kotaro's ire. The stare he delivered to the group of women was harsh and brutal.

"What's going on here?" asked a voice from farther down the hall, grabbing everyone's attention. When they looked, there stood Arman, an expression of bewilderment on his face.

Arman's gaze wandered over everyone standing petrified, fell to Ruri on the ground, and then stopped at the two women standing in front of her. He fired a sharp glare their way.

Rin flapped her tiny wings over to the Beast King, addressing him. *"Hey, Beast King. Is this how you educate the people in your castle? Throwing dirty water over the head of a Beloved after they tried to trip her? All right in front of us? Are they trying to pick a fight? Because I'll give it to them ten times what they're dishing out."*

"Ten times isn't good enough. Make it a hundred," said Kotaro.

"Can we go get them?"

Arman grimaced as the two spirits readied themselves to strike at any moment. "I see. You have my apologies. I assure you that I'll handle this matter." He looked over to the two women who were baselessly attacking Ruri. Both his look and his tone were reproachful as he said, "Explain yourselves, the both of you."

The two women flinched momentarily, but they quickly curled their lips into a flirtatious pair of smiles and approached Arman. "Oh my, Your Majesty, explain what?"

"What were you both doing? And by that, I mean, what were you doing to the young lady over there?"

"There were rumors among the harem that you summoned a new bride from the Nation of the Dragon King. We were just giving our romantic rival a bit of a *warning*; that's all," said the first woman.

"But never mind that, Your Majesty. I'd like it ever so much if you were to stop by my room today," said the other woman in a coquettish voice as she tried to cuddle her voluptuous body against Arman.

Arman shook off her advances. "A new bride? What are either of you talking about?"

"Oh dear, why might you be so upset? You never try to interject when the queens normally quarrel."

"Does she suit your fancy that much?"

The two women glared straight at Ruri. Their pensive faces, altogether different from how they greeted Arman, made Ruri wince in surprise.

"Do either of you know what it is you've done?" Arman asked, giving both ladies a stern look.

"Why, what do you mean?"

"She isn't a new bride; she's the Beloved of the Nation of the Dragon King, under our care by request of the Dragon King himself. So, I ask again, do either of you know what it is you've done to a Beloved of the spirits?"

The ladies didn't understand what Arman was saying at first as they stared at him with blank looks, but they gradually wrapped their heads around his words. They looked at Ruri, then at Arman, and then back at Ruri again. Their faces drained of all color and their lips trembled as the realization finally set in.

"Wait… That can't be…"

"A Beloved? This whelp…err, I mean, woman?"

"That's right. She is a Beloved, just like Celestine."

The two ladies appeared to be scared—*terrified*, in fact—as they gasped and immediately dropped to their hands and knees, prostrating themselves before Ruri.

"O-O-Our humblest apologies!"

"Please, forgive us, milady!"

The two of them apologized profusely, practically rubbing their foreheads against the floor as they quaked in their shoes.

Arman looked down at them with a piercing gaze. "Do you think you can just apologize for trying to harm a Beloved? You'd both best prepare to face a suitable punishment to quell the spirits' rage." Both of them yelped in fear, bowing their heads and pleading with Arman, but he simply looked at Ruri and heartlessly asked, "Ruri, what do you want to do?"

Ruri found it difficult to speak up right away. "By that you mean...?"

"Dealing with these two. Since they've assaulted a Beloved, I think torturing them, lopping off their heads, and sticking them on pikes near the castle gates would be a proper punishment, but..."

Ruri's eyes widened in shock once she heard Arman call that a "proper" punishment. "No, no, no! That's way overboard for just tripping me and splashing some water on me! Not only that, but they didn't even succeed. If they just apologize and swear never to do it again, I think that will—"

Before she could finish her sentence, Arman interrupted her. "No, we can't do that. Even if it was a misunderstanding, they assaulted a Beloved. If I didn't punish them at all, then it would set a bad example for anyone else. I told you that we're a devout nation, didn't I? Anyone who tries to inflict harm on a Beloved becomes an enemy in the eyes of everyone in the nation. If they were to get off scot-free, it would incite riots."

"In that case, please give them a more moderate punishment—one less *bloody*, okay?" Knowing that heads would fly over something so insignificant wouldn't sit well with Ruri's mental health. She had been in such a good mood after taking a dip in the springs that it was a shame that nothing she did now could keep her mood from plummeting into the ground.

"Moderate, eh? That isn't going to be easy. Hmm, I know. You're both banished from the castle. I can't very well have you sitting as my 'queens' when you'd lay hands on a Beloved."

Both ladies slumped their shoulders in disappointment, but it was better than losing their heads.

"And the both of you will be offered to Kahste and Dobza instead. And divorce will *not* be an option."

The moment those names were mentioned, not only did the pair of women gasp and go deathly pale, but so did all of Ruri's attendants.

Noticing that something in the air had changed, Ruri looked around at everyone's faces. The people of the Nation of the Dragon King seemed to be just as clueless as Ruri was, but they could figure out that neither person mentioned was good news based on the atmosphere.

Once they heard they were being given away, the pair clung to Arman.

"No, please! Anything but that! Please, send us to anybody aside from them!"

"We don't want to go there! Please!"

Arman looked down at the two women pleading on top of one another with a cold stare as he apathetically continued, "Then, should I throw you both out into town? You're major criminals now that you've attacked a Beloved. Once all the believers in town eventually catch word of what you've done, they'll surely punish you—likely ripping you both limb from limb."

Ruri thought that Arman was being far too severe over something that left Ruri unscathed, but to the people of the Nation of the Beast King, it wasn't severe enough. A huge number of citizens saw spirits as religious figures and were extremely devout, meaning their respect and adoration for the spirits and Beloveds was immense. Anyone harming a Beloved was practically a disaster to them. It was an act equal to treason, and anyone playing a part in it would be considered a major criminal—an enemy to the people. That meant that even if they acted on another nation's Beloved or the plot ended in failure, a pack of devout followers would literally tear them apart.

"Eek!" they yelped.

"Choose," Arman demanded.

Their lives were clearly more important. Neither even needed time to think as they both quickly accepted their fates.

"As you command, Sire," they said, bowing.

Ruri was curious as to why the two people mentioned were so disliked. She whispered to a nearby caretaker, "Hey, so what are these people like if they're disliked *that* much?"

The caretaker whispered back an explanation. "Well, Master Kahste and Master Dobza are both nobles who serve the castle, but..." She hesitated a moment. "Master Kahste is what you would call a 'mama's boy' and does whatever his mother tells him. And his mother is quite a nasty...erm, *strict* individual. She nitpicks and heckles into submission any bride that comes her son's way, so his divorces range into the double digits. Once she finds out that the new bride bestowed to her son caused harm to a Beloved, she will inevitably bully them until their dying days. Since Master Kahste is completely loyal to his mother, he would likely come *defending* her rather than his own wife."

"Yeesh, he sounds terrible."

"Master Dobza, simply put, is a miserly individual, extraordinarily obsessed with saving money. He scrimps and saves everything in spite of being a nobleman. Due to his hyperfixation on saving, he leads a life more destitute than even the most common of commoners. I believe it would take a huge toll on someone coming from the lap of luxury as one of the king's queens."

"They are the two people that absolutely *no one* who works in the castle wishes to marry," added another of the women.

The caretaker women clamored in agreeance, none of them sparing any sympathy for the two women slated to marry such husbands. No one seemed to consider this punishment for simply tripping someone too extreme.

"However, I'd say they're quite lucky that this is their only punishment for harming a Beloved."

"Yes, I quite agree."

"Boy, not even a day in without a mess on our hands," said Ewan as he walked closer to Ruri.

Ruri just stared at him in the face.

"What?" he asked.

"Well, I was just thinking that I'm glad you're not from the Nation of the Beast King, Ewan."

"Where's this coming from?"

"Well, I mean, in this nation, heads fly if I so much as trip over someone. If this were you, you'd have lost your head—three times, might I add."

Ewan paused. "Yeah, maybe so," he said with a mortified look, nervously rubbing at his neck.

They were friends now, but Ewan used to snap and hurl all sorts of abuse at Ruri when they first met. If he acted out in such a way in the Nation of the Beast King, he most likely wouldn't walk away with a slap on the wrist. Even if Ruri's tolerance excluded him from being punished, there was always the possibility of a spirit-faithful person assassinating him. In terms of Ruri's mental health and Ewan's well-being, it was probably for the best that they lived in the peaceful Nation of the Dragon King instead.

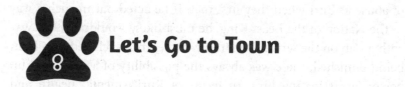

Let's Go to Town

That night after the fight in the hallway, a banquet was held to welcome the guests from the Nation of the Dragon King. It was supposed to be an opportunity to introduce Ruri and make her presence as a Beloved known to everyone. No one, not even Arman, expected that anyone would mistakenly accost her before things could get off the ground.

The women responsible for this mishap were two of Arman's nineteen wives. Both of them were sent off to the houses of their new husbands. And while they didn't directly involve themselves, their attendants were sent to work hard labor without pay.

Arman once again apologized to Ruri. As she shyly accepted the apology, Celestine, who was sitting nearby, scolded Arman.

"This is all your fault to begin with for not telling any of your wives, Master Arman."

"Come on, give me a break. How was I supposed to know they were going to mistake Ruri for a new wife? I swear, who was even spreading that kind of misinformation?"

"From what I've heard, since you prepared Lady Ruri's room close to your own, your wives assumed you were ushering in a main wife, an assumption that ended up spreading to everyone else in the harem."

Arman had many wives, but they were all part of the harem. He still hadn't decided on a main wife. Because of that, his queens would brashly knock one another down a peg on a daily basis.

"That's most likely why they quickly tried to put the woman who might be your main wife in her place."

Arman let out a deep sigh.

"You never rebuke your wives for their actions, which leads to some of them being quick to fly off the handle like that. I assume they did what they did because they knew you wouldn't reprimand them, as always."

"Is this a common occurrence?" asked Ruri.

Celestine looked at Arman with a glare as cold as the tundra. "Quite so. Master Arman here finds the spectacle of his wives vying for his affection *fun*. Tasteless, if you ask me."

"Hey, listen, all my wives just so happen to be strong-willed, and they don't take defeat lying down, so it's fun to watch them go at it," Arman explained.

"A source of fun that ended up being quite the inconvenience for Lady Ruri, yes."

"I know, and I'm sorry for that. Either way, now that we've properly introduced her, I doubt anyone will make the same stupid mistake again, so just relax." Arman's wives were also in attendance at this banquet. Since Ruri was given a proper introduction, the misinformed rumors would likely cease.

"While you have the opportunity, you should instruct your wives to act in moderation from now on. Otherwise, I don't want to see you when they end up bullying the woman you eventually do want as your main wife into running away. You will come to regret not acting sooner, I assure you."

"Oh brother. Okay, okay. I get it. I'll make sure to talk to them," Arman replied. It seemed that not even the mighty Beast King could keep face before Celestine.

Some time had passed since Ruri arrived in the Nation of the Beast King, and she had spent all of it hopping around to all the hot springs in the castle—the mineral sand bath, the steam bath, the outdoor bedrock bath, the cascading bath... That combined with the full-body treatments and massages made it feel like a real vacation to Ruri. However, the daily immersion in the hot springs was starting to wear thin for one individual—Chi.

"*Say, I'm sick and tired of hot springs now. Let's go to town!*" he said, rolling on the floor and flailing his arms like a spoiled child.

Ruri figured that Chi, being the bundle of curiosity he was, would eventually become bored with the hot springs, and it seemed that time had finally come. She could understand how he felt. Now that she had visited nearly all of the springs in the castle, she was starting to feel the urge to do something else. Like, for example, sightseeing, sightseeing, and most importantly—sightseeing. Chi wasn't the only one who wanted to go into town. Ruri felt the same. However, as far as safety was concerned, she couldn't simply go out and about.

"I sympathize, but I don't think it'll fly. The business with the Church of God's Light isn't wrapped up yet, so it'll mean big trouble if I go to someplace filled with people and get assaulted, don't you think?"

"*We'll all be with you, so don't worry. Wind has got his barrier around you, so no mere human could put even a scratch on you. Wind, Water? You guys are coming, right?*" Chi asked.

"*Of course!*" replied Kotaro and Rin in resounding agreement.

"Hmm, be that as it may, I'm pretty sure the Beast King wouldn't approve."

"All you need is permission, right? All righty then, time to go and get it!" Chi said, leading the charge.

"Worst-case scenario, we'll just have to do a little bit of threatening," Rin said ominously.

"Wait a second! Ah, great…" Ruri trailed off before she had a chance to stop Rin. Both she and Chi promptly left the room. Ruri chased after them in a panic, and Kotaro followed behind.

Chi and Rin quickly disappeared from sight. Ruri looked around while asking Kotaro for directions on their whereabouts. When she finally found them, Rin, with her eyes so red and round, and Chi, with his eyes so mean and sunken, were right in the middle of staring down Arman.

"Hey, c'mon, and cough it up!" said Chi.

"Quit complaining and give us permission," said Rin.

"Well, I get that, but, uh…" Arman trailed off, grimacing. He was somewhat pale from the spirits' insistence.

There was a group of people around Arman who seemed to be his aides, but they simply stood in a state of bewilderment, not interjecting in the slightest. Once they spotted Ruri, they threw her a pleading look, practically begging her to alleviate the situation.

Both Rin and Chi menacingly inched closer and closer to Arman—now a hair's breadth from his face.

Ruri sighed in exasperation. "Rin, Chi, don't inconvenience the Beast King."

Though Rin and Chi seemed to have noticed Ruri's presence, their glares remained focused on Arman.

"But, Ruri, he just won't give us permission. He keeps grumbling about it being 'dangerous' and whatnot," Rin explained.

"We're telling ya it'll be fine since we'll be with her, so give us the okay. C'mon, out with it."

"Yes, but, Ruri would be going to town with you, wouldn't she?" Arman pleaded.

"*Well, of course she would,*" stated Rin. "*You said it yourself that the matter with the Church of God's Light isn't resolved yet, so there's no way we'd leave Ruri unattended when danger could be looming at every corner. If we go, so does Ruri.*"

"In the interest of avoiding any danger the Church of God's Light might pose, we'd like it if Ruri stayed safe behind the castle walls," offered Arman.

The Church of God's Light was after Beloveds. There was no real problem with the spirits taking a leisurely stroll around town, but Ruri going out seemed to be an issue.

"*What are you talking about?*" Rin refuted. "*That raider infiltrated this very castle and assaulted your Beloved, didn't they? In that case, it doesn't make a big difference if she's behind the castle walls or out and about in town.*"

Arman's face twitched at Rin's comment. It seemed that hit him where it hurt. However, it was true that a raider not only descended upon the castle but made it all the way to Celestine, the person with the heaviest security detail. While their means of entering the castle was uncovered and dealt with, it was still unknown as to how much that helped circumvent. The thing that provided the most *definite* protection for both Ruri and Celestine was the sturdy barrier Kotaro put in place.

"*The safest place for Ruri isn't in the* castle, *it's with* us," Rin said.

"*Hear, hear. Also, Wind's got his barrier in place, so goin' into town should be absolutely A-OK. So, we can go out, right? Right~?*" Chi said, agreeing with Rin.

Arman silently contemplated this for a bit. Then he scratched his head and let out a long sigh of resignation. "Fine, then. But I want to assign soldiers to protect Ruri as well, so give me about an hour, please."

"*Sure thing. We can wait,*" said Chi.

"*Hooray!*" exclaimed Rin.

As Ruri watched Chi and Rin practically jump for joy, she worriedly asked Arman, "Are you positively sure about this?"

"My hands are tied. A *free* spirit is the only kind of spirit. They aren't worried about human affairs nor can they be bound by anyone. That's simply how spirits operate. They only had enough consideration to come here and get my permission."

"True. 'Freedom' does seem to be everyone's middle name."

Spirits were self-centered and acted to satisfy their own interests. They were very clear about their preferences and never concerned themselves with human matters. The only person a spirit cared about was a Beloved or their contract-bearer. Chi and Rin only came to Arman because Ruri said she couldn't leave the castle without his permission. It was out of consideration for Ruri, not Arman.

"Perhaps I should disguise myself, just in case? If I just bring Rin, Chi, and Kotaro and leave the other obvious-looking spirits here, then no one should realize that I'm a Beloved. That might lessen concerns about me being targeted a little."

"Right," agreed Arman. "But if we go with hiding the fact that you're a Beloved, then I'd like it if Lord Kotaro could stay behind, if possible. With all due respect, he *does* stand out in both size and appearance. It doesn't seem like many in the Nation of the Beast King know that the Beloved of the Nation of the Dragon King keeps a large white wolf—nor many in the Nation of the Dragon King itself, for that matter. So, based on that, I think it should be fine, but…"

"*I refuse to be the only one left behind!*" Kotaro interjected promptly, not wanting to be abandoned.

Ruri and Arman both looked as if they expected this reaction.

"I'll try to make it so that you can walk through town as safe as possible. Granted, I doubt you'd have any issues with that many supreme-level spirits attending you," said Arman.

"*Of course we won't. No danger shall befall Ruri while I am around,*" Kotaro said, his head held high.

Ruri had confidence in Kotaro in that regard, but the uncertain element here was actually Chi. He had a habit of following where his curiosity took him and ending up lost. Regardless of whether Kotaro was there, searching for him in a completely unfamiliar place was going to be extremely difficult. Ruri decided to pay careful attention to him—*very* careful attention.

The Effects of Dragon's Blood

9

While Arman was stationing his troops in the city, Ruri was getting herself ready. She put on her pair of glasses, her brown wig, and a robe that could completely hide her from head to toe. She also draped Kotaro in a hooded cloak as well since it would cause a huge commotion if anyone realized that he was a sacred beast from the Nation of the Spirit King.

Ruri and her crew were now all set, but there was again discontent—this time coming from the smaller spirits. Once she told them that they had to stay at the castle because it would immediately out her as a Beloved, she was met with a chorus of "ugh"s and "I wanna go"s. She only managed to convince them to stay by saying she would buy them all a present from town.

With everything settled and their preparations finally set, they headed out to town. Their group consisted of Kotaro, Rin, and Chi, as well as Joshua and Ewan. All things considered, it looked like a trio of travelers from the Nation of the Dragon King and their merry band of pets. The other dragonkin were there as well, but they were apparently keeping guard incognito.

Ruri went into town quite nervous and on edge, but unlike Celestine, who was a familiar face in these parts, Ruri's presence didn't garner any attention in particular. If anything, Joshua, Ewan, and Kotaro with his huge body were drawing the most amount of eyes.

The vast majority of dragonkin were specimens of beauty, and Joshua and Ewan were no exceptions to that rule. As they strolled around town, most of the ladies eyed the attractive pair. However, it seemed the dragonkin presence emanating from their bodies made it hard for people to approach them. The several ladies, their cheeks flushed, kept their distance and looked only from afar.

With humans, they either had weak mana or no mana whatsoever, so their ability to perceive mana was just as weak. Few humans who stood before dragonkin were left fearful or awestruck by their presence. The Nation of the Beast King, however, was a land inhabited by demi-humans. Perhaps it was because most of the people around sensed the presence of dragons about, but not a single person even tried to come up to them. In fact, they kept a set distance away. Thanks to that, it was extremely easy to notice if anyone up to no good was trying to approach.

The differences between the Nation of the Dragon King and Beast King's royal capitals were endless, but a point they shared was in how active and bustling both cities were. As you would expect of a tourist attraction, there seemed to be a lot of sightseeing travelers around.

Ruri found that the shops offered a large selection of souvenirs, but what stood out the most were the standing banners that read "Beloved Approved" or "Beloved by the Beloved." While this made sense for items like clothes and jewelry, items like bread, confections, dishware, and cosmetics—any and everything that Celestine ever consumed or used—were being paraded as Beloved-related merchandise. But it didn't stop there. There were cookies baked in the shape of Celestine's face and even "Beloved Candies" with the same shade of green as Celestine's hair. Droves of people were taking their pick and buying it up.

"This is kind of, uh, how do I put this? This kind of feels like they're putting *too much* of her private life on display. It feels icky."

It wasn't clear how this information had been leaked, but everything around seemed to be the type of stuff you could only know if you knew about Celestine's daily life. The thought of other people knowing everything from what you had for breakfast that morning to your everyday necessities left Ruri feeling averse to the idea.

"It is what it is," Joshua started, "since the Nation of the Beast King attracts people in with their hot springs and their Beloved. And the Beloved is pretty tolerant of the bandwagon merch if it helps the nation prosper. This nation is very spirit-religious, so they have a strong adoration for their Beloved and want to use whatever they might use themselves. You have some experience with people doing that, don't you, Ruri?"

"More or less," Ruri replied. She recalled the phenomenon of people buying up everything she ate during her walks through the Nation of the Dragon King's capital. Since she was technically an object of worship, it was bound to happen, but it was probably even more intense here in the Nation of the Beast King.

"It probably won't get as overblown as it is here, but it won't be too long before the Nation of the Dragon King has its own bandwagon merch too."

"I'm not sure how to take that."

The signs were already there. The good luck charms and scent pouches that Amarna sold were good examples. The more shrewd business owners would probably try to capitalize off of the healthy sales Amarna's trinkets brought in by unanimously deciding to sell their own brand of Beloved-based merchandise. Ruri would probably need to make the same kind of allowances Celestine did if she were to ever let that happen.

Ruri and her group proceeded to leisurely stroll without issue. Thanks to that, Ruri was enjoying a comfortable tour around town, seeing the sights and relieving some of the tension from being so on-guard lately.

However, that was when a little girl came out from the crowd and walked up to Ruri and the others—no, more accurately, up to *Ewan*. Perhaps his dragonkin aura had hit her, because there was a twinge of fear on her face.

"Um, are you a dragonkin?" she asked.

"What of it?" Ewan responded. Assuming that she wanted to say something, he squatted down to her eye level.

Her eyes were initially filled with determination, but now she stood in front of Ewan with a pleading stare. "Blood… Give me your blood," she said. Her voice was shaky, but her message was clear.

The message caught Ewan completely by surprise, and he replied, "What are you talking about?"

"Please! Just a little!" the young girl desperately pleaded, clutching Ewan's sleeve. "It doesn't have to be a lot; just a little!"

"Stop this," Ewan said, shaking her off.

Ruri and the others silently looked on, but in the next instant, the girl bit her lip and reached into the bag slung across her shoulder. She pulled out a glinting silver object—a dagger—and swung it right at Ewan.

Ewan, being the dragonkin soldier that he was, wouldn't be caught dead being unable to dodge the attack of a single little girl. He effortlessly avoided the swing of her weapon, and then he grabbed her wrist and wrenched it. She winced in pain and dropped the dagger.

"What are you doing, girl?" Ewan asked, looking down at her with a piercing gaze.

The girl let out a tiny yelp. Her eyes filled with tears until she found herself unable to take it anymore and she broke down in sobs. "Waaaaah!" she wailed as hot streams of water poured from her face.

Ewan was the one who'd been assaulted, but at a glance, it looked like he was accosting an innocent young girl.

"Oh, boy~ You made her cry~" Ruri said.

"Naughty, naughty~" Joshua chimed in.

Ewan flinched at their teasing. "*Me*?! Why is this *my* fault?!"

Unable to stand Ewan's floundering, Ruri walked over to the girl and patted her consolingly on the back. As she did, a woman came rushing over.

"E-Excuse me, but did this girl just do something?"

"She assaulted me. With that knife," Ewan explained, pointing over to where the evidence—the single dagger—lay.

The woman's eyes widened and trembled. She then kneeled before Ewan and bowed her head. "Please accept my apologies!"

"You her mother?" Ewan asked.

Her face paled and she bowed deeply. "Yes, I am her mother."

"You can't just apologize it away," said Ewan. "I would have been fine, but one wrong step and she could have gotten seriously injured. What kind of parenting are you even doing? She tried to kill someone she's never even met."

"I wasn't!" screamed the crying girl. "You're wrong. I wasn't trying to kill you. I just wanted a little bit of your blood; that's all."

"Just a 'little bit'? Why, you…"

"Ewan, hold it," Ruri interjected, interrupting Ewan's angry and exasperated rebuttal before it could get started. "We might want to take this someplace else." They were in the middle of the street, and this mishap was drawing everyone's attention.

"Let's continue this conversation once we've moved," Ewan said after taking a look around them.

"In that case, I humbly invite you to our house," said the mother. She stood up and took the crying child's hand.

The group followed her all the way to her home, a typical one-story house in the Nation of the Beast King.

"Now, get some tea ready for our guests. I'll go check on how your father is doing," the mother said as she proceeded to walk through a door in the back of the house.

Ruri and the others sat and waited for the young girl to prepare tea, and it wasn't long before her mother returned.

She once again bowed her head and apologized. "I am so very sorry for what happened to you. I shall make amends for it, so I humbly request that you forgive my daughter. She simply wanted to help save her father."

"What do you mean by that?" Ruri asked.

The mother's expression turned grim. "Her father is a carpenter. He took a big fall the other day and got pinned under some lumber. He sustained near-fatal wounds and we're not sure how long he has…"

"Oh, no…" Ruri said, trailing off.

"When the doctor told us that he's too far gone to help, he murmured something under his breath. He said, 'Maybe he could be saved if we had some dragon's blood, though.'"

Dragon's blood possessed incredible restorative properties. The medicine made from their blood had the power to immediately cure any wound. It was a fact that Ruri was informed of just recently.

"Of course, there's no way we could ever get our hands on any ourselves. We were told that dragon's blood can't be exported and can't be acquired by anyone—not even those in high authority. But then we overheard some people talking about how there were some travelers from the Nation of the Dragon King. The news must have spurred my daughter to take action. She was convinced that the dragon's blood would save her father, which is why…"

She tried to hurt someone, so it was an utterly brash and hasty decision, but it was hard to be mad at the girl considering her young and immature feelings.

"I am truly sorry." The girl's mother bowed earnestly.

Finally understanding the severity of her actions, the young girl also bowed deeply and apologized in a tiny voice. "I'm sorry…"

With both mother and child bowing before them, Ruri shot Ewan a look. Since Ewan was the one assaulted, it was appropriate that he decide the course of action. The girl seemed to be apologetic, so Ruri figured it was fine to let the matter drop.

Ewan seemed to be in agreement as his expression wasn't angry at all. "If you swear you'll never do something like this again, I'll forgive you," he said.

The girl raised her head and nodded profusely. "I…swear. I'm…sorry."

"Dragon blood is too strong to be used anyway," Joshua interjected. "It has to be processed into medicine first, and only dragonkin know how. Even if you had gotten some, you wouldn't have been able to use it."

Hearing that all of her efforts were ultimately pointless, the girl seemed crestfallen.

Ewan watched the girl slump in despair, and with sympathy he said, "Hey, Ruri, I've got a favor to ask."

"Thought you'd never ask!"

Ruri knew what Ewan was about to say, so she pulled out the goods from her pocket space—the goods being the small bottle of medicine made from dragon blood that Jade had given her. This instant cure-all medicine could help cure her father's wounds.

"Is the injured man in the back of the house?" Ruri asked.

"Um, yes, he is…" replied the mother, confused.

Ruri walked away on her own and proceeded to the door toward the back. Inside the room lay a man covered in bruises, wrapped from head to toe in bandages. He was unconscious and his breathing was shallow. One glance was enough to tell he was in critical condition.

"These are some terrible injuries," Ruri said. She opened the lid of the bottle and brought it near the man's mouth.

Before she poured it in, Joshua warned her, "Ruri, just *one drop*. That should be more than enough to cure him. If you give him any more, it'll end up poisoning him."

"Okay, I won't." She delicately tilted the bottle toward the man's mouth, being careful not to give him too much, and let a single droplet of the crimson liquid fall in.

The results were near instant. His visible wounds started to heal in the twinkle of an eye. The wounds hidden underneath the bandages were most likely closing up in similar fashion.

After getting permission from the little girl's mother, they took the bandages off of him just to be sure. His wounds underneath weren't completely healed yet, but they were on the fast track to recovery.

They all waited and watched in silence. Before long, the man's eyes fluttered a bit before slowly opening.

"Dear!"

"Dad!"

He was still only barely responsive, but the girl and her mother started to cry tears of joy.

Ruri hadn't doubted the effects of the medicine, but she was still astonished that the dragon's blood *really* ended up healing the man's wounds.

"Wow, its restorative powers are something else."

A single drop yielded this sort of effect. Ruri saw the dragonkin's restorative abilities on display all over again.

"If one drop does this, then I wonder what a whole bottle would do. Maybe it'd even bring back someone from the dead." She said it as a lighthearted joke, but there was a hint of seriousness to it as well because of how well the medicine was working.

Joshua heard that and smirked. "No way that could happen. It'd be too strong and they'd do just the opposite—they'd *die* instead. That's why you need to be careful handling that stuff, Ruri."

"Right." Ruri returned the bottle of medicine back to her pocket space and turned her eyes to the bed to see the girl in tears and clinging to her father. She watched the scene unfold, happy and warmhearted.

10 Rumors

"Truly, thank you for all you've done," said the mother.

Her daughter echoed her. "Thank you so much!"

Once Ruri had finished healing the father's wounds, she figured it was time they departed. Both the mother and daughter saw them off with deep, gracious bows. They also loaded her up with a heap of local gifts as tokens of appreciation.

"Oh, you shouldn't have," Ruri said gratefully. "Still, I would appreciate it if you kept the fact that we used dragon's blood a secret. It might end up being trouble later down the road."

"Very well," the mother agreed. "This secret stays with us. We are eternally indebted to you. Thank you *so* much for all you've done. I'm so glad we didn't have to resort to that shady religious group."

"Religious group?" Ruri repeated.

"Yes, after my husband had his accident, a person claiming to be a believer of the religion of something-or-other came to us and said they would help save him. He said, 'Our glorious leader has the power to resurrect the dead, so he can resurrect your husband should he die.' But he added, 'on the condition that you worship our god and swear your loyalty.'"

"Resurrect the dead...?"

"Yes. I certainly thought it was shady, but if my husband were to actually die, then I might've been left grasping for straws and accepting their offer."

Resurrecting the dead? Glorious leader? Those were words Ruri had heard all too recently.

"This religion? Was it called the 'Church of God's Light,' by any chance?" Ruri asked.

"Yes, I believe that was the name he gave."

Ruri, Joshua, and Ewan all looked at one another.

"When was this?! When did that person come to you?" Ruri asked, abruptly and loudly.

The mother flinched but continued. "Let's see. I believe it was about three days ago."

Three days meant there was a good chance they were still here in the capital.

"We should report this to the Beast King, don't you think?" Ruri suggested.

Joshua agreed. "Yeah, let's get back on the double."

After saying their goodbyes to the mother and her child, they made their way to the main street leading to the castle. But that was when Chi started whining.

"Aww, we're leaving already? We barely got to have any fun yet."

"We need to get back to the castle and report this, Chi," Ruri replied.

"Oh, come on, we can be just a little late."

Chi's unwillingness to cooperate was an issue. Ruri looked at Joshua and Ewan in hopes they would have a plan, but Joshua just shrugged and Ewan awkwardly smiled.

"No harm in making a little allowance, right?" said Ewan. "If we drag him back, we're just going to hear his complaints later."

Ruri could imagine Chi rolling around on the ground, grumbling and complaining, so she reconsidered her stance. "All right, but just for a little bit. We can always come back again later, after all."

89

"*Sure thing!*" said Chi.

And so they walked around town, following Chi so they wouldn't lose sight of him—which was a huge ordeal since he was a bundle of curiosity. He would dash over to any and all things that caught his eye. If they looked away for one second, they would immediately lose sight of him.

Fighting back the urge to return and report, Ruri wandered around town with the others until a certain stall caught her eye. The person attending it was someone Ruri had seen before. Shocked, she approached the stall, wondering why this person was here.

"Amarna-san... That is you, right?"

Yes, the one attending the stall was the woman who was supposed to be back in the Nation of the Dragon King's capital—Amarna.

Amarna looked at Ruri blankly, apparently not recognizing her with her glasses, wig, and hood.

"It's me. *Me*," Ruri said, taking off her glasses and sliding her wig off a bit before putting them right back on.

Amarna's eyes widened in surprise. "Oh my, Lady Bel—mgfh!"

Ruri rushed to cover Amarna's mouth before she could utter the rest of the title. She had come here in disguise, so Amarna loudly proclaiming that Ruri was a Beloved would put her in a world of trouble.

"I'm *Ruri*. Not Lady Be-you-know-what! *Understand*?!" Ruri warned. She waited for Amarna to give a couple of firm nods before she released her hand.

"So, Amarna-san, what are you doing here of all places? Did you move from the Nation of the Dragon King?"

"No, I didn't move. I'm here temporarily to study."

"Study?"

"Why, yes! The Nation of the Beast King's royal capital is the leader in selling merchandise with a Beloved's seal of approval, so I'm here, acquiring the know-how on how to sell Beloved merchandise. Once I return to the Nation of the Dragon King, I'll utilize that and rake in profit after profit..." Amarna trailed off into an eerie laugh as the prospect of money started to cloud her eyes.

"R-Right. Good luck with that."

"Thank you very much. Oh, that's right," Amarna said as if she remembered something. She stuck her palm out in front of Joshua with a sweet smile.

"What?" he asked.

"You still haven't repaid me for last time~"

Joshua's face scrunched up into a sneer as he pulled out a few coins and placed them on her outstretched palm.

Amarna looked at the bit of coin in dissatisfaction. "This is too little! Far too little!"

"What're you talking about? It's a reasonable amount. You do realize that those 'Reapers' the other day were imposters, right?"

"And might I ask what *you're* talking about? I said that there were people calling themselves Reapers in the capital. I technically never said they were *real*."

"Don't get *technical* with me."

Ruri wasn't exactly following their argument, but their familiar attitudes with one another suggested that they were already acquainted.

"Do you two know each other?" she asked.

"This is one of the informants I've been using," Joshua explained.

"Informant? Aren't you a vendor?"

"It's my side-job~" Amarna replied. The sweet and smiling woman didn't seem like she would be working a job as shady as an informant.

"I got my intel about the Reapers being in the Nation of the Dragon King and their hideout from her. Well, the Reapers ended up being bogus, but still," Joshua said, glaring at Amarna. He still felt some resentment for being fed fake information.

"I simply told you the information I gained without a single embellishment. What my clients parse from that information is solely up to them~"

"Well, don't *you* just have a way around words? Anyway, I'm not paying you a *single* coin more."

"Aww, is that any way to treat me? Here I am with new information too~"

Joshua looked at her, skeptical. "Don't tell me—*more* fake nonsense?"

Amarna brought her face up to Joshua's and whispered, "It's rumors about the Church of God's Light."

Ruri and the others shifted their brows in intrigue. Joshua gave her a look, prompting her to continue, but Amarna grinned from ear to ear and held out her palm. He was going to have to cough up the dough if he wanted to hear the rest.

Joshua bitterly and reluctantly plopped a few more coins on her palm. Amarna smiled in satisfaction and began to speak.

"Beyond the royal capital is a volcanic mountain called Mt. Ulawoon. One day, there was an incident in a village at the foot of that mountain—all the villagers started to die of unknown causes."

"Was it sickness? Or were they raided?" Ruri asked.

"No clue. I don't have many details. The village has always been closed off without much exchange with the outside world, so the causes are unclear. And considering it might be because of a pandemic, no one has dared to come near the village. They say the corpses were left to the elements and littered every street in the village."

Ruri envisioned that sight and shivered, rubbing her arms in discomfort.

"One year later, assuming the illness had died down, looters went to the village to steal anything left worth of value. When they did, for whatever reason, there wasn't a single corpse to be found and the villagers were walking like normal."

"So, they weren't dead after all?" asked Ruri.

"No," Amarna said, "they definitely died. But there they were—alive. Or rather, brought *back to life*."

"Brought back to life? No way." Ruri looked at her with obvious doubt.

"Do you think it's a tall tale? That village isn't the only one with news of people coming back from the dead. There are a few rumors of other villages where people who died of illness sprang back to life. And it's said that the person responsible for that miracle is the leader of a religion called the Church of God's Light."

"The Church of God's Light?!"

Just as Ruri started to wonder why she was bringing up villagers dying and coming back to life, Amarna linked it back to the Church of God's Light.

"Noah-kun talked about his 'leader' too. He said he could bring back the dead."

First, there was Noah who targeted Ruri in order to resurrect his dead parents. Then, there was the member of the Church of God's Light that visited the carpenter right after he was severely injured. However, Ruri wasn't willing to completely believe Amarna's story just yet. Bringing the dead back to life was something that even Kotaro and the other spirits said couldn't be done.

"So, just how much of that can we take as fact?" Ewan asked.

Amarna simply shrugged and replied, "No clue. I'm only going off rumors; I haven't bore witness for myself. However, the only thing that's for certain is that all of the rumors started from the small villages at the foot of Mt. Ulawoon. The stories have apparently been around for years now, but they never spread since those villages don't do much exchanging with others."

Ruri and everyone stood in silent contemplation. But all of the thinking in the world wasn't going to provide solutions.

"Why don't we try going to this village with the raised dead? We might be able to find some clues about the Church of God's Light," Ruri suggested.

At Ruri's feet, an extremely excited-looking Chi emphatically replied, "*Hey, now that sounds like fun. A village where the dead come back to life? Count me in. I gotta come for this!*"

"First, we go back to the castle and report," said Joshua. "This is the Nation of the Beast King, after all. We can't just act all willy-nilly as reps from the Nation of the Dragon King."

"*All right. Let's hurry back, then.*" Maybe it was because he had his sights set on a new playground now, but this time around, Chi didn't whine over going back to the castle.

"Okay, see you around, Amarna-san."

"Take care now~" Amarna said, waving her hand.

After saying their farewells to her, the group rushed back to the castle.

11 Testimony

After Ruri's group returned to the castle, they headed to Arman to give their report. Arman listened, a quizzical expression drawn over his face.

"A village of the raised dead?" he repeated. He didn't look the slightest bit convinced that what he was hearing was true. Then again, his reaction was only natural. Ruri and the others were half-skeptical themselves. No, actually, if they were to split hairs, they were *definitely* more skeptical than not.

"Yes, from what we were told. Have you heard anything of it, Sire?" asked Ruri.

"No, I haven't," replied Arman. "I do remember something from a few years ago about an epidemic wiping out a village close to the foot of the mountain, but no new reports since then."

"Noah-kun, the child arrested in the Nation of the Dragon King, said something about his leader bringing the dead back to life, so I think there might be a connection. Could we possibly go and check?"

"Hold on, hold on. Slow down there. You expect me to send you to a place where the Church of God's Light might be connected?"

"But, I'm concerned over this 'resurrecting the dead' business," Ruri continued. She was positive it was a downright lie since the spirits refuted the possibility, but she wanted to find out exactly *why* those rumors sprang up in the first place.

"Have you forgotten you were almost *killed*?! Don't just casually prioritize fulfilling your curiosity! And in the event an epidemic really did wipe out the villagers, what happens if you contract the same illness? I wouldn't be able to so much as look Jade in the eyes if something happened to you because you went on some trip to satisfy your interests."

"Of course I haven't forgotten," Ruri replied, "but right now, my *rage* is far outweighing my fear. My rage directed toward the people who tried to kill me by deceiving an innocent child—the Church of God's Light. I want to apprehend them, and fast. And I want to help in that as much as possible. It would also be my way of *revenge* against the Church of God's Light."

"It's not that I *don't* understand how you feel, but…"

"If the Church of God's Light is at the heart of these rumors, then it's even more reason for me to go. Besides, I'll have Kotaro and the other supreme-level spirits by my side at all times. I'll be safe from infection as well. With Kotaro's barrier in place, I'll be able to investigate in complete safety."

"Well, that is true…" Arman conceded, trailing off. Even from his perspective, there was no way he *couldn't* investigate this matter now that it had come to light.

As king, he needed to dispatch his soldiers to the village, but Ruri had a good point—if she went, then she would greatly boost the overall safety and the investigation itself. With the spirits around, she could employ their powers and make searching easier. However, Arman was at odds with himself. He couldn't possibly ask Ruri, the person the Nation of the Dragon King entrusted to him, to do something so dangerous.

"Also, Chi is all set on going, so I think I will be going in spite of your word, Beast King. Seeing as we don't know what Chi is liable to do if sent on his own, you need someone capable of stopping him to go."

Arman looked down at Chi standing below. Seeing the sparkles in his eyes, pleading to let them set off already, it was hard to say no. Even if he did, Chi would most likely pressure him into giving permission anyway. There was no way the Beast King, ruler of a nation devout in their faith for the spirits, could ever refuse. Not even Ruri had a way to contain Chi from going through with this.

Racking his brain, Arman heaved a deep sigh of resignation. "Fine, fine. But I can't just send you all out there by yourselves. I'll get a party of soldiers ready, so you can set off tomorrow. That is my final say. I can't have you going somewhere full of potential danger with little protection. We don't even know how many members the Church of God's Light has, after all."

"Yes, very well. Right, Chi?" prompted Ruri.

"Sure! I was actually hopin' to head out right now, but waitin' a night won't kill me."

"...I swear, I know Celestine is a handful, but this girl is her own set of problems. Why are Beloveds always so active like this? Are *none* of them reserved?" Arman said to himself.

Ruri couldn't take that comment lying down. Chi and the other spirits were the ones trying to act. She herself wasn't really trying to actively do *anything*—at least, in Ruri's own opinion.

The next morning, the soldiers stood at attention in a row, ready to set off. Arman was also there, along with Celestine.

"Celestine-san?" Ruri questioned, wondering why she was here.

"Would you mind if she came along with you?" Arman asked.

"No, I wouldn't mind, but it might be dangerous," Ruri replied.

"*You're* one to talk. Listen, I'd appreciate it if you could. She won't take no for an answer. I'll increase the number of soldiers to compensate."

Arman was the one requesting that Ruri take Celestine along for the ride, but he didn't seem too keen on the idea. It was probably because Celestine made some sort of request to make this happen.

"If you say it's all right, then I have no objections. But why the sudden desire to come with me?" Ruri asked.

Celestine replied, "I want to assist however I can to apprehend the Church of God's Light. I will put all of my efforts into helping with their arrest, so I implore you to bring me along."

"Well, she's resented being cooped up in the castle because it's too dangerous for her to go outside too. I already told her not to do anything unreasonable, so I would be grateful if you take her along, as a little distraction."

Their safety was practically guaranteed since Kotaro and the other spirits would be there, so Ruri didn't mind Celestine joining in, but she worried this would turn into a troublesome affair nonetheless. After all, Celestine was smitten with Jade. Ruri couldn't gauge from her attitude how much animosity she held out of mistakenly assuming that Ruri was Jade's mate. She really wasn't too keen on the idea of traveling alongside her, but she couldn't refuse Arman's earnest request. Taking her along was the only option.

After everything was settled, the group went on their way. Their first destination was one of the several villages at the foot of Mt. Ulawoon.

The rumors were all said to come from villages at the foot of the mountain, but since it was unclear which of these villages they came from—outside of the village that was wiped out—their plan was to pick one and ask every resident there. Ruri thought it would be a speedy process considering how small the village was, but that was when they ran into a snag. Being an insular village, their wariness toward outsiders was so strong that none of them could even approach any of the villagers, much less ask them questions. Their hostility was especially apparent when they saw Ruri and the dragonkin dressed in apparel of the Nation of the Dragon King.

Given the circumstances, Celestine ended up bearing the brunt of the work. It seemed that even in this insular and overly cautious village, the Beloved of the Nation of the Beast King garnered worship and praise, like some sort of messenger of the gods. The villagers spoke without reservation as soon as Celestine questioned them. Respect and adoration was clear in their eyes, so Ruri thought she could manage since she was a Beloved as well. But when she tried to interject herself into the conversation, the villagers would slam the door to their hearts right in her face.

(*But I'm a Beloved too!*) Ruri thought, a little disheartened.

However, this difference in treatment was obviously due to her outsider appearance. She regretted not changing into local attire before coming. With Celestine solely leading the investigation, Ruri felt she was steadily becoming useless by the second.

They visited one village and then another, but they weren't gaining the insights they'd hoped for. It seemed that since they were all so closed off from outside contact, they didn't even have any information about neighboring villages. In fact, they didn't even know that a whole village of people had died a few years ago around these parts.

Given that they hadn't found even a single clue, they had no other choice but to go around ruling out each village one by one. They traveled around to several villages before they finally found one with some information.

"Wait, you know?!" Ruri exclaimed. After several trips, they were starting to write the whole thing off as a false rumor, but they found their first witness—a person *willing* to give a testimony. Ruri couldn't *help* but interject in the middle of Celestine's conversation with them. However, she quickly regained her senses and pulled back.

Celestine then urged the villager to continue speaking. "Please, tell us more."

"A short while back, an outsider came to this village. He was neither a merchant nor a traveler. He said he was doing missionary work for his religion called the Church of God's Light and was zealously trying to recruit people into his faith. He said that his group's leader possessed the ability to revive the dead, but no one believed him. Since no one gave him the time of day, he up and vanished. However, right after he did, a beast attacked a child in the village and the child ended up dying. Their parents sank into depression over it. Simply dreadful."

Apparently, there were magic beasts around the area, and while it was a shame it happened to a child, beast attacks weren't uncommon.

"That was when the child's parents remembered the person's claims about resurrecting the dead, so they set off in search of him. Everyone tried to stop them, saying it was clearly a hoax. However, neither listened. Granted, I can completely understand how they must've felt."

"And then?" Celestine prompted.

"A few days passed and they brought a group of people back with them to the village—among which was a well-dressed older man. They proceeded to do something or other at their house, but the villagers were too wary to even step close. However, before long—shockingly—the supposedly dead child emerged from the house."

"He really came back to life?" Ruri asked.

Breathing heavily from his nose, the villager forgot about their wariness toward Ruri, and in excitement confirmed, "Indeed he did! I was shocked out of my wits! Everyone in the village was flabbergasted. We all celebrated on that day."

"Was the child really dead?" asked Ruri. "It wasn't a chance of mistaken identity? Or maybe he wasn't actually dead to begin with?"

"No, no. The child's death was confirmed by everyone in the village. The child who stepped out from the house was indeed one and the same. I've known the child ever since they were born, so there's no way I'd mistake him. There he was—standing and walking, although he did go right back inside since they said he was still of ailing health."

Ruri turned toward Joshua and Ewan. Both of them looked rather puzzled. None of them expected to hear a witness confirm the ridiculous tale of people coming back from the dead. This person didn't seem to be lying nor did they have a reason to. However, their statement only led to more questions. After all, Kotaro definitively said that the dead couldn't be resurrected.

"Where is the family of this child?" asked Joshua, deciding it best to meet them in person.

"Aah, well, you see…" the villager said as if struggling to find the words—and *not* because he was wary of Joshua.

"What's wrong?" Joshua prompted.

"I'm afraid the family isn't here."

"They're not? Then where are they?"

"Well, after their child was brought back to life, they left the village with the people from the Church of God's Light. In exchange for resurrecting their child, they said they would serve the God of said church."

"Do you not know where they went, then?"

"No, I can't say I do."

Ruri and her group went around asking other villagers, but none of them knew where the family went. Just when they thought they had a clue, it dissipated right before their very eyes. They probably weren't going to gain anything else from this village. Afterward, they found out about similar phenomena happening in several other villages around Mt. Ulawoon. But in each case, the revived person and their family ended up relocating with the Church of God's Light, shutting down any chances of meeting them.

"I have to wonder, did they really resurrect them...?" Ruri questioned, doubtful it was true. However, the existence of witnesses changed everything. Magic existed in this world, so perhaps revival wasn't out of the realm of possibility.

Kotaro immediately refuted the idea, almost as if he read her mind. "*Resurrecting the dead is impossible. Once a living being dies, the body and soul are cut free from one another. No means can tether them back together. Not even spirits. There must be some sort of trick behind it all.*"

"*That's right.*" Rin added. She flapped over to Kotaro's head and perched on it. "*According to the one villager, they were only able to see the child for a few moments. We won't be able to know the truth unless we meet them in person.*"

"Meeting them would be nice," Ruri agreed, "but that family is with the Church of God's Light, right? And we don't have any idea where the church might've gone..."

"So, the Church of God's Light's goal is to gain believers? They did go to the house of the kid who assaulted Ewan to offer them a place in their church in exchange for reviving the husband, after all," Joshua muttered as he pondered to himself. "So, what's the plan now?"

Ruri looked at Joshua and everyone else. What were they to do? They had found no solid evidence, and they had traveled to nearly all the villages in the vicinity.

That was when someone spoke up amidst the deadlock. *"I want to go see the village that's supposed to be wiped out,"* said Chi.

That was the destination he talked about wanting to see ever since the start. They had been putting it off for a while now, but it was the only place left. After hearing all this talk about people being brought back to life, there was no way that village wasn't related to the Church of God's Light.

"Well, we've visited all the other villages. Maybe it's time we head over there?" Ruri suggested.

With no other leads on the Church of God's Light, they had no other choice but to investigate wherever else they could. And since all of the inhabitants of that village were supposedly raised from the dead, it was possible that people were still staying there.

Ruri and her group then headed straight toward that rumored village—the village with a populace brought back to the land of the living.

Village of the Dead

12

Ruri and the others traveled to the village rumored to be brought back to life after inexplicably being wiped out. They knew the location thanks to Arman, who had received reports from Amarna.

Out of all the villages they visited, this village settled closest to Mt. Ulawoon. The nearer you approached the sanctified ground of Mt. Ulawoon, the sparser traffic became. There was little interaction with others here.

The news that all the residents of that village had been wiped out came to Arman after a few months had already passed. Considering it was only discovered because of merchants, who would only visit the village once every few years, you could say that the discovery was made rather quickly.

The merchants testified that there were no survivors and that the disease was possibly still spreading through the village. Once Arman received the news, he decided not to send any of his soldiers out because of the danger of infection. He instead barred access into the village.

It seemed that would be the end of it, but after a few years' time, the village was said to be alive again. It was as if the entire concept of the villagers dying had been a lie from the beginning.

Ruri and the others touched down outside of the isolated settlement at the foot of the mountain. They stood amidst the dead silence around the area. It was so devoid of human presence, devoid of even sound, that it was doubtful anyone was still here.

Ruri figured that they might as well head inside and start their investigation. She took a step forward—that was when it happened. She felt the strange, startling sensation of passing through a thin film of some sort. The surprise caused her to trip over her feet and tumble to the ground.

"Whoa! Yowch!" Ruri screamed. She managed to avoid colliding face-first with the ground by her snapping her hands out to catch her fall—in exchange for scraping her palms and knees. Blots of blood started to seep from the skinned areas. "Ah, I'm bleeding."

"Hey, c'mon. What're you doing?" asked Joshua.

"But just now...something was there and it..."

Joshua sighed as he stepped toward Ruri, thinking she had tripped over nothing. But he soon stopped in his tracks and knit his eyebrows as he stared at something in front of him. He patted down the air, almost as if he were pantomiming a wall being there.

Ewan looked on in confusion. "What are you doing?" he asked.

"...It's a barrier. There's a barrier here," Joshua said.

Ewan squinted at where Joshua was touching and after a short pause muttered, "Hey, you're right."

You couldn't tell with just a glance, but once you focused your sights, you could see that there was definitely a magic wall in place, cutting off the outside world.

"Oww," Ruri said as she stood up, brushing off the grit on her hands and legs. Kotaro, Rin, and the other spirits all came rushing in.

"*Are you all right, Ruri?*"

"*You got all hurt.*"

"*Any pain?*"

Ruri looked toward the group of smaller spirits and replied, "Yeah, I'm fine. But anyway, this is a barrier?"

"Yeah, and not just any old barrier either," Joshua said. Then he crossed the barrier and touched it from inside. "You can get in from the outside, but you can't get out from the inside. That's how it's set up, and it's in place all over the village."

Ruri agreed that it was a barrier. She had experienced that sensation of passing through a thin layer of film before with the barrier posted around Chelsie's house. That barrier was meant to defend against trespassers coming in, but this one seemed to be set up to keep people from going *out*.

"Then we can't walk out?" Ruri asked.

"No, as long as your mana is higher than the person who put it up, you can walk out just fine," Joshua explained, proving it by going in and out of the invisible barrier himself.

If Joshua could go through it, then Ruri, with her mana on par with Jade, could as well. She breathed a sigh of relief.

"Still, we've got folks who *can't* get out, so I'd better break this sucker down," Joshua stated. He swiftly kicked at the barrier, and with a loud glass-like crash, the barrier shattered all too easily.

"That should do it." After destroying the barrier, Joshua went over to Ruri, poured water over her wounds, and applied some basic first aid.

"But why was there a barrier here in the first place?" Ruri pondered. "I could understand it being used to ward off entry, but preventing an *exit*?"

"Yeah, it's almost like they're trying to keep something bottled up," Joshua replied.

"Something like what?" Ruri asked.

"Well, logically, it'd be the villagers since they're the only ones here, but…" Joshua trailed off, wondering what the need would be to erect such a barrier. "Anyway, let's search the village. Asking the villagers is our best bet."

Feeling a tad uneasy, the group entered the village proper. Just to err on the side of caution, they kept Ruri and Celestine in the center of the pack for protection.

The village was frighteningly silent despite it being the middle of the day. The suspense was growing, and it sent shivers down everyone's spine.

The village wasn't very big, so they reached the center in no time. With as many people as they had coming into town, they should have noticed *someone* around by now, but there was nary a face to be seen.

"Excuuuse us! Is there anyone arooound?!" Ruri cried, her words echoing throughout the silent streets. Right after, a clatter resounded from a nearby house. The soldiers raised their guard.

As they all intently focused their attention on the house, a single man silently walked out from the opposite side. Everyone jumped in surprise.

"Oh, it's a person. Excuse us, sir! Could you spare us a moment?" Ruri called in a cheerful tone, no wariness toward the stranger.

It seemed as though the villagers were alive after all, but something definitely seemed off.

Since merchants seldom came to this village, Ruri didn't expect anyone to be wearing the latest and most fashionable attire. It only made sense considering the people in the other villages donned worn-out attire. Be that as it may, the man before her was practically dressed in rags. He was filthy as well. He was so covered in grime that it was a wonder he had ever washed his body at all. Not only that, but he was horrendously emaciated. His limbs were skin and bones, like a pauper who couldn't even feed himself for the day.

The man's lifeless, deep-set eyes stared vacantly at Ruri and the others as he walked over on shaky legs.

Seeing how radically different he was from any villager she saw up until this point, an indescribable sense of worry came over Ruri as she addressed the man she assumed was a resident.

"Um, are you okay, sir? Maybe you're not feeling too well?"

However, the blank-eyed man simply snarled at her.

"Hngaaaah!"

"Huh?!" Ruri exclaimed.

"Ruri!" Ewan yelled.

The man came charging at Ruri, letting out a bizarre cry. Ruri could only stare in bewilderment.

Ewan quickly moved in front of Ruri while Joshua landed a clean hook on the man. The man went flying and tumbled to the ground.

Because it was such a snap decision, Joshua wasn't able to hold back. He assumed the absolute worst for the man he just dusted. After all, he just took a dragonkin's punch at full force. He probably wasn't dead, but he likely wouldn't be able to move for a while. A little harder and it might've been fatal.

That was supposed to be the case, at least. However, not even the force of a dragonkin hook was enough to flatten the man. He quickly rose up from the strike—a feat that not even Joshua could contain his shock over. The man didn't so much as look at Joshua, though. He immediately set his sights on Ruri and headed toward her again. This time, Ewan delivered a merciless kick that sent him to the ground. But in similar fashion, he stood right back up.

While all of their attention was focused on the emaciated man before them, several people staggered out of the house they initially heard activity from. Then scores of people started flooding out of all the houses in the area.

Were they residents of this village? Their stares were also blank and lifeless. Letting out cries akin to a beast, they all came rushing toward the group. For whatever reason, they paid no mind to Joshua and the others and came after one target and one target only—Ruri.

"Hngaaaah!"

"Why *me*?!" Ruri cried.

"Crap! Hey, protect Ruri!" Joshua yelled, prompting the dragonkin soldiers to rush to her aid.

They were completely surrounded. The soldiers pushed Ruri and Celestine as close to the center as possible. They dealt with the supposed villagers without weapons, so as to not take their lives, but no matter how much punching and kicking they did, the people continued to stand back up and charge at them. Joshua and the others were finding it harder to hold themselves back.

While the dragonkin soldiers dealt with that, the soldiers of the Nation of the Beast King, composed of members of races with weaker combat abilities, were finally forced to draw their swords. Orders not to kill were no longer an option now. If this kept up, their lives could be in jeopardy.

"Hngaaaah!"

One of the soldiers thrust their gleaming sword deep into the chest of a would-be attacker.

"Eek!" yelped Ruri, clenching her eyes shut.

The soldier stabbed the person right through the chest, a fatal blow under normal circumstances. However, this was anything but. The villager let out an unearthly cry and thrashed about as if they didn't care that a sword was sticking out of their chest.

"Wh-What's with this guy?!" the soldier exclaimed.

"This one too!" exclaimed another. Other soldiers inflicted what they thought were fatal wounds, but despite felling them over and over, they repeatedly stood back up—as if the concept of "death" didn't exist.

"What is this?! Are they humans?! Zombies?!" Ruri exclaimed. She was under the protection of Kotaro and the others, but she was unable to keep her cool after seeing everyone stand despite their mortal wounds.

Standing by her side, Celestine was equally shocked, and her face turned pale.

"Lady Beloveds, please stand back!" said a soldier as he sliced the head of an attacker clean off. "How's that for size?" The soldier assumed that the person would cease moving if he separated the head from the body. Not even dragonkin and their amazing restorative abilities could avoid death if their head was lopped off their shoulders.

As the body collapsed in place, the head flew through the air, landed on the ground, and tumbled its way over to Ruri and Celestine's feet. That alone was enough to make them shriek for dear life, but the severed head—a head that shouldn't be able to move—looked over to them curled their lips into a smile. Then the headless body began to twitch, and it slowly crawled toward Ruri and Celestine as if searching for its head.

"Eeeeeeek!"

"GAAAAAAH!"

Unable to contain themselves, the two girls screamed with such intensity that their voices would surely be hoarse later. Incidentally, the dainty, feminine scream came from Celestine, while the primal war cry was courtesy of Ruri's vocal cords.

"They're coming this way!" warned Ruri.

"Eeeeek!" cried Celestine.

Panicked and flustered, the two turned and tried to run away from the severed head, but another headless body lay in their immediate path, so they immediately froze.

"Gaaah! Over here too!" They turned the other way, but that was back the way they came, where the crawling body still remained.

"Eek!"

"Urghh! This way's no good either!" Ruri's face tensed, and Celestine's face lost its color. They looked for ways out, but terror and panic overcame them. They moved here and there—left and right—restless and confused.

"Lady Beloveds, please remain where you are!"

"That's easier said than done!" cried Ruri.

With all their pacing around, it probably made it harder for the soldiers to protect them, but faced with this horde of people, there was no way they could keep themselves still. Plus, they were all targeting Ruri for some odd reason. Even Celestine couldn't help but panic at full force, completely dropping her usual refined and composed demeanor.

The soldiers were fighting to keep Ruri and Celestine safe in the center of their circle, so they were surrounded on all sides by these mysterious undying humans. There was no way out.

The headless body was drawing near. Ruri shot a look over at Joshua and his crew for help, but they seemed to have their hands full with matters of their own. Given the situation, Ruri and Celestine needed to handle this one on their own.

As they stood terror-stricken by the headless body, the spirits around them chattered.

"Whoa, it's got no head, but it's moving!"

"Yikes. That's amazing. What's with them?"

"They're zombies. I've seen 'em in movies before." The spirit that mentioned "movies" was one that had crossed over to this world with Ruri.

"Wow, this is somethin' else!" added Chi. He even sounded somewhat *amused*—but maybe that was a figment of Ruri's frightened imagination.

"A hole! Guys, dig a hole and drop the body in it!" Ruri yelled. She figured if their movements couldn't be stopped, then dropping them down a hole was the next best option.

"Okay!" responded the spirits in unison.

The ground collapsed under the headless body, and it plummeted into the abyss and out of sight, much to the relief of Ruri and Celestine.

Just as holes were forming elsewhere, the ground started to open large and wide, creating a hole so massive and deep that no amount of people could climb out of it. The creator of this gigantic chasm was the Spirit of Earth himself, Chi.

"Hey, you guys! If you can't beat 'em, chuck 'em into here!"

"Chi, good job!"

The soldiers locked in battle with the undying people caught on to Chi's advice and started throwing them down the hole, one by one. They kicked, threw, and even pushed them down the hole, reducing their numbers steadily. Kotaro even used his wind powers to blow them away into the pit.

The villagers didn't seem to be very capable fighters despite their inability to die, so they offered little resistance. They all plunged into the depths. Some tried to wriggle back up, but the hole proved to be far too deep and they simply scratched at the soil, unable to climb the distance.

Once every last one was down the hole, Ruri and the soldiers alike breathed a sigh of relief.

13 Soulless Bodies

"Seriously, what in the hell are these things?" Ewan said, peering down the gigantic hole. He looked exhausted.

Ruri looked down at the people squirming to get out and a shiver of fear ran through her. As deep as it was, she was still nervous they might come back up.

Celestine and some of the others mentioned that they couldn't stand to look at them, so they kept watch over things from a short distance away.

"So, hey, are these the 'revived' villagers?" Ruri asked.

"I'm going to assume so," Ewan replied. "Joshua is out searching the village to see if there's anyone else around, but besides these *things*, there doesn't seem to be any normal people here."

"The rumors said they 'came back to life.' But seeing as they were running around alive even with their heads cut off, they're pretty much zombies, wouldn't you say? They aren't capable of speech, and it doesn't seem like they can communicate via thoughts either," Ruri concluded.

"Looks like asking them for info is out of the question," said Ewan, figuring it impossible to ask for *anything* out of the mob other than their default bizarre screeches.

"Then whoever saw these people weren't assaulted?" Ruri questioned. "The witnesses were looters trying to pillage from the empty village. Makes sense they never bothered to enter the village once they realized it was still populated, don't you think?"

If they had gone in, they would have been trapped by the barrier and the mob of people would have attacked them. The rumors wouldn't have been able to spread.

"Still, I have the feeling they were only targeting *me* back there, but maybe it's just my imagination?"

Even as they crawled around in the hole, the groaning mass of people kept their eyes set on Ruri. In spite of the large number of people around her, they charged straight at her as if she was the only thing any of them could see.

"You didn't do anything, right?"

"I didn't do anything! You should know; I was with you the whole time," Ruri replied.

"Hmm, then it wasn't Beloved related," Ewan said, pondering aloud. He noted that Celestine, who had been right beside Ruri the whole time, wasn't attacked.

There had to be *something* separating Ruri from the others...

Ewan stared at Ruri, thinking of what could set her apart, until his eyes landed on the wounds on her palms and knees, the ones she received when they first entered the village. That was when a preposterous theory crossed his mind. As absurd as it was, he pulled out his sword to test it out. He slid his blade across the palm of his hand. Blood gushed from his freshly carved wound.

This gash was nothing more than a scratch to a dragonkin with fast healing like Ewan, but the sight of him slicing open his hand for seemingly no reason still made Ruri jump in surprise. "Wait, Ewan! What are you doing?!"

"Testing something," Ewan explained.

Once the crimson blood started to drip in trickles from his hand, the mass of people in the hole down below, who had been focusing solely on Ruri, let out their bizarre cries and began frantically pawing toward Ewan instead.

"I knew it," Ewan said.

Although he had confirmed his suspicion, Ruri cocked her head in confusion. "You knew *what* exactly?"

"These things react to *blood*. You got those scrapes, right? That's why they were only ganging up on you."

"But why?"

"How should I know?" Ewan retorted.

"Was the barrier around the village to keep these people from leaving?"

"I'd assume so, but I don't know *who* was penning them up here or *why* they were doing it. Maybe the Church of God's Light? Or maybe someone totally different..."

There was also the mystery as to how the people ended up like this in the first place. It was hard to consider these droning masses who attacked at the sight of blood to be normal humans.

"It's safe to assume these are...*people*, right?" asked Ruri.

Ewan shifted his brows, not saying a word in reply.

It was *extremely* hard to call them "people." Their malnourished bodies and skin lacked any moisture. They were like a wilted tree, and their eyes resembled that of a dead fish. If someone were to tell Ruri they were magic beasts, she would believe it. Still, that didn't change how they *looked* like people.

"*No, those are not people. In fact, calling them living beings would be too far-fetched,*" Kotaro proclaimed.

They all looked down at the squirming people in the hole with somewhat grim expressions.

"Kotaro, what do you mean by that?" Ruri asked.

"*All living beings in this world possess souls—people, magic beasts, and spirits alike. When that being dies, the soul exits the body and enters the next step of the cycle of reincarnation. However, all that's down there are bodies—soulless bodies, bodies that no longer house spirits of their own. Saying they're 'alive' would be a misnomer.*"

"So, does that mean these people died and only their *bodies* revived?"

"I would say less 'revived' and more that some unknown factor is helping these corpses move on their own."

"Wait, then they *are* zombies."

"That would mean the stories we heard in other villages—the ones of people being revived..."

"You should consider them the same. No resurrections, just moving corpses."

Given the testimony from the other villagers, the Church of God's Light's leader was the one resurrecting people. It was probably safe to assume that the leader in question was the one moving the corpses here as well.

"Assuming the leader is behind this, how is he moving these corpses in the first place?" questioned Ruri.

"I'm afraid that's a question not even I can answer," Kotaro said, his tail drooping as if he regretted not knowing the reason behind all of this. Ruri assured him it was all right by petting his furry head.

Not long after, Joshua returned from scoping out the village. "No other people around. Just these guys in the pit."

"I see... Did you find any clues about the Church of God's Light?" Ruri asked.

"Nope, not a one," Joshua replied. "Though, since we know the revival cases in the other villages were the church's doing, I think they're the ones who put this village in the sorry shape it's in right now."

"Then they were the ones who put up the barrier?"

"Most likely, but it's still just an informed guess. We have no definite proof."

They thought they would be able to find clues in this place, but all they found was a pack of zombies. While the discovery was a substantial lead in itself, with nothing concretely connected to the Church of God's Light to be found, there wasn't any point in sticking around.

"What should we do now?" asked Ruri.

"Right," started Joshua, "I say we head back to the castle and report to the Beast King. We've pretty much gone around all the villages in the area, so we're probably not gonna find any more clues pertaining to the Church of God's Light. It's best we fill him in on the state of this village, especially with it being this close to the capital."

Ruri nodded. "What do we do about the zombies, then?"

The people inside the hole were being kept inside the village via that barrier—the same barrier Joshua smashed to pieces. Leaving them wasn't an option because there was a chance they would escape to the outside. And if these things showed up in one of the other towns or villages, it would be a huge commotion. They would most likely attack any and all wounded people they saw.

"I'd like to take these guys back as evidence, but the question is how?"

They were way too violent to safely bind them up with rope. And even if they contained them, they didn't have any carriages to transport them out since this situation was so unexpected to begin with.

Joshua contemplated what to do next, his brow furrowed and his arms folded. That was when Ruri nonchalantly informed him, "Well, I have a cage if you want to use that."

"A cage that's big enough to stuff all those guys inside of it?" Joshua asked.

"Yup, it's in my pocket space," Ruri replied.

"Why do you even have that?"

"Lydia collects any and everything, so there's pretty much anything you can think of in my pocket space. Plus, even though these people are moving, they're basically corpses. So it should be fine to put them in someone's pocket space, right?"

Lydia had warned that any living being that stayed in the pocket space for a prolonged time would start to mentally break down and go insane, but these were simply mindless walking corpses. They couldn't have a mental breakdown when there was nothing there.

"Ooh, I guess that *is* one way of doing it, huh?" Joshua remarked.

"Well, let's get to it, then. I wanna get out of here and fast," prompted Ewan. He didn't want to be around the mystery zombies any longer than needed.

Mirroring Ewan's sentiments, Ruri quickly pulled out a giant cage from her pocket space.

"Hey, you guys. Lend us a hand puttin' these suckers into the cage," Joshua requested, calling out to the Nation of the Beast King soldiers standing by Celestine a short distance away. They needed the extra manpower since the Nation of the Dragon King's troops alone wouldn't suffice.

As the soldiers came to help, Ruri swapped places and went over to Celestine. Kotaro posted a barrier over both of them since it was still possible the corpses could attack.

Once everyone was in place, Joshua turned to Chi and asked him to raise the hole. The huge depression in the ground started to move, rising until it eventually became one flat surface again. Of course, that *also* meant the zombies were now free. However, Ewan self-inflicted a wound to lure them toward him so they wouldn't go anywhere else. The zombies did just that, seemingly reacting to Ewan's blood, without batting an eye at any of the other uninjured soldiers.

"Aaah…" moaned one zombie.

"Ngaaah…" moaned another.

"C'mon, c'mon. This way, you all."

While Ewan diverted their attention, the rest of the soldiers nabbed them from behind and steadily wrangled them up.

Ruri and Celestine looked on from afar, grimacing all the while. After all, the scene was just as frightening far away as it was up close. Ruri didn't want to so much as touch those walking corpses. She felt bad for Joshua and the others who were doing it in her stead, but she just didn't handle ghosts, zombies, or other things of that nature very well. She had watched horror movies before, but knowing that what happened on the screen stayed on the screen gave her peace of mind. Acting out one of them in real life wasn't on her to-do list. It didn't help that she already played damsel-in-distress earlier.

Ruri was dreading going to sleep tonight; she had no doubt that she would be dreaming about zombies chasing her. "Will I even be *able* to go to sleep…?" she wondered.

"*Worry not, Ruri. I will not leave your side,*" Kotaro said, chivalrously.

Ruri was touched by his gallant display, and his words even pricked Celestine's ears.

"Lady Ruri, I have some of my favorite liquor back at the castle—it's quite delectable. I would love it if we could drink the night away together."

It seemed that Celestine was also afraid to sleep tonight. They looked at one another and silently joined hands. The two were on the same page without uttering a single word. Any mixed feelings Jade introduced into the equation had been blown out the window by today's wild turn of events.

 # Drinking Party

The plan was to put the caged zombies into the pocket space. That, however, caused a slight dispute to break out. *No one* wanted to put something like that into their precious pocket space. That made sense. Who would willingly want to put these bizarrely howling zombies anywhere near them?

Everyone bickered and tried to pass the buck to one another. Finally, they decided that since the cage belonged to Ruri and she possessed the largest pocket space out of everyone, the zombies would be placed in *her* pocket space. Ruri was *vehemently* against the decision, but she was met with deaf ears. Though she was on the verge of tears, she reluctantly complied and placed the zombie cage into her pocket space.

"Let's get out of here so I can hurry and get rid of them! I *so* don't want to keep them in here!" The very thought of the zombies squirming around in her pocket space was enough to send shivers down her spine. She was also concerned about how it would affect Lydia.

"Right, let's hit the road, then." Joshua and the other dragonkin turned into their draconic forms and then took off to the skies.

Lydia was monitoring the domain of space as usual. She had been sorting through things in different pocket spaces to leave in Ruri's own pocket space ever since she did so for her first contract-bearer, Weidt. She would also place anything she wasn't familiar with into random rooms. Needless to say, she had grown accustomed to the process.

As she kept up her work, Lydia could tell that something had entered Ruri's room. She knew everything that happened in this domain, including when new objects came into it. However, since she couldn't mind every single one of the countless rooms present in the space, she mainly focused her attention on Ruri's room.

Something had entered her room—something *big*.

Lydia decided to go and check what it was since Ruri would sometimes send her presents from the outside world. She went into the room to determine whether it was for her or not. However, what awaited her there was a gigantic cage. The cage itself wasn't the problem since it belonged in the room—it was what was *inside* of it.

"Hngaaaah!"

"Aaaaaaah!"

"*Eep! Eeek!*"

Inside the cage were people—at least, they *looked* like people, but it was hard to actually tell—letting out bizarre cries. Some were just headless bodies with what was presumably their heads at their feet.

"*Ruriii, what in the world are you putting in here?!*"

Ruri soon received Lydia's protest by way of the spirits, telling her not to put "whatever these are" inside her pocket space. Apparently, their presence had scared Lydia to tears.

Anyone would be reduced to tears if they found themselves in the same space with those things, but seeing how it was too late to bring them out now, Ruri clasped her hands and apologized to Lydia in her mind.

Once Ruri and her crew arrived back at the castle, they went straight to Arman to report. He couldn't contain his utter shock at the cage packed full of zombies. Meanwhile, Celestine stood from a good distance away and watched the events transpire from afar.

"Who...*what* are these...?" Arman stammered.

"Zombies, Sire. According to Kotaro, they're animated corpses without souls," Ruri explained.

"Is this the Church of God's Light's handiwork?"

"We can't be certain of that yet, but we are sure they are villagers the church brought back to life. It seems that not even Kotaro knows how they're actually making the corpses move, however."

Arman placed his hand on his chin. He was no doubt thinking about the next course of action. Ruri's group silently waited, never once interjecting.

There was word of people being revived in other villages as well, albeit not an entire *village's* worth. Given that, it was possible the church could create similar zombies in the future. So long as the fact remained that Ruri was attacked by these unknown creatures, Arman had a responsibility as a ruler to stop the Church of God's Light from making them—not just for Ruri but for the safety of his own people too. It would be one thing if they were harmless, but they reacted to blood and attacked. Arman needed to investigate this matter immediately before they attacked someone else.

"You said they react to blood, right? If you don't mind, we'll take over these things and investigate them. Is that okay?" asked Arman.

"Absolutely," Ruri swiftly replied. She unloaded the zombies off to Arman as if she couldn't wait for him to take them off her hands.

As Arman and his aides thought up their next course of action, Ruri and her group parted ways. Now that Ruri was free of the zombies, she breathed a sigh of relief. She decided to head down to the hot springs to refresh her weary mind and body.

"That reminds me, I wonder if Lydia is all right," Ruri said to herself.

After enjoying her bath, Lydia was the first thing on Ruri's mind as she exited the spring. She *did* put that gaggle of zombies in the pocket space, after all. Lydia probably had some huge mental scars as a result.

Figuring it would be a good idea to check in on her, Ruri entered her pocket space. As soon as she stepped in, there was Lydia waiting on the other side, standing with her hands on her hips and a stern look on her face. She was clearly upset, and tears were welling up in her eyes.

Ruri wanted to turn right back around and get out while she still could, but Lydia wasn't about to let that happen. Before Ruri could even move, the entrance blipped out of existence. Lydia had cut off her escape route.

"Oh..." Ruri blurted out in vain.

"And where do you think you're *going, Ruri?"*

"Oh, erm, well... Ah ha ha!" Ruri stammered her way into a dry, awkward chuckle, hoping to smooth over the mood, but Lydia just stared at her. "You wouldn't happen to be mad, would you?"

"Of course I'm mad! What were you thinking *putting those disgusting things inside of this space?!"*

Lydia's anger was entirely justified; those things popping into here out of nowhere had to be a huge shock. It didn't help that Lydia was all by herself in here, which probably made the whole thing that much scarier.

"But I really had no choice. There was no other place to put them in."

"Well and good, but I was terrified!"

"I'm sorry, I'm sorry. I didn't want to put those things in here either, you see. Everyone kind of strong-armed me into it." Ruri clasped her hands together and bowed apologetically to Lydia, but it wasn't nearly enough to improve Lydia's mood. "I'll bring you some local treats from the Nation of the Beast King to make it up to you," she bargained.

"...One or two treats won't cut it. I want you to come with enough that you're lugging them under both arms," Lydia replied.

"You got it."

It seemed that Lydia had yelled off enough steam to calm down a bit, and she agreed to the offer of an apology gift.

"Anyway, what were those things?" Lydia asked.

"You don't know anything either?"

"Aside from them not having souls, no." It seemed that Lydia knew the same thing Kotaro knew. *"But, yes, if I recall correctly..."*

"What is it?" Ruri prompted.

"Long ago, Weidt told me about how the witches had been researching ways of reviving the dead. Even though that's impossible, that is. Not even spirits can return a soul to its body once it's left."

"Witches... Reviving the dead..."

Including the details behind the bracelet, Ruri felt like she was hearing "witches" mentioned an awful lot lately. It seemed unlikely, but could it be that the Church of God's Light had ties with these witches? As the thought crossed Ruri's mind, she hoped that this matter wouldn't get more complicated than it needed to be.

Ruri had returned from Lydia's place and was sharing dinner with Arman and Celestine.

Since the stories of people being revived were from the villages around Mt. Ulawoon, Arman deployed soldiers to those villages to conduct an investigation. They were also searching the capital since believers of the Church of God's Light solicited there as well, but since they'd done such a good job of conducting themselves in secret, it was probably going to be a while before they learned anything.

The three of them discussed their plans moving forward and exchanged some light banter over dinner, but Ruri and Celestine were eating their meals in an odd manner. It didn't seem to be a lack of appetite, but they were moving their hands awfully slow—almost as if they were *intentionally* taking up time.

Arman, however, had long since finished eating, and he reached for some liquor to cap off his meal. He quickly gulped down his drink and turned to check on Ruri and Celestine—only to find that they were both *still* picking at their food.

Since he had a mountain of obligations to square away, Arman tried to stand up from his seat on the floor and take his exit. He tried, at least, but he was soon stopped by a flustered Celestine.

"Master Arman, we have yet to finish our meal," she protested.

"Yes, leaving your seat in the middle of a meal is bad manners," added Ruri.

"You're taking an eternity. How long do you plan on eating? Eat your food and go to bed."

"This is a perfectly normal pace. I dare say that *you* simply eat far too fast, Master Arman. So don't be so hasty and stay with us longer," Celestine said.

Ruri backed her up by saying, "She's right. It's too early for bed. Let's stay and keep chatting some more."

Arman felt that the both of them were trying to stall him for whatever reason. He quizzically stared at them, wondering *why* they deemed that necessary.

"*Aah, you're both scared, right?*" Rin asked, throwing a somewhat disappointed gaze their way. "*You're scared to go to your rooms after what happened with those things earlier, aren't you?*"

Ruri and Celestine both looked away without an ounce of subtlety. It seemed Rin hit the nail right on the head.

Ruri doubled down and pleaded her case. "But, but, but! How do you expect me *not* to be scared?! I need to be in a place with a lot of people. If I'm someplace quiet, I'll start remembering it again. I can't go to sleep like this. I'll definitely have night terrors. I mean, forget sleep; I can barely turn the lights off at this point."

Celestine vigorously nodded her head in agreement. "So, please, stay with us a little while longer!"

"How long is a 'little while'? Don't tell me you two plan to stay up till daybreak, do you?" Arman asked.

"We'll stay up until we can't anymore," replied Ruri. "Oh right, Celestine-san! You said you had some liquor you've been saving, if I recall?"

"Yes, I'll send for it right away," Celestine replied.

"Let's drink our troubles away! If we drink, then maybe the sandman will pay a visit and we can go to sleep."

"An excellent idea!" Celestine said. She then requested that her favorite liquor be brought in. As soon as she did, the servants lined up a massive stock of bottles before them.

There was enough there to get drunk for sure. However, leaving a couple of Beloveds to get drunk as skunks wasn't a wise decision. Arman was probably the only one capable of stopping a Beloved if something should go awry. Stuck between a rock and a hard place, Arman once again sat down.

"Lady Ruri, do you partake in liquor?" asked Celestine.

"Not really, actually. I can count the number of times I've drank. All small amounts each time too." Ruri was underage until she came to this world and Chelsie never drank, so she'd never had a drop of alcohol in her world or the entire time she lived out in the woods. When she started living in the castle back in the Nation of the Dragon King, she had a few sips here and there at parties and whatnot, but it was always so strong and dry that she could barely down any of it.

When Ruri told Celestine that, Celestine sympathized with her. "Yes, the Nation of the Dragon King tends to favor strong, dry liquors. Our nation is the same, but I'm just as averse to it as you are. That being said, this is a fruit wine made in the Nation of the Spirit King. It's made for light drinkers and is very popular among women. I think this will be right up your alley, Lady Ruri."

Ruri took a sip of the wine, encouraged by Celestine's remarks. The wine was very sweet and she could practically chug it down like juice.

"Wow, this is sweet and goes down so smooth. It's delicious!"

"Please, drink as much as you'd like," Celestine offered.

Off to the side, Arman prepared to drink as well, pouring wine into his glass. It wasn't the sweet concoction that Celestine brought out, however. It was the bitter and dry swill made in the Nation of the Beast King.

He watched Ruri and Celestine both guzzle down the smooth beverage. "Hey, pace yourselves with that stuff. It may be smooth going down and easy on the palate, but it packs more of a wallop than you expect. That goes especially for *you*, Celestine."

"Yes, you needn't nag; I get the picture, Sire," Celestine replied.

"Why are you singling out Celestine, if I may ask?" Ruri inquired.

"Because she's a pain in the rear when she gets drunk. You should be careful yourself. She'll come bugging you too."

One hour later...

"Why, oh *why* doesn't Master Jade accept my feelings for him?! *Tell meee!*" Celestine shouted.

Arman's warning ended up being wasted on Celestine and Ruri—both were positively plastered.

"Nya ha ha ha ha! Jade-sama is head over heels for me! Jade-sama loves soft and cuddly things! So he's head over heels for me. Cat me, that is... Pft, heh heh heh heh!" Ruri cackled, pounding on the table.

Celestine apparently wasn't fond of Ruri's utterance. Her brows tensed in anger and she grabbed Ruri by the collar, shaking her back and forth.

"But why when I'm right *heeere*?!"

"Nya ha ha ha!" Ruri chortled loudly, her head violently shaking back and forth.

"I told you not to overdrink like that..." Arman said, rubbing his temple as he looked at the two dead-drunk Beloveds.

"To think, losing to a brat like...*you!*" Celestine said, her face beet-red and her heart filled with disgrace.

"Grr, '*like you*'?! What do you mean '*like you*'?!"

"My pride will simply not allow myself to lose to an underdeveloped brat," Celestine said.

"Where do you get off calling me underdeveloped?! I am *not!*" Ruri replied.

Celestine looked up and down Ruri's body, stopping at her breasts. She then let out a patronizing and haughty laugh.

"You're mocking meee! *Waaaah!*" Ruri whined. Tears welled in her eyes as she started to cry. Since she was drunk, her emotions went from one extreme to another—one moment she was laughing her head off, the next she was bawling her eyes out.

"You have quite the nerve standing next to Master Jade with such a pathetic build."

Celestine was thin, but she had mass where it counted. She was so shapely that her extremely revealing outfit only complimented her figure, not deterred from it. Meanwhile, Ruri's breasts *did* somewhat suffer in comparison to Celestine's and that was a fact.

"I've just got a slender build; that's all. Don't get all cocky just because you've got a big chest. You can keep those *clumps of blubber* to yourself!" quipped Ruri.

"Hmph! Grumbling like a dog with its tail between its legs, I see. If you're going to be Master Jade's mate, then you should *look* the part. Do you think that your unshapely figure will cure what ails him?"

"It can cure whatever just fine! Jade-sama loves the soft and fluffy. He is always telling me that my cat form is 'so cute' or 'so healing'...so there!"

"My oh my, doesn't that mean *any* cat will do, not necessarily you? If I become a cat, I can be the healing comfort that Master Jade needs. Hand over your bracelet immediately!"

"No way, no how! Comforting Jade-sama is my job!"

Perhaps because of all the alcohol in their systems, neither of them were holding back. Off to the side, Arman sipped away at his wine, looking on in silence. The night was still very much young.

15 Celestine's Feelings

In Sector Two of the Nation of the Dragon King's royal castle, Jade sat in the room serving as his temporary office, locked in battle with the hefty mountain of documents stacked on his desk. He was quite busy. In addition to settling matters with the most recent set of incidents, he had also just received Joshua's report of their time in the Nation of the Beast King.

"The dead being risen, huh?" he repeated to himself.

"What could the Church of God's Light intend on doing?" Claus asked, furrowing his brow as he scanned over the report himself. "Their ties with the witches is also concerning."

"Well, nothing is set in stone just yet. The Church of God's Light seems to be in the Nation of the Beast King, so we'll just have to leave it up to Arman to take care of things," Jade said.

"Yes. It also seems they used the blood already. I believe the report said Ewan was the first to suggest using it," Claus said. He directed his gaze toward Finn, who was standing near the wall reading over the report as well.

Finn grimaced and Jade looked none too pleased himself.

"And after I gave them ample warning to be discreet about using it too," said Jade. "I'm glad nothing happened, regardless."

"I shall reeducate Ewan once he returns to the kingdom, Sire," Finn said, bowing in apology. "It seems it's still too early for Ewan to learn our secret techniques."

Jade gave a single nod. "It would seem so," he replied.

Making medicine using dragon blood was a dragonkin secret technique. Not all dragonkin knew about it, and several conditions needed to be met before one could learn the ways. Ewan hadn't fulfilled those conditions yet, so he didn't know the secret techniques. But after this mishap, he probably wouldn't gain that opportunity for quite some time.

Between the Church of God's Light, the risen dead, and the dragonkin who had gone missing in the castle, there were a heap of problems to be solved. With this many headache-inducing issues on the table, Jade was beginning to crave a healing touch as he longed for that soft and fluffy coat of snow-white fur.

"*Haaah*, I miss Ruri... Are the repairs to the castle *still* not finished?"

"Everyone is working to the best of their abilities, but it will still be a while before they're done," Claus replied.

Jade slumped in his chair. He suppressed his urge to cast his work aside and go to meet Ruri. Instead, he took up his pen, saying, "Well, I just hope she's getting along with Celestine, at least..."

The next morning, after her all-night drinking party with Celestine, Ruri awoke to a terrible headache.

"Ugh- My head is splitting~" Ruri groaned, holding her head. She had yet to get out of bed.

"*Well, yes, you drank too much,*" Rin said as she flapped her arms over to Ruri's side.

"*Ruri, are you all right?*" Kotaro asked. He sounded exasperated, but he was peering into Ruri's face with concern.

Ruri wasn't sure when she had returned to her room; her recollection was a total blank. She remembered exchanging some heated words with Celestine, after which they randomly decided to have some sort of competition to see who could drink the most. She couldn't recall a single thing that happened after that. Someone must've carried her back to her room once she passed out halfway through.

Her overconsumption had also led to quite the nasty hangover. Ruri didn't just have a headache; she felt sick in general. A hangover was unavoidable for anyone at that point—especially if they hardly ever drank, didn't know their limits, and spent a whole night drinking their weight in booze. The pain in her head and the general discomfort prompted her to solemnly swear off alcohol for the rest of her days.

Ruri took some hangover medicine, but she still found it hard to get out of bed. She finally managed to get up some time after noon. With no appetite to speak of, she downed some easy-to-stomach soup, took a moment to regain her bearings, and decided to head to the springs to revitalize her mood.

Once she undressed in the changing room, Ruri hopped right into the bath. That was when she spotted Celestine there as well. Time stood still as neither of them made eye contact. Given how sickly Celestine looked, she was probably just as hungover as Ruri.

Ruri remembered the heated words she exchanged with Celestine last night. Even though she felt awkward about it, she was already too far in to turn back now, so she stayed in the bath. Thankfully, the tub itself was massive, like a public bathhouse, so there remained a bit of distance between the two of them.

Silence fell and the tense air made it difficult to stay in place. Ruri was about to get out of the bath early, but that was when Celestine's voice rang out.

"...Lady Ruri, when did you fall in love with Master Jade?"

Ruri was at a loss for words. "No, um, err..." she stammered, remembering that the misunderstanding still hadn't been cleared up. She attempted to say something to finally clear the air once and for all, but Celestine interjected before she could get a word out.

"I've loved Master Jade since childhood. It was love at first sight from the moment I laid eyes on him, and my heart has not wavered since. At first, I was wrought with indecision. Master Jade, the Dragon King; I, the Beloved of the Nation of the Beast King. Marrying one another would create a great many issues."

The Nation of the Beast King was mostly wasteland. Cropland was in scant supply, so its harvest greatly depended on the existence of their Beloved. Not only that, but the proceeds the nation received from the extensive sale of Beloved-related merchandise was quite substantial. If Celestine were to marry Jade and join him in the Nation of the Dragon King, it would severely impact the Nation of the Beast King in a number of ways. The Nation of the Dragon King wanted to avoid souring relations with the Nation of the Beast King as well, which stealing their Beloved would absolutely do. It was a union that neither side wished to happen.

"Nevertheless, even though I knew it would cause problems, my heart remained the same. I tried the best I could. I took great care so that my personal appearance would be pleasing, and I learned how to act graceful and refined, all so Master Jade would choose me—all so I could stand by his side. And yet... And yet here I am, with some girl fresh out nowhere snatching him away from me," Celestine said, glaring daggers straight toward Ruri.

Ruri's face tightened. Apologizing would come off as strange, so she didn't really know *what* to say. Actually, Ruri's conscience nearly drove her to apologize, but that seemed like a surefire way to hurt Celestine's pride.

"Up until now, I've used my status as a Beloved to eliminate any woman that hung around Master Jade, but I can't necessarily do that if I'm dealing with another Beloved. I would have *long* since taken measures otherwise," Celestine said with eyes that spelled regret and frustration.

Ruri was sweating bullets, thankful that she *was* a Beloved and not just a normal girl in this situation. She also shuddered to think just *how* Celestine went about "eliminating" people.

Celestine breathed a sigh to regain her composure and removed her gaze from Ruri.

"...I understand. I understand that Master Jade sees me as nothing more than a friend or maybe even a younger sister. However, while Master Jade always awkwardly turned me down, he never flat out refused me; that is a facet of his kindness that I've taken for granted."

"Celestine-san..."

The normally strong-willed Celestine now seemed faint of heart. She must have really been in love with Jade. Ruri could feel how much her affection was tearing her up inside.

She decided to clear the air about this once and for all as she said, "Um, Celestine-san, you've been mistaken. Jade-sama and I aren't mates at all. Jade-sama just fawns over me because I can turn into a cat and he's a lover of small animals. Rest assured, he only considers me a pet, so there's nothing going on between us."

After saying everything she needed to say, Ruri breathed a sigh of relief and looked over at Celestine—to find that she was shooting a somewhat angry glare her way.

"...Why might you be glaring at me, if I may ask?"

"You say there is nothing between you and Master Jade?"

"Y-Yes. That's correct," Ruri replied, hesitantly nodding her head in the face of Celestine's intensity.

But Celestine was not satisfied with that answer. In fact, it only made her even angrier.

"Then what is that necklace about?! Master Jade gave it to you, did he not?!"

"You mean *this* necklace?" Ruri took the glass orb housing Jade's scale into her hand. Jade gave it to her as a good luck charm, so she kept it on while in the springs.

"You don't just blatantly show off something like that if there's *nothing* between you and Master Jade!"

Ruri was confused. Why was Celestine getting so upset over this trinket?

"Um, is there something about this charm that I'm missing?"

Celestine glared at her. "You're doing this on purpose, aren't you? Are you trying to feign ignorance to disarm the situation?"

"No, I really don't know what you're talking about…" Ruri answered, completely clueless.

"That's Master Jade's dragonheart and you know it!"

Ruri cocked her head in confusion. Dragonheart—she felt as though she'd heard that word somewhere before. It was the symbol of courtship that dragonkin bestowed upon their mates.

"No, this is a good luck charm. Jade-sama told me it was when he gave it to me."

Getting the sinking suspicion that Ruri's confusion was genuine, Celestine calmed herself and asked, "You received that scale from Master Jade, did you not?"

"I did."

"And there is truly nothing between the two of you?"

"No, nothing," Ruri said, nodding her head. She maintained direct eye contact in order to convince Celestine that her statement was in no way false.

"Do you know where he pulled that scale from?"

"Um, around his heart, if I remember correctly. I noticed it was the only part of him that was a different color, and when I pointed it out, Jade-sama plucked it out for me, saying it was a good luck charm."

Celestine winced for a second as if fighting back a sudden pain and said, "That is, without a doubt, a dragonheart. A single scale of different color growing atop his chest—the same color as his eyes. What you are wearing around your neck right now is Master Jade's dragonheart."

"His... Huh?" Ruri was about to laugh it off as being preposterous, but Celestine's face was dead serious. She swallowed her words and slowly looked down to Jade's scale hanging from her neck.

She was in utter disbelief. However, her mind immediately went toward doubt. After all, there was no way Jade would give her something so important. It made her suspect what Celestine was telling her.

"Master Jade does *not* see you as a mere pet. If he did, he wouldn't possibly give you that."

"Um, I find that hard to believe."

"I'm not sure if you're aware, seeing as you weren't even aware that was a dragonheart, but Master Jade always feeds you during meals, does he not?"

"Yes, he does."

"That is called 'partnerial allofeeding,' which is a courtship custom performed by male dragonkin."

Ruri's eyes widened. "No, that was just him feeding his pet…"

"Male dragonkin only personally feed their mates and their children. Seeing that was enough for me to recognize that you were Master Jade's mate."

Ruri had never considered there was any deeper meaning to Jade's actions. She'd always believed he was simply doing something akin to feeding a pet, but her conceptions were shattering at Celestine's words.

Despite the evidence, Ruri still couldn't bring herself to accept it. She thought it unbelievable—*infeasible*.

She might have been unconsciously trying to dance around the subject, feeling that her relationship with Jade might change if she accepted it. There was a part of her that didn't want to think about it. The times Ruri spent with Jade were gentle and affectionate, but not in any sort of romantic way. They were calm and peaceful times that Ruri adored.

What would even happen if the element of romance were added to their relationship? Wouldn't it be impossible to maintain the same gentle mood they always shared? Those doubts ran across Ruri's mind, and she couldn't rebuff them. She could do nothing other than stubbornly deny what Celestine was telling her.

"No, but…"

"I don't know how you think of it, but Master Jade has been treating you as his mate, beyond a shadow of a doubt."

"That just can't be…"

"This might be a prime opportunity for you. Master Jade views you in a completely different light than me. That is how big the gap is between his mate and everyone else," Celestine said, closing her eyes as if to suppress her emotions. The splashing of hot water accompanied her out of the bath as she left Ruri to sit in a dumbfounded daze.

After Celestine left, it wasn't long before Ruri started to feel overheated from sitting in the hot water too long. Once she stepped out and returned to her room, she collapsed onto her bed to cool off her flushed body.

Her mind was occupied by one thing: the conversation from earlier. Dragonhearts, partnerial allofeeding—all of these things spun around in her head, driving her up a wall.

"Say, Rin, guys? Did you know? That this was a dragonheart, that is."

"*Yes, we sure did,*" Rin nonchalantly answered.

"Why did none of you ever tell me?" Ruri asked, shooting her a rebuking look.

"*We knew you'd figure it out eventually.*"

"Fat chance! There's still *a lot* about how things work in this world that I don't know. I've heard about dragonhearts before, but this whole 'partnerial allofeeding' stuff is news to me."

Celestine said that feeding someone was a form of courtship, but Jade had been doing it for quite some time now. Which would mean that, ever since then, Jade had been treating Ruri as his...

"...Does that mean Jade-sama has feelings for me? You know, not as a pet?"

"*Well, he wouldn't have given you his dragonheart otherwise. A dragonheart is absolutely precious to a dragonkin, after all.*"

Ruri didn't want to believe her ears. It was inconceivable. She had been like a pet to Jade and his fluffy animal-loving ways, which was why he would always fawn over her so much—at least, that was what she thought.

Never in her wildest dreams did she expect Jade saw her as his mate. From when exactly? He definitely treated her like a pet at first. When did he start seeing her in a different light? None of this made any sense to Ruri.

"*Just so you know, you're the only one who never caught on. All the king's aides and all the dragonkin knew about his feelings for you. You* are *the only one who didn't.*"

"Are you kidding me?!" Ruri exclaimed. She sprang up to a sitting position and looked Rin right in the face.

"*I'm serious. With him practically doting on you this entire time and partnerial allofeeding right in public, anyone with eyes would notice. While you were overcome with naive joy at receiving the king's scale as a gift, the king was disappointed you didn't realize he actually gave you a dragonheart.*"

"Really? You say that so matter-of-factly, but remember I'm *not* from this world. How was I supposed to know?"

"*Be that as it may, it clearly showed in his attitude. Male dragonkin only devote themselves that much to one person—their mate. There's also his attempts to keep you by his side morning, noon,*" *and night. And let's not forget how he's always concerned about your whereabouts whenever you're out of sight. Try telling the dragonkin that work in the castle that there's 'nothing between you two.' Why, their jaws would all drop to the floor."*

Ruri was shocked. Everyone had been forming this assumption right under her nose.

"His aides are the only ones who know you're not lovers. Everyone else has long since assumed you two are an item."

"...Am I really that *dense*?" she questioned. Everyone around her knew, but she'd been oblivious despite being so close to Jade.

"Quite so, yes."

"Urghh~ But, but! Jade-sama never said anything to me, not once!"

"I believe he's said plenty *to you. You've just been construing it all as talk toward you as a* pet, *haven't you?"*

"Urk, I suppose that's true."

She hadn't thought Jade saw her as a member of the opposite sex. He often told her that she was "cute," but she figured it was all directed toward her *cat form.*

"Well, what now, Ruri?"

"Huh? About wh-wh-wh-what?"

"About the king. If you have no feelings for him, then you need to return that dragonheart, don't you? However, you should carefully consider before doing so. The king's future hangs in the balance."

"What do you mean?"

"Once a dragonkin finds a partner, their dragonheart changes color. And that scale can only be given to the person who caused the color change. If that dragonkin were to get turned down before they removed it, then it would revert to its natural color once they sorted through their emotions. However, once they pull it off, it's already too late. Should the person who changed the scale's color refuse it, then

the dragonkin will never be able to hold a mate ever again. Dragonkin can also only produce offspring with the person they've given their dragonheart to. Accepting one requires commitment."

"Wait, really?!" Ruri exclaimed. The scale suddenly felt *much* weightier than before.

Why would Jade hand her this and lie about it being a good luck charm? He left Ruri in the dark and gave it to her without any clear proof she would even accept it. If she returned it now, Jade wouldn't be able to have a mate ever again. It was hard to tell what his intentions were.

"Ruri, what do you think of the king? From my perspective, you seem to have affection for him."

"Well… Unghh…" Ruri said with a groan, racking her brain.

If asked whether she liked Jade, well of course she did. As for whether she liked him in a *romantic* way? That left her unsure.

With his gentle gaze and his professed "doting," Ruri couldn't help but feel affection for him. He was also physically attractive and had a great personality. However, she had tried not to think of anything beyond that. She kept telling herself that his conduct was between a man and his pet, not a man and a woman.

Even so, Ruri knew it. She knew that the moment she found herself trying to contain herself—setting barriers between the two of them so that Jade's views of her wouldn't get conflated—her feelings for Jade would go *far* beyond simple, platonic affection.

She had thought Jade never saw her as a member of the opposite sex this entire time. Ruri had said things like wanting a new family and wanting a boyfriend in this world, but the reason she didn't include any of the dragonkin in that equation was actually because she was being mindful of Jade.

Jade apparently thought of her as his mate, which seemed to make the decision easy—no need for overthinking. But weakness started to rear its ugly head. Doubts started to bubble up to the surface. She questioned why he chose her and whether it was truly all right for her to accept him.

"Aaah, what should I do, Rin?!"

"*Well, some calm consideration for starters. You have time to do so.*"

And so a problem more troubling than the Church of God's Light put Ruri through the wringer for several days on end.

16 Mismanagement

It was the wee hours of the night and everyone was sound asleep. Every corner of the corridor was cast in darkness and draped in silence. The only ones still awake at this hour were the soldiers on patrol.

As the silent night ticked away, that was when it happened. Furniture started to rattle and clatter before a thunderous tremor shook the ground.

"An earthquake?" Ruri asked, waking up in no real panic, as she calmly watched the furniture tremble around.

Kotaro and Rin woke up soon after and huddled over to Ruri's side. Chi, on the other hand, showed no signs of waking up as he remained conked out with his gut hanging out.

Even though the Spirit of *Earth* should've been the first one to react to an *earthquake,* Chi remained unfazed. Ruri was all the more impressed at the depths of his lackadaisical attitude.

"*Are you okay, Ruri?*" asked Kotaro.

"Yeah, I'm fine. Feels like a four in intensity—by Japanese standards, at least." Ruri didn't live in the Land of the Rising Earthquakes for nothing. This small set of tremors wasn't nearly enough to spook her.

It wasn't long before the quake died down and Ruri went back to sleep—that is, until a violent knocking assaulted Ruri's door, one not caused by any earthquake.

Ruri jumped up from her pillow in surprise. "What? What? What?!" She rushed out of bed and opened the door to find Ewan and Joshua there, both looking tense.

"Are you all right?!" Ewan asked, a frantic look on his face.

Ruri thought he was going overboard, but she saw that even the normally jolly Joshua looked serious.

"Well, yeah. That little quake was nothing special. Most it did was wake me up out of a good night's sleep."

"Wait, why are you being so nonchalant?! The *ground* just *shook*!" Ewan replied.

"I mean, earthquakes aren't really a rare occurrence, are they?"

As soon as she said that, she heard an awful commotion.

"Make sure His Majesty and Lady Beloved are safe!"

"This is unthinkable! The ground shaking, of all things!"

"Who in the world angered the spirits?!"

A chorus of flustered voices rang outside Ruri's door. Things were devolving into a bit of a panic.

While earthquakes weren't at all uncommon for Ruri, she finally realized that might not be true in this world.

"I'm guessing this is a pretty big deal, then?"

"Sure is," Joshua explained. "I don't know the deal in your world, but here, earthquakes rarely happen. In this world, they're known as the 'wrath of the spirits,' and they're said to be triggered by spirits, so everyone is freaking out right now."

Not only were earthquakes infrequent, but because science hadn't developed in this world like it had in Ruri's, the reasons behind why they occurred were naturally ill-defined. It was no surprise they'd assume they were derived from some unknown force, given that fact. Then again, since this was a realm where magic existed, she couldn't deny there might've been some factors that lacked a scientific explanation.

All of a sudden, Arman came running into Ruri's room with his aides in tow.

"Ruri, is there something wrong with Lord Spirit of the Earth?"

"Chi? He's fast asleep over there."

"So Lord Spirit of the Earth *didn't* cause the earthquake," Arman said, his face a mix of relief and apprehension.

Assuming that Chi, a supreme-level spirit, was behind an earthquake was most likely normal in this world.

"I don't think so. Chi does some outrageous things when he's bored, but he's calm when he sleeps. Even if he were awake, he wouldn't do anything to cause trouble for others."

"I see. Celestine said there was nothing wrong with the other spirits either. I suppose we'll just wait and see what happens."

Just as Arman, who was now feeling more assured, went to leave Ruri's room, the ground started to quake once more. It was a very small tremor, but it seemed to be enough to instill terror in the hearts of everyone not acclimated to earthquakes. Frightened screams could be heard from everywhere.

"Hmm, aftershocks?" Ruri wondered aloud, the only one remaining calm.

The weak earthquake continued to persist. As Ruri was eating breakfast the following morning, the tremors started once again. The caretaker women all shrieked and crouched down in fear, but Ruri continued to eat unaffected. That was when she finally realized that these quakes had been happening a little *too* frequently. Some aftershocks were fine by her, but it could be the threat of a bigger earthquake to come.

She tried asking Chi since he was the Spirit of Earth, but he said he hadn't done anything.

As Ruri pondered over other potential causes, one that crossed her mind was the landmark that lay far off in the distance—Mt. Ulawoon. She remembered it being a volcanic mountain. It wasn't an extinct volcano either; it was very much active.

According to one of the caretaker women she asked, it last erupted a thousand years ago. A terrible thought crossed Ruri's mind, but she decided not to think about it, assuming it was probably a baseless worry.

Ruri had spent quite some time in the Nation of the Beast King. At first, she was extremely reluctant to have so many people acting as her caretakers, but now she had grown fully accustomed to it. Her caretakers had been waiting on her every need, hand and foot—so much so that she worried whether she'd be able to return to life as usual, tending to her needs on her own, once she got back to the Nation of the Dragon King.

She had grown accustomed to all of the spice-laden dishes and was able to stomach them without issues, but the constant supply of spicy foods was making it hard to stave off the craving for the Nation of the Dragon King's cuisine. Whenever she got the urge, she would eat the food she'd brought with her as she wondered what Jade was doing back in the kingdom—the thought of which made her somewhat sad and lonely.

It seemed she was getting homesick. She wondered when she'd be able to go back.

As her urge to return and see Jade again grew, Joshua came to her one day and asked her, "Hey, Ruri. You remember that mother and child who used the dragon's blood?"

The father cured by the dragon's blood along with his wife and daughter were still fresh in her memory, so Ruri had a very clear recollection of them.

"Yeah, of course I do," she replied.

Both her and Ewan developed a look of satisfaction as they remembered their good deed from that day.

"Sorry to burst your bubble, but we've got a situation."

"What do you mean?"

Ruri and Ewan both scratched their heads.

Joshua then proceeded to take them to the house of the mother and child from before.

"Come on, gimme some too!" yelled a man.

A woman declared, "My poor child is sick! I beg of you!"

"Don't hog it all for yourself, dammit!" shouted another man.

In front of the mother and daughter's house was a mob of people all raging in unison and pounding their fists at their door so hard it seemed likely to break. But no one was coming out. They were most likely too afraid to do so due to all the angry yelling.

The sight of all this was filling the air with a vague sense of dread.

"What's all that about?" asked Ruri.

"...Those are people who came looking for dragon's blood."

Ruri and Ewan both gasped, their eyes widening in shock.

"A young girl assaulted Ewan, a dragonkin, for dozens to see right in the middle of town—screaming about giving her blood. And right after, that girl's father goes from being on death's door to good as new. Seeing that, people thought she must have convinced said dragonkin to treat him. Of course, the dragonkin cure that readily came to mind was dragon's blood. The people in front of that house are out for blood—dragon's blood, that is. And they're asking for the family to put in a good word if they don't have any to spare themselves."

"Why did it all turn out like this…" Ruri murmured.

"Personally, I figured it'd turn out this way," Joshua replied in a very pragmatic manner.

Ruri and Ewan both turned to him in surprise. "Why…?" they asked, neither understanding what he meant.

Joshua looked at them both with exasperation, like you would a couple of confused children.

"That's just how big of an effect dragon's blood has. It's pretty obvious that anyone would want medicine that cures any ailment in the blink of an eye. You can't just go using it in front of people or else it stirs up chaos like what you're seeing. I specifically told you to be careful how you use it, didn't I? That also meant to be mindful of any situations that'd come as a result."

"Right…" said Ruri in reply.

"That goes for you too, Ewan. You need to think hard about why we don't allow this medicine outside the kingdom, or sell it, for that matter. It's to avoid situations like this. A single drop of dragon's blood could very well start a war. That's why dragonkin don't just go sharing it with people."

"Yeah…" said Ewan in reply.

Both of them hung their heads, crestfallen. They understood the terrible situation their compassion helped cause, albeit too late.

"And giving someone who attacked you dragon's blood? That's pretty much an open invitation, saying it's all right for anyone to assault a dragonkin in the future. Are you both trying to expose dragonkin to danger?"

"We're not!" they both replied.

"I wouldn't be surprised if your thoughtlessness sparked something like that, though. People might try to use any means they can to get blood from us, playing the sympathy card and whatnot. And if we refuse, they'd probably call us heartless for not forking it over. But dragon's blood isn't an infinite resource, and it's not something we can just hand out to everyone across the world. So, I'm warning you both—think about the repercussions before you act from now on."

"...Yes, sir," Ruri replied, slumping. She was disheartened.

"Yeah, all right," Ewan said as well, his shoulders following in suit.

Joshua rustled their hair as if to say he was done lecturing them.

"But you're not right at all, Joshua," Ruri proclaimed. She looked up at Joshua, sulking. "Why didn't you warn us of this happening *back then*? You just let Ewan and me run free and get excited without saying a *single* word."

When Ewan had asked to use the dragon's blood and Ruri had accepted, Joshua said nothing. He simply watched the two do what they did and told them about how to use the medicine. If he had given a proper explanation at the time, then neither Ruri nor Ewan would have even attempted to use the medicine.

"I figured it would be a good lesson for the two pushovers, getting all moved by that sob story. Sorry 'bout that."

"You're terrible. How can you be so dismissive?"

"Okay, maybe not the best way to put it, but you hear that kinda stuff all the time. Are you going to heal every single person in a similar situation? How? Processing dragon blood into medicine *isn't* easy, you know."

"Really?"

"Yeah, really. It would take months to make the amount in that small vial you were given."

That revelation shocked not only Ruri but Ewan, a dragonkin himself, as well.

"Wait, really?" Ewan asked.

"Wait, you're asking? *You* don't know how it's made, Ewan?" Ruri asked.

Ewan winced as if she hit a very sensitive area.

"They still haven't taught Ewan yet. There are some requirements to meet in order to learn the secret techniques. The most important of them are being trustworthy and keeping tight-lipped. You can't teach secrets to someone who'll give away medicine that's not supposed to be distributed to anyone who tugs at their heartstrings. And I'm sure this little incident will help ensure he's kept out of the loop for even longer."

Ewan slumped in disappointment.

"Well, anyway, what do we do about *that*?" asked Ruri, referring to the mob that was still in front of the house. If they didn't do something soon, then the family inside would have to sit in fear of the mob eventually busting their door down.

"Ah, right. I should probably straighten this out."

"You can?" asked Ruri.

"Just sit back and watch," Joshua said before briskly walking toward the mob.

Ruri and Ewan watched on discreetly from behind a corner.

Once the screaming masses shouting and banging at the door caught a glimpse of Joshua, they seemed to identify him as a dragonkin based on the aura he exuded alone. They ceased yelling and turned their attention toward him instead.

Ruri watched with bated breath, but Joshua simply gave his usual charming smile as if nothing was wrong at all.

"You're a dragonkin, ain'tcha? Gimme some dragon's blood, please. You gave it to the guy who lives here, didn'tcha?" demanded a man.

"Please, give me some as well. I'll pay you good money for it!" pleaded a woman.

Joshua looked around at the people, each giving their individual requests, and spoke to them. "Sorry, folks, but dragon's blood *isn't* what helped cure the guy who lives here."

"Don't tell lies! Explain how someone that badly injured is good as new, then!" refuted the woman.

"Yeah! Explain!" said the rest of the mob in agreement.

Showing no signs of backing down, Joshua continued to elaborate. "It's the truth. The Church of God's Light healed the guy here."

"God's... Huh? What's that?" Everyone in the crowd looked dumbfounded.

However, among the confused masses, Joshua's words seemed to jog a single elderly woman's memory as she said, "...Come to think of it, the lady of this house said something about a believer of some sort of church dropping by, offering to help them in their hour of need."

The woman's words prompted the others to finally start listening to what Joshua had to say.

"The Church of God's Light healed the good sir here. Apparently, they save all who worship and swear loyalty to their god. They might still be in the capital, so why don't you guys go looking for them?"

Hope started to set into the people, amazed that such a group existed. They had the power to cure the very sick and injured. No one knew what these people looked like, but everyone now seemed eager to search for them. But...

"Hey, instead of buying that bullcrap and searching for some mystery person, we could be having *this guy* give us his blood right now!"

Joshua had managed to divert the subject, but one man in the crowd snapped the rest back to their senses. Their eyes became frenzied, ready to pounce on Joshua at any moment, as tension flowed through the crowd.

However, Joshua kept his same smile, completely unconcerned about the bloodlust looming in the air.

"What? You guys wanna go? Against me, a dragonkin?" he asked.

Although Joshua was grinning, his powerful presence triggered the mob's instincts and they quickly faltered. Joshua could tell that their bloodlust was starting to wilt away. The person they were up against was a dragonkin, the race at the top of the hierarchy. The fact that not even their combined forces as a mob stood a chance against him was embedded in their demi-human instincts.

"Instead of trying to do the impossible and fight me, I'd recommend you do something that *is* possible—namely, looking for the Church of God's Light."

Joshua intimidated them out of their will to fight. They looked around at one another before they started to leave the area one by one—either to go in search of the Church of God's Light as Joshua said or simply because they'd given up.

Ruri, who had been watching the situation on edge, looked at Joshua as he came back to where she was hiding with Ewan. She breathed a sigh of relief, thankful that the people dispersed without conflict.

"I didn't know *what* would happen there," Ruri admitted.

"No way I'd let a bunch of wimps like that take me."

Joshua was probably right, but she was still worried, regardless.

"I'm glad you're safe, but should you have said that back there? You know, lying about the Church of God's Light healing that man?"

"It's fine. They'll probably start searching hell or high water for the Church of God's Light now that I've told them that. And if the guys we're after actually are in the capital, we might just get some kind of intel out of it."

"Yes, but, what if they find out you lied?"

"I'll just feign ignorance and let it be that. Besides, those church guys are on the wanted list in the first place. If the government nabs 'em, then whether they did patch the husband up or not will be a moot point. The people from that mob just now *aren't* going to go asking favors from someone in a jail cell."

Although she still had some slight reservations, Ruri decided to drop it since the mob had safely cleared out from in front of the mother and daughter's house.

"We don't have any clues about the Church of God's Light anyway. If we send out too many soldiers to search, they'll probably go into hiding. But with those regular citizens on the prowl, they'll never see it coming."

According to the info, the Church of God's Light was trying to gain more followers. Considering that they'd made it their mission to offer to revive the dead in exchange for becoming a follower, that logic should be accurate.

"But wouldn't it backfire if they do end up recruiting more followers, especially because you told people about them?" Ruri asked.

"Just gotta catch 'em before that happens. The church might show itself in the capital if we give them an opportunity to gain a bunch of followers. That said, I've got a favor to ask of you, Ruri."

"What?"

"I want you to ask the spirits for help. I'd like for them to pay attention to what people are saying and see if any followers of the Church of God's Light contact anybody in the capital. If the spirits are too obvious, they might get found out, so make sure it's discreet."

"I think everyone can handle that if I ask, but will just watching in secret be good enough?"

"Yeah, we just need to find them. Have the spirits report in and make sure they don't do anything to them. Just catching one member will allow the guys in charge to pass the buck to the small fries. So, if we're gonna do that, I wanna let them swim a little bit and take care of the rest from the root when they least expect it."

If Ruri were to ask the spirits, they would likely agree to her request, gleeful to help. Otherwise, she would just have to ask Kotaro and the others.

"Okay, got it," Ruri replied.

17 The Spirit of Fire

Ruri and the others returned to the castle to find it was filled with busy soldiers, frantically running to and fro. Their voices could be heard shouting all over.

"Hey, hurry up!"

"Call a medic!"

"Get the support troops together. Get to His Majesty's side on the double!"

"Did something happen?" Ruri wondered aloud.

As they went farther into the chaos to scope out the situation, they could see soldiers collapsed on the floor. Not just one or two either. Soldiers lay everywhere along the corridor, as if making a path of bodies.

Ruri checked a nearby soldier, happy to see he was breathing and merely unconscious. Curiously enough, his clothes and hair looked as if they had been singed by heat. Upon closer inspection of the ceiling and walls, they also showed traces of fire damage.

"What happened here?" Ruri questioned, looking to Joshua and Ewan for answers. But since they had been with her this whole time, they naturally had no idea themselves.

Rin, floating by Ruri's side, looked at Kotaro and Chi as if she noticed something.

"*Say, doesn't this presence feel like…?*"

"*Indeed, it is his presence,*" replied Kotaro.

Chi nodded. "*Yup, sure seems that way.*"

The three spirits alone had a grasp on the situation.

Oblivious to their revelation, Ruri and her group followed the path of bodies. It led straight to the royal throne room. Normally, Arman would be there giving orders to his aides. Ruri debated whether to proceed on. Judging from the state of all the soldiers, she could guess that something big must have gone down.

Ruri and her group were torn. They wanted to avoid immediate danger, but they also didn't want to just abandon Arman. However, as the party pondered over their decision, Kotaro and the other spirits steadily marched onward.

After realizing Ruri and the others weren't following, Rin turned around and called out, "*What are you doing, Ruri? You're going to get left behind.*"

"Wait, you're going in?!" Ruri exclaimed.

They were hesitant, but since they couldn't just let Rin and the other spirits go by themselves, they ran to catch up to them. Ruri couldn't hide her anxiety over what could possibly be happening in there.

They rushed into the throne room. Arman could be seen toward the back where the throne rested. In front of the throne, a slew of soldiers stood in a circle with their swords drawn, their faces intensely hostile.

In the center of the circle was a lone man. He was tall, with a mane of bright, waist-length hair and strong gold-colored eyes. Despite being surrounded by a number of threatening soldiers, the corners of his lips pushed up into an amused smirk.

It was plain as day that this person was an uninvited guest. But it was even more shocking that the abundance of soldiers had allowed the man to infiltrate the heart of the castle, where the king assumed his duties, in the first place.

With the literal path of soldiers leading to the throne room, Ruri looked around to see if the invader was accompanied by anyone else. But the red-haired man was the only one there. That was also quite the shock since it meant he made it all the way here by himself. It was safe to assume that whoever he was, he boasted considerable strength.

The mystery man, not paying any heed to the soldiers around him, looked squarely at Arman as he sat atop his throne.

"I presume you're the king?"

"What are you all doing? Seize the intruder!" Arman ordered, ignoring the man's question.

Upon his call, the fleet of soldiers descended upon the man in an instant. He was trapped like a rat in a cage, surrounded on all sides with nowhere to go. Holding one's own single-handedly against this many people was a tall order for anyone that wasn't a dragonkin. However, when the soldiers tried to lay hands on the man, flames ignited high around his body, creating a wall of fire between them.

The soldiers tried to extinguish the flames flying onto their garments as they loudly shouted, "Fire!" and, "Put it out!"

The pillars of flames touched the ceiling, scattering embers and sending skin-searing heat toward Ruri, who was standing a distance away from the action.

"Rin, please!" Ruri shouted, asking for Rin, the Spirit of Water, to assist in dousing the fire. It wasn't long before water cascaded from overhead, extinguishing the flames that had spread throughout the throne room.

Although some scorch marks remained, the massive amount of water killed the fire licking at the soldiers. They likely had a few burns to show from the ordeal, but luckily nothing too serious had happened since the fire was put out almost immediately.

Their relief was short lived, however. The man had somehow gotten close to them and snatched hold of Rin.

"Hm? You're…" the man started, squinting at Rin.

Being a supreme-level spirit, Rin should have been able to easily get away, but for some reason, she didn't show any signs of resisting. Kotaro and Chi looked on, calm and composed. The only one going into hysterics was Ruri, who stepped forward to come to Rin's aid.

"Hey, let go of Rin!" Ruri shouted.

The man turned his attention toward Ruri. He had just infiltrated the castle, but there wasn't a hint of hostility or bloodlust in his eyes. He seemed to be simply looking Ruri over as if to ascertain her identity.

He winced for a moment before glaring sharply. "Who is this bratty little girl?"

"Never mind me. I'm telling you to let Rin go!"

"Rin?" repeated the man, quizzically looking at the supreme-level spirit in his hand.

"*Yes, that is my name. A perfectly fine name at that. I had Ruri pick it out for me.*"

"Ruri? By 'Ruri,' are you referring to that pug-nosed little brat over there?"

"Pug-nosed…" Ruri was miffed at the man's choice of words, but she was more concerned over the casual manner in which Rin was conversing with the stranger. She was a supreme-level spirit with a ton of pride. Normally, if anyone just grabbed her out of the air like that, she would fly into a fit of rage and pummel them into the dust.

As Ruri tried to concoct a plan to rescue Rin from his clutches, Kotaro and Chi both walked up to the man and casually addressed him.

"*It's been quite some time,*" Kotaro said, approaching the man without hesitation.

"*Yo*," greeted Chi. He lifted his tiny front leg like he was waving hello to an old friend.

The mystery man's eyes widened in surprise. "Well, I can't say I expected *you two* here as well. The whole lot of you are in some bizarre bodies. And, well, this is behavior I expect of Earth, but seeing you among all these people is a rare sight, Wind."

"*I'd rather you use my name. It's Kotaro.*"

"...*You let a* person *name* you?" the man asked, extremely shocked.

Kotaro nodded proudly. "*Indeed. A fine name, is it not? Ruri gave it to me.*"

"Ruri..." the man trailed off, finally showing something other than disinterest. He looked at Ruri again. You could tell from his eyes what he felt—curiosity.

He made a beeline straight for Ruri, but knowing they couldn't just let some unknown individual approach her, Joshua and Ewan stood before her in an attempt to protect her.

"Move out the way," said the man.

"Not on your life, pal. Who in the hell are you?!" replied Joshua.

Joshua and Ewan glared at the mysterious man, refusing to budge an inch. The man furrowed his brow and slashed his hand across the air. Soon after, a roar exploded around them. It blew both dragonkin away, and they smacked hard against a wall. Though they were on their guards, they weren't able to take the man down. In fact, they weren't even able to defend themselves. They both just sat on the floor, reeling, their expressions sour.

"Joshua! Ewan!" Ruri shouted in concern.

The sight of two dragonkin—two natural-born elite fighters—falling so quickly and unceremoniously was unheard of. Everyone's eyes bulged out of their sockets, and they all stared at the man as fear coursed through their veins.

Now with the obstructions removed, the man came to stand before Ruri. He was naturally looking down at her due to his height, giving him an imposing demeanor.

"You're the one who named those two?"

"I did. You have a problem with that?!" Ruri replied bravely, but secretly she was scared witless. He had incapacitated both Joshua and Ewan, two powerful dragonkin, with little effort, so eliminating her would be easier than taking candy from a baby.

Kotaro snuggled up to Ruri as if he could sense her fear. He tried to reassure her by saying *"It's all right, Ruri. You needn't be scared. They simply have an interest in you; that is all."*

Rin slipped from his hand and floated right up in his face. *"You blew those two away and scared poor Ruri!"* she shouted angrily.

"Nonsense. I employed the proper amount of restraint. I didn't *kill* them, now did I?"

"Well, you need to employ more *restraint. They may be dragonkin, but they're still mortal,"* Rin argued.

"You're always going overboard, Fire," Kotaro added.

"That's the *last* thing I want to hear out of you, Wind."

Rin and the man exchanged words in a friendly manner, and even Kotaro's quip seemed to exude a sense of familiarity.

"Wait, do you all know each other?"

"Indeed, this is one of our brethren. He is the supreme-level Spirit of Fire," Kotaro said, his voice echoing throughout the silent throne room.

"Huh?!" Ruri exclaimed.

Ruri, however, wasn't the only one to show surprise. Ewan and Joshua, still sitting on the floor, and Arman atop his throne all looked on, eyes wide.

The soldiers, however, proceeded to turn deathly pale. It was for good reason too. They had pointed their blades toward a spirit, the object of their worship. Not just *any* spirit either—a *supreme*-level spirit.

Everyone in the room dropped their swords and collapsed to their knees. Arman couldn't blame his men for losing their will to attack. While he was still skeptical, there was no way he could possibly tell them to attack now that he knew the offender was a spirit.

"What is the supreme-level Spirit of Fire doing here...?" Ewan questioned.

"Yeah, and as a sidenote: *yowch!*" Joshua exclaimed.

Ruri ran over to them as they staggered to their feet, asking, "Are you both all right?"

"Supreme-level spirits really are no joke..." Joshua commented. "I don't think I've ever taken a beatdown *this* bad before, especially without putting up a fight."

"I have, but only from brother," Ewan clarified.

Out of all the people who served in the royal castle, Joshua and Ewan were some of the youngest, but both of them were immensely capable individuals. That was obvious from the fact they were the ones always serving as bodyguards to Ruri, a Beloved. In spite of that, both had been quickly dispatched. Neither outwardly showed it, but it was safe to assume they were shocked. Fortunately, while they seemed to be in pain, neither were completely incapacitated thanks to their sturdy dragonkin bodies.

"Mere mortals shouldn't try to impede me," remarked the man in a brazen, offhand manner.

That comment annoyed Ruri, but the spirit seemed to be the type to attack others at the drop of a hat. His temperament was also a mystery, so it was probably wise not to make any thoughtless remarks. Knowing this, Ruri repressed her urges and stayed silent. Mentally, however, she was slinging all sorts of heated words in his general direction.

"All of you are contracted to this little girl?"

"*Darn tootin'. Well, for now, at least,*" Chi replied.

"*Not just us. Time is also under contract,*" Kotaro added.

"With Time as well? Who is this girl?"

"*And why, pray tell, is it you don't know? Didn't you hear from the other spirits?*" asked Rin. Rin and Chi both came to see Ruri based on the stories from the other spirits.

Spirits had the ability to mutually communicate their thoughts, so they could hear each other's voices even if they were at a distance from one another. That was why, if the man was the supreme-level Spirit of Fire, he should have heard *something* about Ruri already. She had four supreme-level spirits conscripted to her, making her so famous that there wasn't a single spirit around that didn't know who she was.

"I've been sleeping here for the past thousand years. I just woke up the other day."

"*Early to rise as usual, I see,*" Rin quipped.

Judging from Rin's unsurprised reaction, this news didn't seem to be a one-off occurrence. Apparently, he had a loose grasp on time.

The four spirits then started to engage in some rousing chitchat with one another. They probably had a ton of things to talk about, but Ruri wished they would pick a better time and place.

Arman and the soldiers wanted to speak up, but they couldn't bring themselves to do so as none of them had the courage to dare interrupt a conversation between a pack of supreme-level spirits. The only person capable of doing that would be Ruri, the contract-bearer of Kotaro and the others.

She could feel the silent pressure coming from Arman to straighten things out. Ruri also felt hesitant to interject, but she reluctantly did so, regardless.

"Sorry to interrupt the festivities, but could I have a moment?"

The conversation screeched to a halt, and all eyes fell upon Ruri.

"What, brat? You have some nerve to interrupt our conversation, being the mere mortal that you are."

"Stop calling me 'brat.' I have a name and it's 'Ruri'!"

"What's wrong with calling a brat a brat?"

"Rin, make him *stooop!*" Ruri turned to Rin for help since nothing she said was getting through to the man.

167

"Oh my, weren't you supposed to be a lover of ladies? You're being rather harsh to Ruri despite her being one herself," Rin commented.

"Hmph! Even I have my preferences. A bratty little girl like this is so far removed from my tastes that I scoff at the thought. Beautiful women with feminine features are more my type. If you want me to treat you nicer, then I'd brush up on being a better woman if I were you, brat. You lack what it takes."

Ruri clenched her fist, seemingly ready to snap. Socking him across the jaw wasn't going to cut it for her. She must've had a terrible look on her face because Ewan hooked his arm through hers to stop her.

"Contain yourself, Ruri. You're trying to square up against a supreme-level spirit here. Act rashly and who knows what'll happen to you? He's not like the spirits you've contracted."

"Supreme-level spirit or not, I've had it up to here!"

"Keep that scowl on your face and you'll send men running for the hills, brat. That is, if there's any man crazy enough to pick you in the first place."

Just as Ruri ran out of her last bit of patience, Arman finally stepped in. Faced with the Spirit of Fire, the spirit who had invaded his castle and left dozens of soldiers in his wake, Arman looked to be a tad bit nervous, to say the least.

"I am the Beast King, Arman. I extend my most sincere apologies for drawing blades against you, Lord Spirit of Fire. However, I would like to inquire as to why you have come to my humble castle, if permitted."

"Oh, right. Nearly forgot. I want you all to eliminate the Church of God's Light."

No one present expected to hear that response, especially Ruri whose eyes bulged wide at the supreme-level spirit's words.

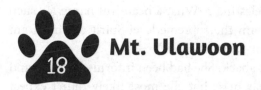

18 Mt. Ulawoon

The supreme-level Spirit of Fire had dropped the name of the Church of God's Light.

Once everyone had settled down, they decided to move to a more suitable place for conversation. Not only were there a ton of soldiers suffering from burns, but the entire room was flooded from the mini waterfall that had drenched the flames. It wasn't the ideal place to talk at length.

Arman, Ruri, Kotaro, and Chi sat atop a tapestry. Rin perched on top of Chi's head. Meanwhile, Joshua, Ewan, and Arman's aides all stood alongside the walls.

Thinking it was better for Beloveds to be together when dealing with a spirit, they also sent for Celestine, who opened the door and entered the room shortly after.

Celestine was in her usual, slightly revealing outfit that complimented her incredible figure. Once the Spirit of Fire caught a glimpse of her, his eyes widened and he shot straight up from the floor. He walked over to Celestine, took her hand, and took a knee.

"And what might your name be, O Beautiful One?" The Spirit of Fire flashed a smile so sweet it was hard to believe it was from the same person as earlier.

Confusion tinged Celestine's face for a moment, but she deduced he wasn't some sort of deviant considering the company he was keeping, so she answered in bewilderment, "My name is Celestine. And you are?"

The Spirit of Fire repeated her name like he was etching the letters into his mind. "Celestine... What a beautiful name for such a beautiful individual. I am the supreme-level Spirit of Fire. I am currently in material form, as you can see."

Celestine was taken aback. She had been informed beforehand that the Spirit of Fire was here, but she most likely didn't expect him to be in *human* form—especially when the other supreme-level spirits with Ruri were all in beast forms. Although, since Kotaro and the others were simply borrowing their bodies, it didn't matter whether it was beast or human so long as it served as an adequate vessel. It wasn't too far-fetched that some spirits would assume human form, in that case.

"Oh, so, you're the Great Spirit of Fire. A thousand apologies for my manners," Celestine said as she started to kneel so she could prostrate herself before the Spirit of Fire.

However, he stopped her before she could, saying, "That won't be necessary, O Beautiful One. Come now, let us take a seat over there." The Spirit of Fire escorted Celestine by hand over to the gathering spot. He wrapped his arm around her waist and sat them both between Ruri and Arman.

Ewan grimaced at the sight of the Spirit of Fire wrapping his arms all around Celestine, but Joshua was the only one to notice.

The Spirit of Fire was all smiles, and he treated Celestine kindly, which shocked Ruri. Of course it would; the gap in his attitude toward her and Celestine was as clear as day.

"Why does *she* get the warm reception?!"

"Quiet, brat. You and this beautiful woman aren't the same. Know your place," the Spirit of Fire bluntly said. It was so unabashed it was actually somewhat refreshing, to say the least.

Nevertheless, Ruri cuddled up to Kotaro, rubbing her face against his fluffy fur in order to console herself. "Ugh, the jerk! I hope he goes bald."

"*Don't worry, Ruri. Fire has always been like this,*" Kotaro assured.

"Unghhh, Kotaro~" Ruri whined.

"Uh, yes, mind if we get to the heart of the discussion?" Arman interjected, aiming to change the topic, albeit hesitantly. His remark seemed mainly directed toward the Spirit of Fire, who had become so preoccupied in fawning over Celestine that he might've just forgotten what he came to speak about. Apparently, the stories about the spirit being a ladies' man were true.

"Lord Spirit of Fire, you mentioned the Church of God's Light back in the throne room, but would you mind elaborating on what you meant?" Arman directly addressed him, finally drawing the spirit's eyes away from Celestine.

"Yes, it was a millennium ago. After my visit with the Spirit of Trees in the Nation of the Spirit King, I came here to the Nation of the Beast King. Mt. Ulawoon produces power that fire spirits favor, so I've often used it as a sleeping place. I slept there for a thousand years but woke up once I noticed some sort of commotion. I had *planned* to keep sleeping another century more, but here I am."

Everyone in their heart of hearts wanted to point out how *obscenely* long he slept, but none of them dared interject aloud for fear of breaking the flow of his story.

"Being jostled from my slumber already put me in the worst mood imaginable. And the Church of God's Light ended up putting me into an even *worse* mood on top of that. They fiddled around at Mt. Ulawoon, absorbed the mountain's powers with Spirit Slayer, and started making those soulless, walking corpses as well. Thanks to that, they've been strutting around the mountain like they own the place."

"They *what*?!" Arman exclaimed.

This was the lead to the Church of God's Light they had been looking for.

"The Church of God's Light is in Mt. Ulawoon?" asked Ruri.

"They are. The Spirit Slayer they're using is making it so the other spirits can't stay there. More importantly, the presence of the dead there is a huge eyesore. That is exactly why I've come all the way here to tell you to get the lead out and fix things."

"Huh? But I didn't hear anything from the spirits about someone using Spirit Slayer or the Church of God's Light being up there," Ruri said. The spirits should have known she was looking for the Church of God's Light, in which case, they would have told her if they found any clues.

"Did you explicitly ask them if the Church of God's Light was at Mt. Ulawoon? Or if someone was using Spirit Slayer?" asked Arman.

"Well, no, I didn't..." Ruri couldn't ask something she didn't know, after all.

"I swear, you're pathetic," the Spirit of Fire interjected. "You call yourself a Beloved, and you've made contracts with supreme-level spirits, but you don't know a thing about spirits, brat. Lower-level spirits are like infants. Their interests wane by the hour, and things go straight into the back of their memories all the time. If you don't explicitly ask them, they won't give you any answer."

"*We normally have to limit the amount of voices we can hear as well,*" Kotaro added.

"*That's right. It's just too much to listen to* all *of their little chatterings,*" Rin elaborated.

Kotaro and Rin's explanation lay open a glaring hole in Ruri's communication with the spirits. She had thought that if one spirit found something, they would share it among all of them.

But that was a faulty assumption, much to Ruri's surprise. Apparently, however, spirits had the ability to look into another spirit's memories after the fact, so they could check at a later time.

"Mt. Ulawoon... Well, no one would be going there, that's for sure. Perfect spot to do something in secret. These are the same cretins who claim all religions other than their own are heresy. They probably don't care about stepping foot on a mountain we consider sacred ground. That was a blind spot we didn't cover," Arman said, looking extremely displeased.

Celestine was convinced as well, saying, "The rumors of the dead being revived came from around that mountain as well."

"Now that we know where they are, let's go there right now and apprehend them!" Ruri suggested, leaning forward. She was brimming with enthusiasm over knowing where the Church of God's Light had been hiding after all this time.

"Now, hold on there," Arman said, stopping her. "The mountain is huge. I'd like to ask exactly where on the mountain they are."

Conducting a reckless search might raise too much suspicion, and then the suspects would run away. But if they knew exactly where they were, all Arman would have to do was send troops there to handle matters.

However, the Spirit of Fire answered with a rather blunt reply. "No clue."

"Huh?" asked Ruri.

"I said I have no clue."

Ruri stared at the Spirit of Fire with an expression that could only be described as *dumbfounded*. "Pardon? How can you have no clue when you just said they're at the mountain?"

"I'm certain they're somewhere on the mountain. I'm a fire spirit, however. I'm not suited for conducting searches."

"Then maybe if we ask Kotaro or Chi…"

"I just said they used Spirit Slayer all over the mountain, did I not? With that in the way, it'll be hard looking for them even *with* Wind or Earth's powers."

"And there's nothing else you know? Like whether they're to the north or south? If you could at least narrow down the scope a bit, that'd be great. Otherwise, they'll likely get wise and run away right in the middle of our search."

"I was asleep until just the other day, so how do you expect me to know that?"

"Jeez, you're useless!" Ruri inadvertently exclaimed.

The Spirit of Fire furrowed his brow in displeasure. "You'd best watch your tongue, brat. Who do you think you have to thank for knowing where the Church of God's Light is?"

The Spirit of Fire was angrier than she expected, and it caused Ruri to shrink back.

"That's right, Lady Ruri. You should not be so rude toward the Great Spirit of Fire," the extremely spirit-religious Celestine said in his defense.

The Spirit of Fire had a lovestruck smile on his face, as if his anger from before had dissipated. He then held Celestine's hand, his heart touched. "Your beauty is only matched by your overwhelming kindness. I've grown more smitten with you than ever. Learn by example, you bratty whelp."

The Spirit of Fire was indeed every bit the lady lover the rumors stated.

As Ruri let out an exasperated sigh, something suddenly came to her mind. "That reminds me. What should I refer to you as? Spirit of Fire is a mouthful. Do you have a name like Kotaro and the others?"

"What, you want to call me by my name? You're quite the impudent brat. Well, since you are the contract-bearer of my brethren, I wouldn't be opposed to you referring to me by name, but unfortunately, I've yet to be named. And I'm certainly not about to let you name me upon request. But if it's just a general nickname you're after, then do as you wish."

Although phrased in a very annoying way, he was essentially saying it was fine to call him something.

"...Uh, okay, then. How about Heat-sama? Kotaro and the others call you 'Fire,' so 'Heat' isn't too far off," Ruri suggested. She added the honorific because she knew he would get annoyed if she addressed him without a title like with Kotaro and the other supreme-level spirits.

"An overly simplistic and feeble-minded nickname using some strange suffix? That's all very befitting a strange brat such as yourself, indeed. Well, so be it. I will allow you to call me as such, but only as an exception."

"Yes... Thank you, I guess," Ruri said in resignation, realizing that this was just how he was going to speak to her and there was no changing it. Sometimes you just needed to know when to give up.

"Let's get back to the subject," Arman said, bringing the derailed discussion back on track. "We know they're at Mt. Ulawoon, but without any details, we can't mobilize any troops. And there's a chance they might catch on to what we're doing and flee before we can even catch them."

"What do we do, then?" asked Ruri. "If we can't go to the mountain to search, and we can't use the spirits to look either, then we'll never figure out where they are."

"There is one way," interjected Joshua, who was standing near the wall.

"You have an idea?"

"There are rumors circulating around town right now that our church friends will cure the sick and wounded."

Those rumors likely came about due to Joshua name-dropping the Church of God's Light the other day to distract the mob from the family Ruri and Ewan gave dragon's blood to.

"The Church of God's Light must be reaching out to people. After all, they're in the business of looking for more followers."

Arman seemed convinced. "I see. So, we have two options. We either catch them while they're making contact and force them to divulge their hideout, or we tail them to find it. Still, we don't know who they'll reach out to or *when*."

"Ruri's got the spirits in the capital keeping tabs on town, so they'll come reporting once they see them make any moves."

"Why, you. Going off on your own like that…" Arman looked at Joshua, frustrated that the young man took action on his own, but he wasn't necessarily angry. If he were any other dragonkin, Arman would have questioned why he was doing whatever he wanted in a nation other than his own, but Joshua was his nephew. Seeing as he was family, Arman seemed willing to forgive this minor issue.

"Regardless, it's a good plan, isn't it?" Joshua said.

"Well, we don't have any other options, it seems… Still, involving civilians in this matter is an issue," Arman argued.

"In that case, all you have to do is slip some soldiers into the mix of people looking for the Church of God's Light, right?" Ruri suggested. "If they dress in regular clothes, no one will ever know. And if they interact with one of them, it'll be even better."

Arman nodded in agreement.

"Also, we know they're capable of *raising the dead*. I doubt they'll come reaching out if we search for someone to heal the sick or injured, but it might be a good idea to search while letting it be known that our people are looking to *specifically* raise the dead. And I would make sure to instruct them to put on a sad act to really trick them, as well," Ruri added.

"Yes, good point. I'll make arrangements right away. I ought to recall the troops I sent out to search the area around Mt. Ulawoon while I'm at it. We don't want them getting wise to us."

The discussion was brought to a close. The only thing left was to wait patiently until the spirits reported in.

19 The Church of God's Light's Hideout

Several days had passed since Ruri and the others remained on standby at the castle. The spirits hadn't reported in. The soldiers in civilian attire scoured the capital in search of the Church of God's Light on a daily basis, but there was still nothing. It was a complete dead end, and it made everyone even more impatient.

In the midst of that, the only one pleased as punch was the Spirit of Fire—aka "Heat." The ladies' man that Heat was, he flirted with every woman worker in the castle and enjoyed little stints with them.

The women were confused at first and questioned who this flirty stranger was, but as soon as they heard he was the incarnation of a supreme-level spirit, the spirit-religious women started to fawn over him, looking at him with respect and adoration instead.

Heat was getting such a big head over this treatment that he didn't just hit on young girls; he hit on *every* girl under the sun—children and elderly alike. It was causing some issues that were difficult to clear up. Although he said that age wasn't a matter for spirits, Ruri had to put her foot down when it came to flirting with kids.

Heat would flirt with any girl who entered his sight so much that Ruri wondered if anything female with two legs was good enough for him. It also made her question why he was giving her the cold shoulder. It was frustrating to watch. He'd said she wasn't his type, but he obviously wasn't picky in the slightest.

Ruri decided to voice her complaint to him. However, he replied, "I have preferences that laymen just wouldn't understand." It seemed he wasn't planning on changing his attitude toward her any time soon.

Heat was currently in the middle of living it up with Arman's queens in the throne room. With an abundant assortment of food and wine, he sat in the middle while Arman's many wives circled him, all scrambling for a chance to snuggle against him and pour his wine. Heat gleefully accepted the affection with a dopey look plastered on his face.

Arman had been so busy with the Church of God's Light incident that he hadn't had time to see his wives, but Arman's harem seemed to be turning into *Heat's* harem. Arman's jaw would probably hit the floor if he saw what was happening right now. If they didn't wrap up matters with the church quickly, Heat was likely to take over the entire harem.

As all of this flirtatious merrymaking went on, some long-awaited news finally reached Ruri.

"*Ruri, we found them~! The Church of God's Light!*" reported a spirit.

"Really?!"

"*Yup, the others are keeping an eye on 'em right now.*"

Ruri rushed straight into Arman's office.

"Beast King, Sire! The Church of God's Light has been found!"

"Yes, I've just received reports myself," Arman replied. "It seems they reached out to a soldier of the kingdom."

The soldier in question had recently been dumped by his girlfriend, meaning that his sad performance was most likely extra convincing. They hadn't caught on to the fact that this was a sting operation yet.

"What should we do? Apprehend them? Leave them at large?" asked Ruri.

"We'll leave them at large for the time being. We'll tail them back to their hideout and pinpoint their location."

"So, just be careful we're not detected, correct?"

"Yes. I've ordered the soldier to say he wants to meet their leader and to ask them to lead him to their hideout in town. If that doesn't work, well, then we run into an issue."

"What kind of issue?"

"Trailing them is fine within the confines of the capital. The huge population makes it easy to hide among the crowd and tail whoever. But if you take one step outside the capital, then you'll be met with desert wasteland. There's barely anything to take cover behind until you reach the mountain, so they're bound to notice anyone tailing them. I'm not sure what we should do…"

Since the amount of people thinned out the closer you approached the mountain, the church was guaranteed to be on high alert if found out. That being said, given the surrounding topography, it was difficult to tail them without being seen.

"In that case, what about transforming into animals and trailing them? I'm sure there's no shortage of demi-humans here in the Nation of the Beast King. The church wouldn't be suspicious of their beast forms if they found them, right?"

"That won't work. While you have a point that they might not suspect a beast, a well-trained eye can tell a transformed demi-human from a real animal. And if our men are found out, then all our hard work will go up in smoke."

Just like how catkin in cat form had two tails in comparison to a real cat's one, there were differences that a trained eye could spot. It made using demi-humans for this operation dangerous.

Ruri pondered over it for a bit before proposing an idea she knew would be shot down.

"Then, why don't I go instead?"

Arman blinked. "You?"

"Yes. Well, since Kotaro and the others are spirits inhabiting the bodies of beasts, they should be all right even if they are found out, shouldn't they? And with Kotaro's wind powers, we'll be able to trail them even at a distance."

The desert wastelands lay between the capital and the mountain, and there was nothing to use as suitable cover. Trailing the church under those circumstances would be a recipe for disaster. That was where Kotaro's powers would help. Kotaro could keep them safe as they trailed their targets into the mountain, where the Spirit Slayer hampered their search.

"What are you going to do, though? You'll be spotted in human form."

"I'll turn into a cat with my bracelet. It'll be all right. I'll use a ribbon or something to hide it and pretend to be a runaway house cat. They'll be none the wiser."

The Church of God's Light possessed bracelets that transformed the wearer into rats, so there was a chance they'd realize Ruri wasn't a cat if they saw the bracelet on her paw. She needed to make sure it was concealed. Hiding it with a ribbon was a good way to throw them off and convince them that she was just someone's pet that ran away from home.

Accompanying Ruri would be Kotaro, Rin, and Chi—a wolf, a clione, and a capybara respectively. It was a rather odd assortment, but they shouldn't suspect that a bunch of animals were hot on their heels.

"Still, it's too dangerous," Arman said with concern.

"It'll be fine, Sire. I'll just be tailing them to find their hideout, so I'll be a safe distance away. I assure you, there won't be any danger."

"And why don't you just stay at the castle and give the bracelet to someone else to use?"

"That's an option, but will someone else be able to stop Kotaro and the other spirits if things turn ugly? The Church of God's Light are responsible for my assassination attempt, so they've earned much of Kotaro and Rin's ire. Faced with my would-be killers, they might give in to their rage and tear them limb from limb."

"...Yes, I can see that being an issue. Be that as it may, I can't put a Beloved in harm's way."

"I have Kotaro's barrier around me at any given time, so there's no risk of someone accosting me like with the fake Reapers. I think Kotaro and the others were a little too overconfident back then. They never expected something like that would happen right under their noses. But now Kotaro keeps an eye out around the clock, so I sincerely doubt they'll be able to exploit any gaps in defense like last time."

It was hard to tell if Arman found it difficult to refute Ruri after hearing Kotaro and the others would accompany her or if he simply decided that Ruri's plan was the most sound. Either way, Arman reluctantly agreed.

"...Just be certain not to get too close. If it looks like danger, you are to leave *immediately*. Also, do *not* leave the supreme spirits' sides."

"Yes, I know. I'm too afraid to go off on my own with zombies wandering about."

"You're just following them. Clear?" Arman said for clarity's sake.

Ruri nodded, replying, "Once we find the hideout, we'll come right back."

With that, Ruri left the room.

It wasn't long after their discussion that Ruri was on her way—not to the town in the capital but to the skies far above the outside gates of the town. Now in her cat form, she rode atop Kotaro as they flew through the air, the capital spreading far and wide below them. There they waited for the Church of God's Light's member who had reached out to the undercover soldier.

According to the lookout spirits, after the church member talked to the soldier in a pub, they interacted with several other people seeking help from the Church of God's Light as well. Some of them were simply inquiring, but a few seriously pleaded for help in exchange for becoming members themselves. Ruri needed to settle this quickly or the church was likely to make even more zombies.

"*Ruri, they're coming out now,*" said Kotaro.

After a few moments of mid-air waiting, a single man appeared from the city gates. The soldier in on the sting was going to ask the member to take him to his leader, but it seemed that didn't pan out. Ruri would have backed down if the soldier had found the hideout through conventional means, but since that wasn't going to be the case, Ruri was forced to act.

Rising further overhead, they trailed behind the man. They locked on to their target using Kotaro's powers, but they made sure to keep enough distance so that no one would suspect them.

Ruri and the others preemptively descended as they approached the mountain. Taking cover in some shrubbery, they all watched as the man ascended the mountain from a spot devoid of the sentries permanently stationed there.

He appeared to be wary of his surroundings; he kept glancing around as he proceeded onward. Ruri and her group followed him, being careful not to make any noise.

Kotaro and Chi were having problems keeping track of him—possibly due to the Spirit Slayer. It wasn't just in one isolated area either. It affected the whole mountain. They made sure to keep their eyes planted on the man so as to not lose sight of him.

Higher and higher up the mountain they ventured. As soon as they passed a certain point, they felt the sensation of passing through an invisible layer like in the past.

"This is the barrier that was up in that village of the dead," Kotaro stated.

"The one set up so no one can get out?" asked Ruri.

"One and the same."

This barrier practically confirmed that something was up ahead.

Ruri's party proceeded with caution until they noticed a tree rustling off to the side, opposite of where the man was. Out of nowhere appeared the one presence that Ruri couldn't help but fear—a zombie. "Ngyaaaah!" her cat voice rang out in panic.

"Who's there?!" the man exclaimed, naturally realizing that someone was behind him.

Once Ruri came back to her senses, she quickly poked her head out from the grass and cried, "Meooow."

"Oh, just a cat…" the man said, his doubts quelled. He began to walk again.

Ruri and the others let out a collective sigh of relief.

"Ruri…" said Rin in a scolding sort of tone.

"I'm ashamed of myself…" Ruri replied, drooping her tail.

The zombie was still there, looking at Ruri and the others, but it didn't react, most likely because of the lack of blood. With a blank stare, it started to wander off elsewhere.

They encountered a few more zombies after that, but Ruri managed to contain her screams. She also walked with caution so she didn't accidentally hurt herself. If she was to spill even a drop of blood, the game of tag with the zombies would commence and losing their target would be the least of their worries.

As such, Ruri and her party walked carefully, trailing behind the man in secret, until a giant cave came into view ahead. People were standing at the entrance, but the man waltzed right past them and went inside.

"So, is this the Church of God's Light's hideout?" asked Ruri.

"I would assume so, yes," answered Kotaro.

Ruri's group continued to observe the entrance and noticed that there weren't many people coming in and out. Only two people stood guard outside the entrance, both dressed in the same white robes. And according to Kotaro, there was a different barrier surrounding the cave, one which was designed to keep people from entering, unlike the barrier from earlier. It was the type that required either mana stronger than the barrier master or the permission of the barrier master themselves. It was probably to keep the zombies from getting in.

It was impossible to tell how big the cave was or how many people were inside just from the exterior. The villagers said to have left with the Church of God's Light could also be inside as well.

"I'm going to go check," Rin said before separating from the group.

"Huh? Wait a second, Rin!" Ruri exclaimed.

"The rest of you stay there."

"Stay here? What you're doing is dangerous! What if you're spotted?"

"It's okay. I'm hard to spot since I'm so small."

Granted, even if they *did* find Rin, it wasn't like she couldn't handle herself. Ruri's concerns really lay with the people inside.

"*...Just look. Don't do anything out of the ordinary,*" she cautioned.

"*Yes, yes. I know,*" Rin said. Then she slipped past the eyes of the guards and headed inside the cave.

"*And there she goes...*"

"*Should I go along as well?*" asked Chi.

Chi's size made him easy to spot. Plus, he seemed likely to do something off the wall to satisfy his curiosity. Ruri doubted he'd *just* go scope out the situation.

"*No, Chi. I don't know* what *you might do.*"

"*Tch, you're no fun.*"

After a few worrisome minutes of waiting, Rin came out of the cave, safe and sound.

"*Great, you're back, Rin. Looks like nothing happened.*"

"*No, they didn't notice me. But there seems to be an issue.*"

"*What kind of issue?*"

"*...There was a dragonkin soldier inside.*"

"*A dragonkin? Wait, a soldier of the Nation of the Dragon King? Why?*"

"*Let's return to the castle for now. I'll give you the details there.*"

Clueless about the situation, Ruri made her way out of Mt. Ulawoon with her pack of beastly spirits in tow.

20 The Lost Soldier

After Ruri returned to the castle, she asked the main people involved in the case to assemble in Arman's office in order to give her report and Rin's account. Ruri had difficulties pulling Heat off of his amassed harem, so Kotaro did the talking for her and they managed to bring him along.

Arman was the first to speak.

"So, what did you find?"

His tone was severe, indicating he wanted to clear this matter up as soon as possible. Considering that some mysterious, godforsaken creatures—zombies—were being created in his kingdom, it was only natural he would feel that way.

"We found their hideout. Two guards were at the entrance, and zombies wandered the perimeter. There was also a barrier posted around the cave in order to ward off intruders."

"Did it look breakable?"

"Well, um…"

Ruri didn't personally know whether that barrier was breakable. Seeing that Rin went right inside like business as usual, it meant Rin's mana was strong enough to penetrate it. Then again, that too was only natural; she was a supreme-level spirit, after all.

Ruri looked over to Kotaro, asking for an answer. He simply nodded in confirmation.

"Apparently, it is," said Ruri.

"All right, then. If we conduct a raid, it's best to do it under the cover of night so we aren't spotted. Let's do this as quickly as possible. Although, I do wish we knew how many of them we're dealing with... The layout of the cave too, while I'm at it."

"Oh, well, Rin was able to sneak a peek inside. It's not much, but it's something. However, there's a problem that needs to be addressed."

"What might that be?"

Rin fluttered up to the center of the group to give her report. *"There was a dragonkin soldier inside the cave."*

"A dragonkin soldier?! Are you positive about that?!"

"Quite positive. They were in dragonkin soldier's garb. Their aura was also unmistakable."

Although dragonkin soldiers served under the banner of the Nation of the Dragon King, they wore different attire to set them apart. One look at their clothes was all it took to identify them as a dragonkin soldier as opposed to a normal one.

"Given what Rin said, there's a chance that..." Ruri paused. "You know what I'm getting at, right, Joshua?"

"Yeah. That might be our man who went missing in the Nation of the Dragon King."

Amidst the panic incited by the Church of God's Light and the fake Reapers, a single dragonkin soldier went missing. If there really was a dragonkin in their hideout, then it stood to reason that they were the lost soldier.

"How was he in there? What was he doing, exactly?" Joshua asked with a rather stern expression. His serious change in demeanor was because the soldier was suspected of being a traitor due to his all too convenient disappearance.

However, Rin's answer kicked those doubts straight to the curb.

"I'm not sure if he was sick or sedated with some sort of drug, but his face was pale and he was knocked out. His hands and legs were shackled together and it seemed like he was their prisoner."

"Wow, seriously...?" The soldier in question was said to have been sick from poisoning at the time. However, kidnapping a dragonkin was difficult even if they were ill. Given that, he was suspected of having secret ties to the Church of God's Light, but Rin's description seemed to prove he was indeed kidnapped.

"Seems they sucked out his blood."

"His blood?" Joshua asked.

"I overheard the people inside talking about how they needed dragon's blood to resurrect the dead."

"Resurrecting with dragon's blood?" muttered Arman. "Hold on. They're really just animating the dead, which isn't the same, but is that *possible*?"

Ruri and even Ewan looked to Joshua, hoping for answers. Ewan hadn't been indoctrinated into the specifics behind dragon's blood yet, so he was also in the dark.

"I've never heard of anything like that. Dragon's blood can stimulate cells to heal wounds, but animating a corpse? I doubt it... Even if that were possible, how would the Church of God's Light know that? Dragon's blood isn't just something you can pick up off the street."

Also, the tales of the dead rising had been springing up for a few years now. This soldier went missing just recently. If they claimed they were bringing back the dead with dragon's blood, then it couldn't have been happening over the past few years. It would mean that their group had been using dragon's blood for that long.

"So you don't know, huh? At any rate, I'd like you to report this to the Nation of the Dragon King, Joshua. I'm certain Jade is also searching for this lost soldier. As for *how* they're bringing back the dead, we can get that information straight from the source once we arrest them."

Arman gave the orders to those around him for a raid on the hideout, but that was when Joshua raised his hand.

"The dragonkin would like to participate in the raid as well. They've captured one of our own. We want to save him personally. Plus, they've employed Spirit Slayer. You might not be able to use magic in the area because of it. A dragonkin's strength would be necessary in that case."

None of them knew what the forces of the Church of God's Light were capable of in battle. There was also the Spirit Slayer to consider. It was unknown what they were using the power they sucked out of the mountain for. And if magic was unavailable, it was best to have a surplus of capable fighters at the ready instead.

Arman nodded. "That's fine so long as you all follow my orders. You'd better consult Jade as well, just in case."

"Will do."

The group talked about their upcoming operation while Rin continued to give details about the interior of the cave. Once their meeting was wrapping up, Ruri spiritedly raised her hand.

"Excuse me! I'd like to help as well!"

"You are to *wait here!*"

"Aww…"

Not willing to send a Beloved out into danger, Arman swiftly shut her down.

It was the night of the operation. A tepid breeze blew through the trees of the forest. Everything was engulfed in darkness, the moon's light nowhere to be seen. The dusky forest only made things more ominous, and the thought of those zombies lurking nearby caused shivers to run down everyone's spines.

The soldiers shuddered at the occasional strange groan from around them, but it was hard to call any of them *cowards*— downright impossible, actually. Still, they scrupulously checked for injuries so that none of them would attract any zombies by blood.

As they silently traversed the forest, taking care not to get nicked by a random branch, they encircled the cave that Ruri and her spirits found. Bonfires sat at both sides of the entrance, fluttering in the night winds.

Hiding in the darkness, Rin tossed a small bag into the flames. Under the veil of night, the clione's actions went undetected.

Inside the now burning bag was a potent sleeping powder. The powder burned and turned to ash, spreading its way over to the guards standing watch, lulling them into a deep slumber.

Kotaro then proceeded to break the barrier posted over the cave. With that obstacle gone, the group tied up the unconscious guards and placed them out of the way. Then, on a soldier's signal, everyone stormed the cave.

Chi gleefully strolled inside the cave with the raiding soldiers, so Ruri asked Rin to keep an eye on him so he didn't do anything out of the ordinary.

Ruri watched the raid unfold from the top of a tree. She was actually told to stay behind at the castle with Celestine, but Chi whined about wanting to go, so she was there to keep him in check. After all, no one was willing to talk back to a supreme-level spirit— no one aside from Ruri. Even Arman found himself stepping back when they were present. Ruri was the only one who could act as an intermediary when they made unreasonable requests.

Ruri had been given strict orders not to enter the cave until things were completely wrapped up, so she patiently waited. Ewan waited with her, acting as her bodyguard instead of joining the raid. He was pretty dissatisfied with his role, but since Ruri would've needed a bodyguard even if she had stayed back at the castle, he likely wasn't going to be part of the raid either way.

There was one other who was none too happy as well—Heat. He had been ripped from his new harem and forced to come along. He leaned against the tree and peered at the cave in dissatisfaction.

"Why did I have to come as well, pray tell?" Heat asked.

"Well, there was no other choice," Ruri explained. "Neither water nor wind affects those zombies. Burning them with fire is the only way to beat them. The other fire spirits can't enter the mountain because of the Spirit Slayer, so we need you, Heat-sama, and your supreme-level powers."

"I swear, for a mere mortal, you sure have *some nerve* bossing me around."

"You say that, but weren't you the one who happily agreed once Celestine-san asked you?"

At first, Heat firmly rejected all of Arman and Ruri's requests, refusing to budge. But once Celestine nicely pleaded with him, he made a complete about-face and eagerly accepted.

"I couldn't refuse the pleas of a beautiful woman."

"By that, you're implying that I'm *not* beautiful, aren't you?"

"Hmph, that goes without saying, brat."

(*I am going to sock him so hard one day. Just you watch,*) Ruri swore from the bottom of her heart.

"Nevertheless, time is wasting here. The beautiful, waiting arms of the queens are calling, so I must get back posthaste."

"Heat-sama, just to fill you in, those ladies you're pining after are the Beast King's *wives*," Ruri admonished. He was speaking as though they were his wives.

"Such trivial matters mean nothing to me. Wind, come here for a moment."

Kotaro walked up to Heat, and Heat proceeded to nimbly straddle his back. Then he pulled Ruri's hand and set her atop Kotaro as well.

"Whoa! What are you doing?"

"We're going to take care of the walking dead."

"We're *what*?"

They were supposed to wait and deal with the animated corpses once the cave was successfully occupied and day had broken, but Heat wasn't sticking to the script. Instead, he was taking matters into his own hands. Ruri wanted to tell him off for not keeping to the plan, but he wasn't likely to stop even if she said anything. Besides, if she gave him a piece of her mind, he would give her ten of his own right back.

"Where are you going, Ruri?! You need to stay here!" Ewan exclaimed.

"Don't tell me. Tell Heat-sama!"

"Wait, don't go! Halt!" Ewan continued to shout below them as they took to the skies, but it didn't deter Heat in the slightest.

After a while of riding on Kotaro, Heat said, "Here will do." Kotaro stopped in place.

Ruri wondered how he was going to search and burn zombies in the pitch dark, but Heat suddenly pushed Ruri and sent her tumbling to the ground.

"Yow!" It wasn't a very big fall, so she didn't sustain any injuries, but it hurt nonetheless.

"Wind, loosen the slack for just a second."

"Wait, what are you... Oh, God, it's cold!" Ruri was about to complain, but a mysterious fluid splashed all over her before she could finish. "Wait, what is this?"

Although it was too dark to see anything, she sniffed the liquid drenching her hands. It had a metallic smell to it.

"Heat-sama! What is this?!" Ruri asked, anger seeping into her voice.

Atop Kotaro, Heat nonchalantly replied, "It's animal blood."

Ruri glared at Heat. "Why did you pour that on me...?"

The zombies reacted to blood, and they were currently in an area swarming with the undead. They weren't going to look her way if she kept still, but things were going to get dangerous at this rate.

"What are you doing? If you throw that on me, I'm bound to get attacked! What are you even thinking?!"

Ruri raged at Heat as he sat overhead. However, he simply looked down at her with a frigid stare, unwilling to put up with her outburst, and said, "Brat, I suggest that before you start complaining, you run."

"Huh? What are you talking..." Ruri hadn't finished her sentence before she heard rustling in the nearby tall grass. She flinched and turned around.

Out from the grass emerged a zombie, bellowing like a savage beast. Its hollow eyes set their sights on Ruri and it pounced at her.

"Ungooooh!"

"Eeeeeek!"

"Go on, now, be quick and run. Otherwise, you're zombie food."

"Unghaaaaah!"

Ruri shot straight up and took off away from the zombie.

"I'm going to use you as bait to lure out these creatures, so run like you mean it."

Ruri sprinted in the desolate darkness, relying solely on her night vision. The zombies chased after her, bizarrely crying all the while. Not only that, but they kept gradually multiplying in numbers, attracted by the smell of the blood on her body. She turned back to make sure, but it was too dark to see much of anything. However, from the sheer amount of growls she heard, she knew that a considerable mob had formed behind her. The sheer thought of being surrounded by that many zombie threats was absolutely terrifying.

Heat leisurely watched from a safe spot atop Kotaro in the sky.

"You're a fiend! A devil! An egotistical and ill-adjusted *jerk*!" Ruri cursed.

"If you can run your mouth, you can run your legs. Now, keep it up!"

"You're an evil *bastaaaard*! Screw *yoooou*!" Ruri screamed as she continued to move. She was done for if she stopped.

In the dark forest, the zombie's strange cries and heavy footsteps trailed behind Ruri.

"Aaaaah!"

"Gyaaaah!"

"Agah, agaaah!"

"Oh God! Stay back, you freeeaks!"

The wailing horde of zombies skyrocketed Ruri's fear to the absolute limit. She could feel her heart practically beating out of her chest. She could barely see anything around her. The fact that she had to rely on their cries alone amplified her terror. Kotaro, who was supposed to help her if danger ever befell her, wasn't coming to her aid at all, but Ruri was too panic-stricken to mind that. She dashed on, on the verge of crying her eyes out.

"Whyyyyy?! Why is this happening to meee?!" she screamed.

Ruri wasn't a dragonkin, however. Her normal human stamina wasn't going to last for much longer, and she could feel herself steadily running out of breath. It wouldn't be so bad if the zombies felt fatigue themselves, but seeing as they were just corpses, it wasn't clear if they could. But judging by how easily they were catching up to her, it was safe to assume that they couldn't.

Finally, after much running, Ruri's legs stopped dead in their tracks. The zombies—the literal horde of zombies—encircled her. Running past all of them would be no easy task.

"K-Kotaro..." she stammered, Kotaro no longer in sight.

The zombies slowly approached her until they were just a stone's throw away. Then they lunged at her all at once.

With nowhere to flee, Ruri had no choice but to hold her head and cower where she stood. She braced herself for the onslaught of pain and shock, but the next thing she knew, the entire gathering of zombies was set ablaze.

"Huh?" The flames raged in front of her face, shining bright and shredding through the veil of night.

The light from the fire allowed her to see exactly how many zombies there were. There were dozens of them, probably close to a hundred. All of them went up in flames, oddly howling all the while.

It was a sight horrific enough to exacerbate her terror even more. But oddly enough, despite being right next to the burning flames, Ruri couldn't feel any heat radiating from them. As she wondered why that was, she spotted both Kotaro and Heat. These flames were probably Heat's. There was a lot that Ruri wanted to say—she wanted to lay right into him—but she was too relieved to even get angry.

The fire soon died down, leaving only the charred remains of the zombies in its wake. Kotaro and Heat slowly descended to the ground.

"You moved well, brat," Heat said. His satisfied grin stretched ear to ear.

"Aah, you flatter me…" Ruri said sarcastically, annoyed and exhausted. Her fatigue occupied every corner of her mind so much that she couldn't even muster up a scathing remark to throw Heat's way.

"*Are you all right, Ruri?*" Kotaro asked in concern as he looked at Ruri's face.

"Kotaro, how could you?! Why didn't you come and save me?!"

"*Because Fire stopped me and said it wasn't necessary. I had my barrier around you the entire time, so they wouldn't have been able to lay a finger on you. I did loosen it a bit upon Fire's request when he poured that blood on you, though.*"

"Oh, now that you mention it…"

Kotaro had kept a barrier around Ruri ever since they came to the Nation of the Beast King. Even if Heat hadn't done anything, the zombies wouldn't have been able to hurt her.

Ruri's shoulders slumped. She had totally forgotten about that.

Heat had also realized there was a barrier around Ruri—he'd known she was safe from attack. But to add insult to injury, he threatened that she would be "zombie food" if she didn't run away. It was just a twisted joke. There was no need for her to run like her life depended on it.

However, even if she had remembered she had a barrier protecting her, her legs probably would have moved on their own anyway.

"I am *so* not getting any sleep tonight…" Ruri said, sure that zombies were going to haunt her dreams. She silently cursed Heat for using her as bait without even a moment's hesitation.

21 Eruption

Once the dreadful game of zombie tag was over, Ruri reunited with Ewan, who had remained near the entrance of the cave.

"You can't just go running off like that!" Ewan scolded her.

"Save your complaints for Heat-sama. *I'm* the victim in all this," Ruri retorted. She was an exhausted mess.

"I swear, imagine if something had happened…" Upon closer inspection, Ewan noticed red stains all over Ruri's face and clothes. He jumped in surprise and yelled, "Hey, wait! What happened?! Did you get hurt?!"

"No, Heat-sama did this to me. He made me zombie bait, the louse! I'll make tears pour from his eyes one day!"

"Oh, I see. Well, good luck with that," Ewan replied flippantly, not seeming to care so long as Ruri was safe. He probably didn't want to get wrapped up in any messes himself either. "Anyway, they're done raiding the cave. You can go inside now."

Apparently, everything had concluded while Ruri was out giving the horde of zombies the runaround. Many of the soldiers stood in front of the cave, while others waited on standby further down the mountain.

"What about the members of the Church of God's Light?"

"They apprehended all the members inside the cave, including their leader. Our soldiers weren't able to use magic due to all the Spirit Slayer around, but seeing as they were up against a bunch of regular people who could barely fight, they didn't have a tough time at all. Actually, they said for all the trouble they caused, they went down pretty anticlimactically."

"They didn't attack them with the power they siphoned using Spirit Slayer?" Ruri asked, remembering how Nadasha crafted a magic tool that exploded using Spirit Slayer. She was wary of that possibly happening again.

"No, they're investigating what the church was using the stolen power for, but they didn't put up too much of a struggle. They apparently *did* whine up a storm, though."

"Did they find the captured dragonkin?"

"Yeah, they did. They drained a lot of his blood, so he's pretty weak at the moment, but he's not in any mortal danger. They said he can even answer questions."

"I see. That's great news," Ruri said, relieved that the soldier was safe.

"The soldier is already in transit to the castle. Once he's in better shape, they plan on questioning him. Though, he is a dragonkin. Our bodies are built out of sturdy stuff, so I'm sure he'll recover in no time."

"That means the case is closed, then?"

"Not yet. Joshua has been looking for you. There are some of the dead in there, so he said he wanted to ask the Spirit of Fire to lay them to rest."

Ruri nodded. "Right, okay."

While she wasn't too keen on seeing any more zombies, Ruri reluctantly entered the craggy cave with Heat and Kotaro in tow. The interior was much bigger and more intricately laid than she expected. The cavern was neatly organized, almost as if man-made. Soldiers stood all around, some of them holding lights that brightly illuminated the inside, so Ruri and her crew knew they were on the right path.

They spotted several people dressed in matching robes, all of them with their hands tied behind their back. It was safe to assume they were members of the Church of God's Light. Old, young, man, woman—there didn't seem to be any restrictions to becoming a believer of their religion.

They walked on until they eventually reached a huge, open area, presumably the central room of operations. There were more detained members here than anywhere else in the cave. Dozens of them sat wrangled in the center. Including the members they saw along the way, there were at least a hundred in total.

Soldiers stood around the cluster of captured members. In the center of the cluster was a large cage with people inside of it. Standing in front of that was Joshua.

"Hey, Joshua," Ruri called out, "Ewan said you were looking for me."

"Oh, hey, you're here. I was… Wait, why are you a mess?! Did you get hurt?!" Joshua exclaimed, caught off guard by Ruri's bloody appearance. Possibly in reaction to the blood, the people in the cage started to clamor.

"Don't worry. I'm not hurt," Ruri said. She went on to explain her terrifying game of tag with the horde of zombies.

Joshua looked at her with sympathy. "Well, I'm just glad you're not hurt."

"Me too. But, anyway, since these people in the cage are reacting to me, are they zombies? They kind of look more human than the ones outside."

The zombies outside the cave had lifeless eyes and emaciated limbs. They looked like dry husks devoid of any kind of moisture. But the people in the cage, while exhibiting the same lifeless eyes and pale complexions, were clean and healthy-looking. Their flesh was vibrant; they didn't look much different from a living human being.

"Apparently, the ones in this cage haven't been dead for very long. That's why. But they're the same as the ones outside. They're not alive."

"Oh, I see. Then we need to burn them up as well?"

"Yeah, we can't leave the dead here like this. We need to give them a proper send-off."

"That's true. We sure can't leave them like this."

They resembled regular people, but they weren't alive. They moved, but they had already passed. Giving these people a proper cremation was for their benefit.

"Heat-sama, please, if you could."

Heat scoffed harshly at the prospect of Ruri giving *him* an order, but he walked over to the cage nonetheless. One of the caged people suddenly caught fire, and it wasn't long before the blaze spread to each and every one of them.

Even if they were technically dead, seeing people immolated was still hard to watch. Ruri averted her eyes. Just as she did, a host of sorrowful cries rose up in response to the fire.

"No! Please, stop!" one younger woman begged.

"You have to put out those flames, please!" pleaded a man.

"Those people are still alive!" screamed another woman.

The cries were all coming from the captured members of the church. Tears rolled down their faces as they petitioned Ruri and the others not to burn the zombies. It was safe to assume that the zombies were their lost loved ones, and they had all joined the Church of God's Light in the hope they could be reunited with them.

"You can't really blame those people, can you?" Ruri commented, knowing they just wanted the people they held dear back.

"Got that right. The leader and the original members are to blame here. From what I've heard, the people who joined the church to pay for reviving their loved ones are pretty much in the dark about the inner workings of the organization. The mastermind and the perpetrators of all this are the leader and his original followers."

"What in the world were they trying to do?" Ruri asked.

"We're interrogating them now. We need to get to the bottom of why they were using Spirit Slayer—and why they wanted dragonkin blood too."

The Church of God's Light assaulted Celestine, a Beloved in the spirit-religious Nation of the Beast King. The soldiers probably weren't going to use kid gloves when interrogating the captured members. However, these people had to reap what they sowed. They manipulated Noah, a mere child, into becoming an assassin for their cause, so even Ruri wanted to give them a piece of her mind and then some.

"By the way, where are Rin and Chi? They were at the front of the pack coming in here, weren't they?" asked Ruri, looking around to find both spirits missing. She had been worried the entire time about them doing something out of the ordinary and inconveniencing the soldiers.

"Yeah, they were. They said Spirit Slayer was in use here. They wanted to hurry and dispose of it for the other spirits, but these guys wouldn't give up the location, so they went looking for it."

Just as Joshua was explaining, Rin and Chi came out from the depths of the cave. They had found the source. Beckoning everyone to follow them, they led Ruri's party even deeper into the cave. However, they eventually came to a dead end. There was nothing there.

"Where is it?" Ruri asked.

"*Here. Right here,*" Rin insisted, pointing at the cave wall.

Ruri curiously put her hand on the wall and lightly pushed. The wall started slowly moving inward.

"Ooh! A secret room," Ruri exclaimed as she started to step inside, but Joshua stopped her before she could.

"Wait a sec, Ruri. I'll go in first." After he checked that it was safe, he let Ruri come in as well.

The room itself wasn't very big, but instruments and apparatuses lay all around like it was some sort of laboratory. There were also what appeared to be vials containing a red liquid that sat in long rows next to each other.

"What is this stuff?"

"From the color, it looks like medicine made from dragon blood. Here. Take a look at this," Joshua said, looking down at a magic circle drawn on the floor. Directly above it on the ceiling was a gigantic stone that resembled a lens. And atop the magic circle was a glass filled with a liquid much redder than what was in the vials.

Joshua carefully picked up the glass and sniffed the contents. "Yup, it's blood. Blood drawn from the dragonkin soldier they held captive, I'm guessing. This might be what's allowing them to resurrect the dead. But what about this magic circle…" Joshua trailed off and looked at Rin and the other spirits.

"*The stone on the ceiling is a magic tool enchanted with Spirit Slayer,*" Rin explained. "*They've been using it to funnel the mountain's power into the magic circle and infusing the blood sitting atop it with that power. That triggers some sort of reaction, allowing them to create something that can raise the dead, as far as I can tell.*"

Joshua sighed. "So, we'll have to get the details out of *them*, huh? Well, we're gonna have to take this all in as evidence. There's a lot of stuff here, so I'll get some help."

Joshua rushed out of the room and returned shortly with several soldiers. They started to carefully collect the vials and instruments for evidence, but they ran into a problem—namely, the huge stone affixed to the ceiling. It was still sapping power from the mountain even as they spoke.

"Should I put this whole thing into my pocket space? I did practically the same thing before."

Ruri had put the volatile stones Nadasha used into her pocket space before. Since they couldn't chance the stone triggering an explosion by destroying it, throwing it into the pocket space was probably the safest option. It at least wouldn't be able to steal any more power from inside there.

"That's right. If we bust it up and something happens, it'd be bad news. But, uh, ain't this magic circle active? Is it safe to just take it off the wall?" Joshua asked.

Ruri didn't have any answers, so she looked to Rin and the spirits.

"*I believe you can stop the flow of siphoned power as long as you destroy the magic circle,*" Rin explained.

"*Ooh! Then I'll do the honors!*" Chi raised his paw and volunteered himself, looking like he was having the time of his life. Humming a little tune, he used his earth powers to move the ground the magic circle was drawn on, lumping up the surface and breaking down the shape of the circle.

"*Okay, destroying the magic circle stopped the flow, but we can't stop the stone from stealing power, so hurry up and put it in the pocket space,*" Rin said.

"Got it," Ruri replied. She asked a few of the soldiers to help her take down the stone. Then they swiftly tossed it into her pocket space.

Just as they sighed in relief, happy that the Spirit Slayer was gone and magic was available again, Heat shuffled up, having finished his zombie cremation.

"I heard you found the Spirit Slayer, but you didn't destroy it, did you?"

Something about Heat's words caused Ruri and the others to freeze in place. They slowly turned to look at him.

"Oh, um, we destroyed...the magic circle, at least. And we put the Spirit Slayer into my pocket space, but were we...not supposed to do that?"

Heat heaved a sigh. "Don't blame me for what happens next."

"Okay, that's *really* ominous. What's that supposed to mean?" Ruri asked, her face filling with worry.

"The power balance of this mountain has been thrown off after all the years of the Spirit Slayer siphoning off its energy. Since I'm a supreme-level spirit, I was able to regulate that balance by remaining asleep. However, now that I'm awake, there's no one left to regulate it. On top of that, if you suddenly destroy the Spirit Slayer, all that power it stole will shoot right back to the mountain."

"And if it does, what happens?"

Just as Ruri asked that question, the ground quaked more than it ever had in recent days. Then a thunderous sound and shaking akin to an explosion assaulted Ruri's party.

"Wait, wait, what is this?" Ruri asked, panicking.

"I just told you. The power returning to the mountain triggered an explosion—an eruption, if you will."

"An *eruption*?!"

22 The Quelling

"Wait, eruption?! What are we supposed to do?!"

"You haven't seen the signs? This isn't the first time the mountain has shown instability since I've awakened."

"Oh, do you mean the tremors as of late? So, that *was* because of the volcano after all."

Frequent tremors had been happening for a while now. As everyone clamored in fear, thinking it was the "rage of the spirits," Ruri worried about the nearby volcanic mountain, Mt. Ulawoon. It seemed her fears were justified. Heat had been asleep for a millennium, and the volcano erupted a millennium ago. There had to be a correlation.

When she asked to clarify her suspicions, Heat replied, "I assume even you know that any land with spirits grows stable and fertile, yes? Well, seeing how I'm the supreme spirit of fire, as long as I'm around, this literal hotbed of fire power will naturally remain stable. Ergo, this mountain has yet to see an eruption."

"Oh, that makes sense."

"Well, not that it matters much now. This mountain was already unstable due to the church's handiwork, but you bunch have essentially finished the job. This is what happens when you do things without consulting me first."

"How were we supposed to know this would happen, though?! Rin and the others never told us! And, actually, *you* should've told us earlier yourself, Heat-sama!"

"The power of earth strongly influences the power of fire. Water and the others couldn't have known what would happen since they didn't know I was keeping things regulated."

"In that case, you should've—"

"Hey, we don't have time for all this leisurely chitchat," interjected Joshua. "If this place is gonna blow, we need to evacuate pronto."

"Oh, right," Ruri muttered, coming back to reality. "Let's hurry and get out of here."

They needed to evacuate quickly since the cave was no longer safe, but there were still many people inside—not just soldiers but members of the church as well. Ruri didn't know how large the eruption would be, but she wasn't certain they had enough time for everyone to escape.

They soon exited the cave, telling everyone they passed to evacuate themselves. Now outside, they could see a trail of smoke billowing from the peak of the mountain. Volcanic debris fell from the sky, making the area dangerous.

"Yikes, this isn't good. Did the soldiers and church members evacuate?" Ruri asked as she watched the volcano erupting before her eyes. She turned back to Joshua in concern. They needed to get everyone out before the smoke made it hard to see.

"There's a lot of people to move. It's still going to take some time to get everyone away from the mountain." People were scrambling out of the cave, but the church members were moving slower since they were bound. "Still, it's not going to be a big eruption, so all we need to do is get to the base of the mountain—"

Immediately after Joshua spoke, another loud explosion came from the top of the mountain.

"Eeek!" Ruri screamed as she ducked for cover.

Rocks came lagging behind the explosion, hailing down from the sky. Fortunately, they were smaller than pebbles, barely big enough to cause issues even if they did hit anyone. However, none of them could rest easy since bigger rocks could come flying out at any moment.

"Hey, there's a bigger one on the way," Heat said in the most nonchalant way imaginable.

If an even bigger eruption was in store, the damage from the lava and pyroclastic flow could become a serious issue—not just for the mountain but the capital as well.

"Hey, Heat-sama. If the power imbalance is causing this eruption, couldn't you stop it since you were the one regulating in the first place?"

"Yes, I suppose I could."

"Then, please!" Ruri asked, practically yelling her request.

"And why would I ever need to do that, pray tell?" Heat responded, bitterly dashing her hopes. He wasn't refusing her request just to be mean; he honestly couldn't comprehend why he should do what she asked.

Ruri was befuddled. "'Why'? I mean, people might get hurt at this rate."

"What does that have to do with a spirit such as myself?"

"But, you've been regulating it this whole time, haven't you? Wasn't it to prevent an eruption?"

"You seem to have been mistaken. I can't very well sleep with eruptions going about. I merely did that to ensure myself a sound slumber," Heat said in a horribly apathetic tone.

Apathetic as it was, however, that was how spirits truly operated. They were self-centered beings by default. Humans didn't influence their actions one way or another. Spirits prioritized their own feelings above all else. Kotaro, Rin, and the other spirits treated Ruri with care because she was both a Beloved and a contract-bearer. If she wasn't, their line of thinking would be no different than Heat's.

"But at this rate..."

"Wind and Water may fawn over you, but I do *not*. I will not act unless it will yield me a profit."

"A profit. Profit..." Ruri murmured, desperately spinning her gears to find something that would motivate Heat.

"I could bake you cookies..."

"Unnecessary."

"If you want money..."

"Do you think I, a spirit, need money?"

"Well, I...don't." The only other things her jumbled brain could come up with was writing him up a "One Free Shoulder Massage" or "Slave for a Day" coupon. She was so pressed for time she couldn't think of anything remotely decent.

"Are we finished here? In that case, I'll be going."

"Wait a second! Um, how about... Oh, I've got it! What about a beautiful banquet with a hundred *beautiful* ladies?!"

Ruri shouted out the first thing that hit her desperate mind to the self-proclaimed ladies lover. His reaction was, in a word, stellar. Heat's eyes lit up with so much vested interest that he looked ready to take off at any moment.

"A *hundred* beautiful ladies... Hmm, yes, if that's your offer, then I certainly can't say no."

"Really?!"

"A *hundred*, understand? No homely-looking ladies and no cooking up the numbers."

"Right, right! Deal!" Ruri furiously agreed.

209

Heat had a dopey smile on his face, possibly imagining himself surrounded by a bushel of beauties.

Ruri quickly said yes to Heat because she wanted him to help, but Joshua and Ewan were apprehensive about Ruri's conduct.

"Hey, hold up, Ruri. Are you sure you should be making promises like that?" Joshua asked.

Ewan added, "You do realize that if you end up going, 'Oops, on second thought, we can't do that after all,' he's going to be pissed beyond belief, right? Do you have connections?"

"It's fine. I'll put it all on the Beast King's lap. If a hundred beautiful girls will save his kingdom from peril, I'm sure he'll handle matters. I'll go around and ask girls myself too. Heck, I'll beg, if I have to."

The castle had a glut of extremely pretty female workers, no doubt due to Arman being just as big of a Casanova as Heat himself. Ruri figured that if she asked around the castle, she could at least gather up a hundred of them. In fact, once they learned it was a supreme-level spirit's desire, the devout spirit-religious people of the Nation of the Beast King would likely happily fulfill his wish. After they got the ladies, they just needed to convince Arman to prepare a suitable venue for the banquet.

"All right, then. Wind, bring me up to the crater! I want to hurry this up and get back. My bevy of beauties await!"

Heat was brimming with so much enthusiasm that you couldn't tell he had been opposed not even a second ago. It seemed he was that eager to meet his beautiful welcome party.

He hopped on Kotaro's back with a smug face, instructing him where to go, and Kotaro dashed off. As the two of them reached the cusp of the active crater, they both disappeared into the smoke.

"I sure hope this works out," Ruri muttered, not because she didn't have faith Heat could do it but because she was worried he might change his mind and quit.

It wasn't long after the two departed that the weak, intermittent tremors settled and the outpour of smoke from the crater started to subside.

"…Is it under control?" asked Ruri.

"Looks like it," answered Joshua.

Realizing that they should get out while they had the chance, Ruri's party started descending the mountain. It took time to escort the restrained church members down the rugged mountain path, but they couldn't undo their bindings in case they tried to make a getaway. Luckily, there weren't any more eruptions to follow, so Ruri came to the conclusion that Heat must have gotten the volcano under control.

Flakes of ash rained down and piled up on the ground around them, but Ruri's group made it safely down the mountain without incident. Everyone breathed easier…until they spotted Kotaro coming down the mountain by himself.

"Kotaro, where's Heat-sama?"

"If you mean Fire, he dove into the crater."

"Wait, what?! Is he going to be okay?!"

"He's not the Spirit of Fire for nothing. The heat of flames causes him neither pain nor discomfort."

However, Heat was in a human body. Ruri was more worried about the body itself, but it was likely safe to assume he would be fine even if his outer human shell was burnt away. After all, the worst-case scenario would be that he lost his body and had to change into a new one.

"He'll make his return soon enough. Let's return to the castle," Kotaro suggested.

"Right, let's," Ruri agreed.

Fortunately, no one sustained any notable injuries other than the rescued dragonkin soldier. The leader of the Church of God's Light and his followers were successfully apprehended.

The leader and the senior members involved in assassinating Beloveds and raising the dead underwent intense interrogation. As for the other members who were deceived into joining, they were also questioned, but since they weren't involved in the particulars, their interrogation wasn't nearly as severe.

Apparently, once it was explained to them that their loved ones didn't actually come back from the dead, most of them easily complied. Most of them, at least. There were some who weren't willing to believe and raised a fuss, but they were few and far between. After all, they probably held doubts before this. After seeing their loved ones revive looking totally different from when they were alive, it was no wonder. Nevertheless, they likely tried to convince themselves to believe in the church to hold out hope.

After returning to the castle, Ruri took off her bloodstained clothes and washed her soot-covered body in the relaxing waters of the hot springs. Once her bath was over, she waited for Heat to make his return, but he was taking an awfully long time. Ruri quickly passed out from exhaustion.

One day passed into another and Heat still hadn't returned. On the morning of the day after that, Ruri awoke to a stifling sensation on her chest. Convinced that Chi was sitting on top of her again, she slowly opened her eyes to see—a close-up of Heat and his mane of bright red hair.

Ruri pulled back in surprise, but Heat had his arm wrapped around her and wouldn't let her go. She tried twisting her way out of his clutches, knocking the sheets off in the process and revealing an even more shocking sight.

"Eeeek! Heat-sama, why aren't you wearing any clothes?!"

Heat was unapologetically nude, and Ruri was trapped in his naked embrace.

"Let me go! I mean, *put on some clothes!*"

"…Hmm, control your voice, brat."

Ruri frantically thrashed against Heat, but his adult male body proved too strong. She struggled, but to no avail.

Still in a sleepy stupor, Heat wrapped his legs around Ruri as well, clinging to her like an overgrown leech. He was pinning her down, leaving her no way to run.

"Wake up and *get off!*"

Seeing Kotaro and the others at her bedside, Ruri pleaded, "Guys, do something!"

Just as she was about to get up, a knock came at the door and someone entered.

"Ruri, I heard your voice so I assume you're awake?"

Ruri looked toward the direction of the speaker. There she saw Jade, his jaw practically dragging the floor. She started to ask him why he was *here* and not the Nation of the Dragon King, but her question was drowned out by Jade himself.

"Ruri! Who is *that*?!" Jade asked loudly. He had stumbled upon a scene that was easy to misinterpret and his shock was immeasurable. He gave them a piercing glare, enraged at the sight before him. Enraged for good reason too. Ruri was cavorting with a naked man.

Kotaro, Rin, Chi, and the other spirits stood off to the side, but Jade's eyes were focused solely on the man and Ruri.

"A man…" Jade stated, his tone icy.

"Huh? No, that's not it. This totally isn't my fault. I mean, when I woke up, things were like this. Heat-sama and I aren't like that to one another!"

Ruri finally understood what this all must've looked like. She hastily tried to explain it away, but the more she attempted to clear up the misconception, the more it sounded like poor excuses in an attempt to hide the truth.

"Ruri, sleeping in the arms of a naked man you have *nothing to do with*?! Sharing a bed with another man…*without my permission*?! Should I challenge that man to a duel? Or should I warmly congratulate you? No, I can't bring myself to do that. What should I do?"

"No, no, no! You don't have to *do* anything!" Ruri protested.

"Oh, things sure sound fun in here, huh?" Joshua said, popping his head into the room. He immediately recognized the situation once he saw Jade and Ruri, so he decided to pop back out and observe from the sidelines.

Ruri felt sorry for Jade, whose rage had shifted into sorrow, but this was a complete misunderstanding. At least, that was what she wanted to explain to him, but doing so with a nude man clinging to her didn't make for the most convincing of arguments.

As she pondered a way to somehow get Heat off of her, she felt his legs loosen a little bit. Not letting this opportunity pass her by, she kicked Heat off with all her might, finally freeing herself from his embrace. Then she jumped out of bed and rushed to Jade.

"Jade-sama, this is a misunderstanding!"

"Ruri, do you prefer that man to me?"

"No, I'm telling you, you've got it all wrong! Heat-sama is the *Spirit of Fire*!"

"What? You're romantically involved with a *spirit*?!"

"Uh, no, you've got it wrong again…"

It would take a good while to dispel Jade's misconceptions, but Kotaro and Rin eventually intervened and managed to clear the air.

Details of the Incident

It took a while, but Ruri finally cleared up Jade's misunderstanding. Once that was out of the way, she launched her anger toward the now-awake Heat. He was sitting with just the bedsheet thrown over his naked body, yawning, without an ounce of shame.

"Why were you sleeping with me naked, Heat-sama?! You've caused a *huge* misunderstanding!"

"Did you expect me to dive into the mouth of a volcano and come back *with* my clothes intact?"

"Wait, you walked all the way back here from the volcano stark naked?!"

"Of course I didn't. I borrowed some of the sheets that just so happened to be in the Church of God's Light's hideout."

Ruri was relieved to hear that at least he wasn't running around committing indecent exposure. It seemed even Heat had the good sense not to walk around outside in his birthday suit.

"So, how did you end up sleeping next to me?" she asked.

"When I returned, I saw that you were sleeping quite peacefully. I had grown tired myself, so I slept right on the spot. I would have preferred a beautiful woman beside me, but my fatigue proved too much. Consider it an honor to share a bed with me."

"I don't consider it anything but a *nuisance* since it only gave Jade-sama the wrong idea. I'm just lucky I was able to straighten things out."

It had been hard work trying to clear the air on that little mishap. Seeing Ruri in the naked arms of another man was bound to set Jade off. Ruri wouldn't be so easily trusting if she were in Jade's shoes either.

Even now, though the misunderstanding was resolved, Jade *definitely* seemed wary of Heat. He held Ruri in his lap with his arms around her this entire time, and he wasn't showing any signs of letting go. It wouldn't have been an issue had Heat been in an animal form like Kotaro and the others, but the fact that he looked like a human affected his opinion greatly.

"So is he your lover? How very strange. To think he would pick a whelp like you out of all the beauties in the world makes me not only commend his valor but question his tastes. You're quite the lucky one, girl. You'd best hold on to this one. Otherwise, you'll never find another man in your lifetime."

"Thanks but no thanks for the life advice. You're always running off at the mouth *way* more than you should, Heat-sama! Jade-sama doesn't do that!" Ruri said, mumbling that last part under her breath.

Ruri had been fretting over how to face Jade the next time they met due to their circumstances, but thanks to this mishap, none of that even crossed her mind. The fact that she was able to interact with him far more normally than she expected was a lucky break. Nevertheless, Ruri still wondered if Heat was acting oddly arrogant toward her or if it was a figment of her imagination.

"Anyway, what are you doing here, Jade-sama? Is the Nation of the Dragon King all right?"

"Yes, we're done cleaning up the aftermath, and the repairs to the castle are finished, so I've come to pick you up. Oh, I've also heard that the Church of God's Light has been apprehended, so I came to talk with Arman while I was at it."

"I think you've got your priorities backward there..." Ruri quipped.

"What are you talking about? There's no priority higher than you, Ruri," Jade said without even a hint of embarrassment.

Jade had always been forthright with her, but now that Ruri knew how he felt about her, she couldn't just pass these statements off as affection for a pet like in the past. Her cheeks were starting to blush.

"Quit your flirting, brat. Anyway, what about my beautiful women? I take it you haven't forgotten our deal, correct?"

"Don't worry. I've got everything set up." She had already told Arman about the promise she made—a banquet with beautiful women. It seemed Arman couldn't turn her down if it helped prevent a potential eruption from taking place.

"I see. Good. In that case," Heat said, his lips stretching into a slovenly grin. He was probably picturing himself surrounded by the bevy of beauties.

"Heat-sama, hurry and do something about your clothes. People will start thinking you're just a streaker."

"Hmm, yes, I suppose I can't very well meet with a room full of beauties in the buff, now can I? Very well, I'll take my other form until I prepare a new outfit."

"Other form?" Ruri questioned.

Before she could process what he said, Heat suddenly vanished into thin air. Ruri jumped. That was when she noticed something rustling under the sheet he'd been using. Out from the linen popped a figure—a penguin.

"Huh? A penguin...?"

"Hmm, yes, I can't say I'm a fan of this merry little body."

"Is that you, Heat-sama?"

"Who else would it be? You're too young to be going senile, you know."

His appearance was adorable, but his tone was just as uppity as ever. That was how she knew for sure it was him.

"Well? No problems should arise if I'm in this form."

"Um, well, you raise a good point, but... Huh, I guess your body *was* a demi-human's."

Ruri had been convinced that his body belonged to a regular human, but now that she really thought about it, this was the Nation of the Beast King—a nation of demi-humans. It was likely easier to obtain a demi-human's body than a human's, hence this adorable penguin. But it was beyond weird seeing him in his animal form after interacting with him as a human for so long. A cute penguin with big, round eyes and Heat were two concepts that didn't match *at all.*

"I'm fine with the human form, but this form is far too merry-looking and goes against my image, so I'm not the biggest fan of it."

"Yeah, but I feel it'd be a hit with girls."

"What? This is what girls like?"

"Well, I think most girls like cute things."

"Hmm, is that so? Then I'll check for myself!"

Heat jumped from the bed. He then took little adorable, tottering steps right out the door, probably off to venture for women.

Ruri said he'd be a "hit with the girls," but she couldn't really say for certain here in a kingdom where demi-humans were a more familiar sight. However, dragonkin were popular among men as well as women. Dragonkin like Jade couldn't be any more different from animals of Heat's sort. If Heat were to parade his stubby little legs around in the Nation of the Dragon King's castle, the ladies who worked there would undoubtedly shower him with shrill cries.

Finn walked into the room, passing by Heat on the way out.

"Oh, you're here too, Finn-san."

"Yes, I arrived here this morning with His Majesty. Good to see you again, Ruri. Your Majesty, the Beast King is requesting to partake in breakfast."

"I see. Very well, then."

After dressing and tidying up, Ruri headed down with Jade for breakfast. While it was framed as a meal, its true purpose was to discuss matters of the Church of God's Light. Three days had passed since they apprehended the leader and his members. Arman's preparations for a discussion like this probably meant he managed to pull some degree of new information from the members.

Once their meals were served, they started off by eating. The Nation of the Beast King's style forewent chairs, and instead people sat atop tapestries laid out on the floor. Ruri had grown accustomed to this way of eating during her stay, but she was surprised to see Jade sit cross-legged without hesitation. In fact, it felt a little off to her.

Perhaps out of consideration for their meal, they avoided heavy topics and only exchanged light banter. It was possible they never brought up a single gory, appetite-spoiling subject out of consideration for Ruri as well. However, once they finished eating, the two kings' faces looked as serious as could be.

"How's the Nation of the Dragon King holding up?"

221

"No problems on our end. The castle is fixed, and everything has been the picture of peace after apprehending the raider. Everything aside from the lost soldier, that is. I've heard *you've* been having more issues here."

"Sure have. I never would have imagined that the Church of God's Light was operating in the shadows here in the Nation of the Beast King. And for *years* now, to boot."

"What was their end goal?" Jade asked.

That was the thing Ruri was most curious about. Plotting to kill Beloveds, kidnapping a soldier, animating the dead—these were only a small smattering of their deeds, but there might be many more.

"The leader of the church and a handful of his senior members were pulling the strings. They caused all that grief, but once we got a little rough in our interrogation, they spilled everything."

Ruri didn't know how much "a little rough" was, but after seeing the amused smirk on Arman's face, she was too afraid to ask. Since they'd assaulted Beloveds, "little" to the rest of the world and "little" to Arman was bound to have different connotations.

"Their end goal was the restoration of the Church of God's Light. After losing members and falling into disarray, they were trying to increase their numbers and revitalize the church. The Beloved assassination plots, reviving the dead, kidnapping the soldier—it was all for that."

"*That* was their reason...?" Ruri questioned, a mixture of exasperation and anger. *That* was why they tried to kill her? It made her question why they hadn't just attracted new members *instead* of involving innocent lives if they wanted to restore their church so bad.

"They spread word of raising the dead to gain members and persuaded people who believed their stories to join in exchange for reviving their loved ones. The majority of their following in the cave were people in that very situation. There were some who honestly believed and devoted themselves to the leader, but there were also a lot who were on the fence. Still, the common factor between all of them was that they'd lost their loved ones and were at the end of their ropes."

"And they manipulated their hopes? That's despicable," said Ruri. She thought of Noah, who only wanted the church to bring back his parents. They undoubtedly manipulated other people in similar fashion. She was beside herself, hating how the leader and his crew exploited people's vulnerabilities.

"As for the kidnapped soldier, they needed dragon blood for their revival method, so they used the confusion of the Beloved assassination to abduct a drugged and weakened soldier. The assassination plots against our Beloved and Cerulanda's Beloved were some sort of *purge* against *heretics*, but the assault on the Nation of the Dragon King's Beloved and the other issues were a diversion to abduct the soldier."

The fires in town, the explosion in the castle, the poisoning of the food—they basically did anything they could to cause confusion. Gaining a dragonkin was their goal. Noah and the Reapers were nothing more than decoys to accomplish this.

"What was this whole 'raising the dead' business?" Jade asked. "They apparently needed dragonkin blood, but how do they know of that usage? Did they talk about that?" Jade was particularly interested in that facet since one of his soldiers was kidnapped because of it. It was also an issue for dragonkin as a whole.

"They were processing a certain medicine by infusing dragonkin blood with the power from Mt. Ulawoon. The medicine has the ability to revitalize cells, even *dead* ones. And using that, they created moving corpses devoid of souls. However, the product was incomplete. They conducted their test to confirm the medicine's effects in the wiped-out village, among other places."

"So does that mean it really *could've* resurrected the dead if they'd completed it?" asked Ruri.

"Don't know the answer to that, but the spirits said it was impossible, didn't they?" Arman replied.

"Yes, they did."

"If they say so, then it must be impossible."

You couldn't call them "revived" without a soul. And a soul couldn't be brought back even with the power of a supreme-level spirit.

"How did the Church of God's Light know of that way of making medicine?" Jade asked. "Also, according to what I was told, they've been raising the dead even before the soldier went missing. If they needed dragonkin blood, then where were they getting their supply?"

Jade's doubt was reasonable. The people of that village were wiped away several years ago. If the Church of God's Light was already setting their plans in motion back then, that didn't explain whose blood they used and how they learned to make medicine from dragon blood. Making medicine out of dragonkin blood was a secret technique. It was a processing method only a select few dragonkin knew, so it wasn't something anyone could simply do.

"They said it was a witch."

"A witch?" repeated Jade.

"The person who taught the leader and his followers how to make the medicine called themselves a witch."

"Witches again, eh?"

"They were wearing a hood to obscure their face, but from their voice and height, they seemed to be a man. That man gave them the blood, the recipe for the medicine, and our mystery bracelets."

By "mystery bracelets" he meant the bracelet that transformed the wearer into a rat, like the ones Noah and the fake Reapers used.

"So there are more bracelets?" asked Ruri.

"Yeah, but we've collected all of them," Arman assured.

"Well, that's a relief. Oh, but if that witch has even more of them, there is always the possibility they would circulate them to other people up to no good. Wait a second… You said the witch is a *man*?"

Jade answered Ruri's question, explaining, "Men who use sorcery are referred to as 'witches' as well. Regardless of whether that person was actually a witch or not, there are plenty of witches who live in secret, not belonging to any one nation. They're called 'Rogue Witches.' Either way, it might be hard identifying the specific witch that reached out to the Church of God's Light."

"Yes," Arman replied, nodding. "Plus, the witch only gave them blood, some bracelets, and a recipe for medicine. They didn't actually commit any crime. The Church of God's Light was the one who abused all of those things. We have no reason to arrest them."

The blame was solely on the Church of God's Light for this incident. The witch served as nothing more than the catalyst.

"What will happen to the church now?" asked Ruri.

"The majority of the members we apprehended simply joined the church; they have neither connections nor knowledge of any of the church's actions. Since none of them committed any crimes, we released them to their respective families after questioning."

With the leader apprehended and his followers finally returned to their homes, the Church of God's Light was completely wiped out—a far cry from their plans of restoration.

"But among the handful that did believe in reviving the dead and dedicated themselves to the leader, there were some that lent a hand in his designs. They will be tried along with the leader and his senior members. That's a decision I wanted to talk over with you, Jade. Are you okay with us trying them? The church attacked all of you as well."

The Church of God's Light committed crimes against the Nation of the Dragon King as well as the Nation of the Beast King. It was necessary to figure out which laws they would be tried by.

"I'm fine either way. The Nation of the Beast King can punish them even more severely than the Nation of the Dragon King, after all."

"Oh, is that so?" Ruri asked, clueless to either nation's laws. She had made enough progress in her studies to finally get the hang of this world's written language, but she hadn't progressed far enough to delve into law yet. Even so, there was no way she would know the differences between the two nations.

Jade elaborated, "In the Nation of the Beast King, plots to kill a Beloved are grounds for death, no exceptions. Other crimes have more severe punishments here than in the Nation of the Dragon King. In fact, in light of what happened to you, Ruri, the Nation of the Dragon King will also be enacting the death penalty for any plot to kill a Beloved—be it instigated, executed, failed, or otherwise."

Ruri was surprised by that fact, but Arman seemed to agree with it.

"Actually, you should've put that into place far earlier," Arman commented. "If you had finalized that law quicker, you could have tried that group from before by now."

"Unlike this nation, the Nation of the Dragon King had no Beloved for quite some time. It only stands to reason why the laws haven't been overhauled," Jade explained.

A Beloved would be born in the Nation of the Beast King every so often, but it was said that the Nation of the Dragon King hadn't seen a Beloved in their kingdom since the first Dragon King. Weidt, the First Dragon King, was not only the mightiest of Dragon Kings but a Beloved himself. There wasn't anyone foolish enough to pick a fight with someone of his caliber, which explained why there wasn't a law in the case harm befell a Beloved. Weidt's haphazard way of doing things might have also been a factor.

Arman said it should have been done earlier, but if Jade had instilled that law any sooner, Noah would have been sentenced to death. Ruri was secretly glad it was coming after the fact.

"Well, maybe we should make them parade around town, telling people they plotted to assassinate Beloveds, then? Ha ha ha!"

Arman chuckled heartily, but for the leader and his followers, that would be no laughing matter. The people of the Nation of the Beast King took worshiping spirits very seriously. They would never show anyone who dared touch a Beloved any mercy. They would start stoning the church members or even worse. The Church of God's Light would be ingrained in the public's mind as heinous fiends who tried to kill Beloveds. The townspeople's search for the church would likely come to an end as well.

"So, that's about it for the Church of God's Light," Arman concluded.

"Right. I'd appreciate it if you handled the aftermath. Now that the castle is repaired, would you mind if I took Ruri back home with me?"

"Not at all. In fact, hurry up and take her back. Her presence is more troublesome than Celestine's. Supreme-level spirits are sacred beings, but I don't want them so close all the time. It stresses me out."

Jade smiled wryly, as if he understood how he felt, but Ruri objected to his phrasing.

"How rude. Kotaro and Rin are cute, aren't they? Okay, Chi may have a mean look to him, but still." They were her dear friends, so she didn't want anyone treating them unkindly.

"Getting threatened every time something happens isn't something I can stand. I can't just interact with them as casually as you do. They're supreme-level spirits, after all. Not even Celestine, a Beloved herself, can stop them if something arises."

"They don't make any unreasonable demands. They're free spirits and just filled with a little curiosity, that's all."

"A 'little' is the issue here... But whatever. If you're going back, I'll prepare a lavish banquet."

"Oh, please don't forget Heat-sama's request," Ruri said, reminding Arman since it would be a huge mess if he forgot. If they were short by even one girl, they would probably never hear the end of Heat's complaining. They had to make sure everything was in order, no matter what.

"Yes, I know. I have made preparations," Arman replied.

As such, the turmoil incited by the Church of God's Light tentatively came to a close.

The Banquet

The Church of God's Light had been dealt with, the castle had been repaired, and it was now the day before Ruri and the others were set to return to the Nation of the Dragon King. Heat's long-awaited banquet with a hundred different beautiful women was underway.

The fleet of attractive women was composed mostly of castle employees. Ruri had walked around the castle, carefully picking out beautiful girls for the lineup. Arman's wives also said they wanted to participate, so by adding them to the mix, they managed to assemble a hundred girls.

It seemed that Heat's penguin form hadn't been well received. He was back in his human form with a new set of clothes. Based on his dopey grin, he didn't have any complaints about the girls in attendance. In fact, he seemed to be utterly delighted.

Next door, Ruri's farewell banquet was underway. Since it was a banquet to send off the visitors of the Nation of the Dragon King, Joshua, Ewan, and the others were also sitting in front of the selection of food and liquor. Although they could hear Heat's occasional loud chortle through the wall, everyone was enjoying their food and drink.

Ruri refused to touch the easy-to-drink wine Celestine had laid out, trying to avoid the same pitfall as last time, but Celestine took notice and shuffled up to her. Her face seemed somewhat red; it was possible she was already drunk. And when she was drunk, she became unpleasant. Ruri had a bad feeling about this.

"You don't seem to be drinking at all. I've prepared so much of this wine for you, Lady Ruri."

"I'm very grateful, but I'm not in the mood for another hangover."

"Hangover, shmangover! This is a banquet to see you off, Lady Ruri. What's the point of our guest of honor abstaining from drinking?!"

"No, but, um…" Ruri stammered.

Celestine pouted at her with glassy eyes. She was *definitely* drunk.

"Are you trying to say you can't drink the wine I've prepared?!"

"No, I'm not, I'm just saying—"

"Then, *drink*!"

"Yes, ma'am…" Ruri felt forced to agree now that Celestine was in full-blown confrontational drunk mode. She obediently took the glass that Celestine held before her.

Celestine's personality took a drastic turn when she drank. Ruri wondered why no one stopped her before she got to this point. She turned to Arman, the one person capable of reining her in. However, he was engaged in a friendly chat with Jade, partaking in wine himself, so he was paying no heed to the situation on Ruri's end.

Without any other recourse, Ruri took tiny sips from her glass. She would probably be fine so long as she didn't drink a lot of it. She made sure not to over-consume the sweet, delicious liquor.

This seemed to satisfy Celestine. With that out of the way, she turned her attention to Jade. "Master Jade?" she addressed him as she took a seat next to him. She wrapped her arm around his and slid herself closer.

Jade didn't show much in the way of resistance, but he did smile awkwardly. "Celestine, are you drunk again?"

"The hell? You're already drunk?" Arman asked. "For someone who likes to drink, you're terrible at holding your liquor."

Jade and Arman had seen this song and dance before. However, Ruri was less worried about Celestine and more about Jade, who Celestine was drunkenly hanging on to. Jade was practically letting Celestine have her way with him, allowing her to press up against him with no objections.

What was the big idea here? Ruri was sitting right next to him, yet he was getting all handsy with another woman. She started to question whether what he gave her was *actually* a dragonheart or not.

"...Well, Jade-sama, you seem to be *enjoying yourself*," Ruri muttered with a hint of sarcasm, a bemused look in her eyes.

Jade felt her icy glare descend upon their group and, flustered, he tried to explain himself.

"Oh, uh, no, wait, don't get the wrong idea, Ruri," Jade said. He tried to pry Celestine's hands off of him, but her grip was firm and she wasn't letting go. This was a complete 180 from the situation with Heat earlier.

"Let go of me, Celestine."

"I don't want to."

As Jade argued with Celestine, she drunkenly giggled and clung to him even tighter. Their back-and-forth looked nothing short of flirtatious, which only upset Ruri more and more.

"Well, you seem to be having a ball, all things considered," quipped Ruri.

"Oh my. Well, Master Jade has said that he prefers women who are more *physically attractive*."

"I did *not*! I certainly *did not*!" Jade said, desperately shaking his head as he tried freeing his arm from Celestine's clutches yet again. However, Celestine's slender arms were stronger than they appeared and he couldn't break free. That wasn't to say that Jade *couldn't* pull her off if he went full strength as a dragonkin, but he couldn't bring himself to be that rough with her, so he was left with little options.

As she remained latched to the struggling Jade, Celestine held her head high, boastfully. "Master Arman is always saying that's just how men operate."

Ruri turned her cold glare over to Arman.

"Hey, don't pull *me* into this," Arman said, rushing to his own defense. He knew he was being used as a scapegoat here because Jade also shot him a look—one that chided him for his careless remarks.

"Celestine, I don't pick my partner based on their looks. No matter how beautiful you may be, I don't need any other woman. There is only *one* person I need," Jade said, telling her the facts straight.

Celestine's eyes started to water and her lip quivered. Jade winced, but then Celestine covered her face with her hands and wailed, "Weeeeeh!"

Not even Jade could remain calm in front of a crying girl, no matter how drunk they were. He found himself at a loss and panicked.

"You're terrible! How could you say that when I love you so much?!" Celestine said.

"*Terrible!*"

"*Fiend!*"

"*Heartless~!*"

The spirits by Celestine's side joined the fray, each of them hurling abuse at Jade.

"Even the spirits… Arman…" Jade said, earnestly pleading for help.

But Arman couldn't really do anything either. "Give her some booze and have her drink herself stupid," he suggested.

Following his advice rather to the letter, Jade held out a glass filled with strong liquor to the sobbing Celestine. Celestine weepingly tossed back the drink, and it wasn't long before she was off to slumberland.

Arman smirked as he saw Jade breathe a sigh of relief. He placed Celestine's head on his lap and covered her with his own cape in a display similar to an older brother caring for his younger sister. Given that Celestine had been living in this castle since childhood, Arman probably *was* an older-brother figure to her. He was a lady-loving guy on par with Heat, but it seemed Arman assumed the role of Celestine's protector rather than a love interest.

Jade took a swig from his glass and heaved a sigh before turning his attention to Ruri. They both shot each other amused smirks. The pause they shared was calm and gentle, a moment neither had felt for quite some time. Although it was natural given their long separation from one another, things felt almost nostalgic—and somewhat embarrassing.

"Just so you know, I truly don't have eyes for Celestine," Jade commented.

"Yes, I know," Ruri said. She hadn't meant what she said before. "I just got a little jealous seeing you two so close."

"So I see," Jade said, happily grinning.

"...Celestine-san really does adore you, doesn't she, Jade-sama?"

"Celestine isn't a woman to me; she's like a sister. It might be because I first met her when she was still just a child. That will never change. I should probably be more firm in turning her down, for her sake, but it's not easy."

"You don't want to hurt her feelings, I'd assume."

"She may try to sway my opinion from time to time, and I'm not romantically interested in her, but I will say for certain that I do care for her."

The way that Jade looked at Celestine very much mimicked Arman. It may have saddened Celestine, and there wasn't one iota of romantic affection in it, but he undoubtedly considered her a very important person to him. Celestine must've known that and couldn't bring herself to give up on Jade.

On the other hand, Ruri noticed someone staring at Celestine with passion. Someone else noticed it too—Joshua.

Ruri and Joshua looked at each other and grinned deviously. They then slowly approached the person intensely gazing upon the sleeping Celestine. It was none other than Ewan. Ruri and Joshua looked ready to tease the daylights out of the boy.

"Say, Ewan?" Ruri started.

"Yeah?" replied Ewan.

"You surprised us by leaving Finn-san's side to come with us to the Nation of the Beast King, but how has it worked out since then?" she asked.

"Worked out? What do you mean?" Ewan questioned. He didn't catch Ruri's drift.

"Oh, you know. Right, Ruri?" Joshua said, patting Ewan on the back.

"Yep, yep," Ruri concurred, shooting him a suggestive smile.

Out of the loop, Ewan stared blankly at them.

"Come on, we mean Celestine-san. You have eyes for her, don't you?" Ruri suggested.

Ewan turned bashful and blushed. Finn, sitting nearby, was nonchalantly listening in on the conversation, hoping to hear about his brother's love life. He was most likely intrigued by this as well.

Ruri leaned in, brimming with intrigue herself. "You had a ton of chances to talk to her, didn't you? How did it go?"

Ewan had followed along, foregoing his massive brother complex to travel away from his brother for an extended period of time. He wouldn't have done that if his feelings were superficial. Ruri was giddy to hear what kind of juicy story Ewan had to share.

"Yeah, I managed to talk to her on a few occasions. I also questioned some of the people who attend her."

"Huh? Questioned?" Ruri asked, confused as to whether *questioning* was necessary. She thought maybe he'd been asking about Celestine's likes, but she soon found she was completely off.

"As a result, my intuition ended up being right!" Ewan said, fist clenched. "No other girl is worthy enough to stand by my brother's side! She is the only one to be my older sister!"

"...Older sister?" Ruri repeated.

"Why your *older sister*?" Joshua added.

Ruri, Joshua, and Finn were at a loss as Ewan confidently elaborated, "She is noble, refined, beautiful, and anyone you ask praises her as being a superb individual. She's a tad brash, but a timid woman wouldn't serve my brother. Isn't that right, brother?!"

Ewan's eyes twinkled, but Finn was just confused. How was he suddenly involved in any of this?

"Um, I think it's safe to assume he doesn't know *what* you're talking about, right, Finn-san?"

"...Ewan, I thought you had fallen in love with Lady Celestine and that was why you traveled here to the Nation of the Beast King. Is that not correct?"

"No, I didn't come here for myself. I came here for *you*, brother. I thought a person as flawless as her would be fitting for your mate, and I came here to confirm it for myself!" Ewan said with a look of the utmost confidence.

Ruri, Joshua, and Finn, on the other hand, looked utterly taken aback.

"Um, so, that may be your hope, but did Finn have any say in this? Has Finn said even *once* that he wanted to make her his mate?" Joshua asked, stating the obvious.

"Yeah, really," Ruri agreed.

"Finn-san, if you don't spell it out for him, then our resident brother-complex boy will keep going off the rails. He's likely to confess in your stead and get rejected by her all on his own."

Finn heaved a deep sigh. He had been a tad hopeful that this would end Ewan's brotherly ways. Unfortunately, his brother complex was the whole reason he was here.

"...Ewan, Lady Celestine is in love with His Majesty."

"It's all right. I'm sure she'll fall for your charms soon enough."

It was a wonder where this confidence even came from. A boy with a brother complex was nothing but trouble.

"I'm sure it's the same for Lady Celestine, but I have no attraction to milady. She simply *couldn't* be my mate."

"But she is such a superb individual. I think she would be perfect for you," Ewan argued, still not willing to accept the facts.

In an attempt to reason with him, Finn brought up a realistic issue, saying, "The Nation of the Beast King would never let go of Lady Celestine in the first place. She is their only Beloved. You must understand the benefits a Beloved bestows upon this nation from your stay here, don't you?"

"That's right!" Joshua interjected. "So on the off chance they did become mates, Finn would have to come to the Nation of the Beast King instead. Would you be fine and dandy with the two of you split apart like that?"

"Huh? No, I wouldn't..." Ewan stammered in shock. Apparently he hadn't thought that part through. For someone who loved Finn as much as Ewan did, he would never approve of living apart.

Joshua nodded. "Just give it up. The only way you'd keep Finn in the Nation of the Dragon King is if you brought a new Beloved here. And actually, Finn himself isn't even up for the idea in the first place."

"I know you usually go out of control when it comes to Finn-san, but Finn-san likely has his own tastes in women to explore," Ruri added.

"Right. You're right…" Ewan said, slumping. Disappointment set in and the twinkle in his eye vanished.

Was he really that interested in Celestine? They hadn't really interacted much, but was it sort of like love at first sight?

Ruri and Joshua started to whisper to themselves so Ewan couldn't hear.

"He said he was doing all this for Finn-san, but Ewan basically likes Celestine-san, right?"

"Looks it. Saying he wants her as his big sister is pretty, well, I dunno, just like him? Not sure why he won't just admit he wants to make her his mate, though."

"Do you think it can develop?"

"Psh, not at this rate it won't."

It wasn't clear if Ewan would realize it or not moving forward, but it was clear he had interest in Celestine. And even if Ewan did pick up on it, he was dealing with one tough customer. He would probably have a difficult time winning his way into her heart.

"Finn-san will find a good woman even without you getting involved. Cheer up," Ruri said.

"Yeah, pull yourself together and drink, drink, drink!" Joshua suggested, offering booze to help lighten his mood.

Just then, Ruri heard the sound of Heat yelling angrily.

"Brat! What is the meaning of this?!"

The abrupt shouting made Ruri shudder in surprise. She looked for the source and saw Heat angrily stomping her way.

"What's the matter, Heat-sama? Why are you shouting? I thought you were having fun drinking with all the beautiful girls?"

"You didn't uphold the bargain!" Heat protested.

"Which part?" Ruri questioned.

"You said there would be a *hundred* here, but I've counted a dozen times and only found *ninety-eight*. Where are the other two?!"

Heat made a thorough count after all… His adamance for women was absurd—and annoying.

Ruri thought that ninety-eight was fine since it was only two off, but true to his initial words, Heat wasn't letting a single girl go unaccounted for and he was furious. But Ruri had anticipated him throwing a fit if he realized the numbers were off, so she made sure there were one hundred ladies there.

"What are you talking about? There are one hundred exactly. Are you sure you counted right?"

"I counted repeatedly, but you're still *two* short."

Ruri scanned over the ladies sitting around where Heat had been and then looked over to the sleeping Celestine.

"Did you count Celestine-san?"

"What?"

"She's a pretty woman, is she not?"

Heat looked over at the unconscious Celestine and nodded in agreement. "Hmm, indeed. I had overlooked that. But that still leaves one…"

Ruri smiled sweetly and nudged her finger at herself. "Why, it's *m-e*."

"Uh, come again?"

"I just told you, it's me! *I'm* the hundredth!" Ruri spelled it out, glaring at Heat.

Heat immediately grimaced. "*Pardon me*?! I said I wanted *beauties*, not *brats*. *You* do not fall under the category of the prior!"

"How rude. I'll have you know, my mother is regarded as beautiful and I've been told I look like her!"

"Hmph, as if your parents count for anything."

"Aah! You're badmouthing my parents now? My mother is a beautiful woman and that's a fact!"

"If she is, then saying you bear resemblance is mere platitude at best. Humans *are* creatures who thrive off of empty platitudes and compliments. If you all lived as honest as us spirits, then such misunderstandings would never come to be."

"Grr, you're still saying that?"

On bated breath, everyone watched Ruri and Heat butt heads. That was when Jade stood up and placed his hand on Ruri's shoulder.

"You needn't worry, Ruri. You're more lovely than any woman here."

"Jade-sama…" Ruri's face instantly lit up as she embraced Jade and glared sharply at Heat.

"Well, Heat-sama, why don't *you* learn how to be a gentleman like Jade-sama?"

"Don't compare me to some man who's so blind he thinks you're the most lovely in the room. He is in the minority. Now, bring me the last beauty this instant."

"Quit being unreasonable. It took us so much work to get this many together; there's no way we could bring you another just like that."

"Hmph, well then, introduce me to a beauty when I go to the Nation of the Dragon King. I'll call things even then."

"You're coming with us to the Nation of the Dragon King?!"

"I am."

Ruri was shocked. Heat declared this like it was a natural progression of the conversation. She thought that since he was so fond of Celestine he would stay here in the Nation of the Beast King, but he went against the grain…

"I object, I object! I firmly object!" Ruri strongly opposed this idea, mainly for the sake of her own sanity. She could just hear his smarmy remarks every time they crossed paths.

"It doesn't matter if your 'object' or not. I go wherever I please."

"But what about Celestine-san? Didn't you have eyes for the girls of this castle too?"

"I've talked with almost all the girls here. That's why it's time to move on. Dragonkin are an attractive race, after all. I'll be getting to know some of the Nation of the Dragon King's local ladies."

"Whaaa?"

Arman looked relieved to hear Heat would be leaving as that meant he would be getting his wives back. The dragonkin in attendance, however, were all grimaces. This was what was coming to the kingdom. No one knew *what* kind of commotion he would cause at the castle.

No one wanted him to come along, but no one was brave enough to look a supreme-level spirit straight in the eyes and tell them no like Ruri had. They were thinking it *really* hard in their minds, though—in their minds and definitely not aloud. Kotaro and the other spirits were no problem since they were obedient to Ruri, but Heat wouldn't listen to her at all. In other words, there would be no one around who could stop him if need be, which put the nation in a predicament.

Ruri looked over to Kotaro and Rin for help, but they both collectively shook their heads. Once a spirit made up their mind, that was it. Even if one of their own interjected, they wouldn't change it. Heat's visit was practically set in stone.

Ruri slumped in disappointment. She had no other recourse but to give up and accept fate.

A day had passed and it was time for Ruri and the others to return to the Nation of the Dragon King. Ruri was up bright and early, preparing for the trip back, and Celestine—hungover and groggy as expected—gave her a hearty supply of her special wine.

"Thank you very much for this, Celestine-san."

"Make sure not to drink too much at one time now," she said without a hint of irony as she battled her own hangover. Ruri thought it was advice better saved for Celestine *herself*, but she nodded her head regardless.

Once that was done, Celestine suddenly extended her hand. Ruri hesitantly reached out and grabbed it, thinking it was a farewell gesture, but Celestine's grip was so tight Ruri's eyes widened in surprise.

"I'm hopeless. I can't control my emotions when Master Jade is before me. I don't see myself giving up on him for quite some time. Even now, I wonder why *I* wasn't the one."

"Ha ha..." Ruri nervously chuckled, not knowing how to reply. She could almost feel a bit of animosity in Celestine's grip.

"Well, at this point, I'll just have to try my darndest until I can't any longer. It seems you two aren't an item just yet, so I'd suggest you try your best to keep me from snatching him away," Celestine said, boldly declaring war on Ruri in a move that reflected her prideful nature.

She stared at Ruri, fiercely and without reserve. Not wanting to be outdone, Ruri also upped the intensity of her stare.

"Yes, I'll certainly try," she said.

Celestine smirked confidently in the face of Ruri's powerful gaze. If it weren't for Jade, the two girls might've gotten along surprisingly well.

"Ruri, it's time to head out," Jade said.

"Coming~! Okay, Celestine-san. Till next time."

"Yes, safe travels. Till we meet again, Lady Ruri," Celestine said with a bow.

Ruri ran off toward Jade and the others. She tried to ride atop Kotaro, but Heat and Chi were unfortunately occupying his back. She would feel sorry for Kotaro if she made him carry any heavier of a load.

"May I ride on you, Jade-sama?"

"Of course, I don't mind." In fact, Jade seemed pleased that Ruri had come to him.

Jade and the other dragonkin transformed into their dragon forms one after another. After Jade had transformed into a black dragon, Ruri settled herself on top of his head. Once he took to the skies, the other dragons soon followed.

Ruri gave a big wave to Celestine and Arman, both waving below them, as she departed the Nation of the Beast King.

Sitting on Jade's draconic head, Ruri thought to herself as she gazed vacantly into the passing sky—thinking to herself about what Celestine had said.

"Um, Jade-sama?"

"*What is it, Ruri?*"

Ruri began to speak but stopped herself. The words were on the tip of her tongue, but she wasn't sure how to phrase it, so they disappeared back down her throat.

"...Ungh, unghh~ On second thought, never mind."

"*What's gotten into you? Heh heh heh,*" Jade chuckled.

Ruri wanted to ask about the dragonheart—whether Jade gave it to her with designs on her being his mate as Rin told her—but she stopped herself before she could. She wasn't quite ready to get to the big question just yet. In fact, she wasn't sure what she should even say to begin with. She could cut straight to the chase and ask if he liked her. Or maybe it was better to verify whether what she had was a dragonheart.

Maybe it actually was a simple good luck charm, something that she mistook for a dragonheart all along. It wasn't out of the realm of possibility. After all, Ruri didn't know the way dragonkin operated. If she asked if he liked her and she was mistaken, she wouldn't be able to live with the shame. And if that happened, she wouldn't be able to look Jade in the face ever again either. She would probably have to run back to Chelsie's house in the forest.

She contemplated all of this, nervously wondering what she would do if she was under the wrong assumption. She'd finally caught on to Jade's feelings. If she were wrong about this, it would rock her to her core.

She wished she *hadn't* caught on had she known it would be this stressful. She might be able to maintain how things had been so far, but she felt as though she would worry over Jade's every move from now on.

Did Jade really like her romantically? Since when? Why? Since Celestine and Rin were the ones to tell her that and Jade hadn't confessed to her in clear terms, she had no idea what the answers were. A variety of thoughts circulated through her mind, confusing her.

(*What should I do...?*)

There were eyes all around them. Telling herself that now wasn't the best time to ask Jade questions, she decided to put the matter aside, waiting to talk until after they returned to the Nation of the Dragon King.

To be continued...

Side Story: Lost in Thought

With the cleanup from the fake Reapers incident coupled with his normal workload, Jade had been busy every day since Ruri left for the Nation of the Beast King. He holed up in his royal office and dealt with the veritable mountains of paperwork stacked on his desk.

To be quite frank, he was fed up with looking at it. And his hand was starting to ache from holding his pen for so long. If he were Joshua, he would have undoubtedly planned an escape route, but he had a serious personality and would never choose to run. He'd definitely had his fill, though.

He suddenly stopped writing, put down his pen, and massaged his temple. His eyes were exhausted from the sheer amount of paperwork he had read through so far.

Claus noticed Jade's weary display and paused his work as well. "Your Majesty, might I suggest you take a short breather?"

"As much as I'd like to, there's still work to be done," Jade said wearily as he looked upon the persistent stacks of documents.

"Yes, but running yourself ragged will do you no good either, Sire. Why not go for a brief stroll? I believe viewing the progress of Sector One will serve as a nice change of pace."

Frequently checking on the reconstruction efforts in Sector One was a good idea. Jade nodded in agreement. "You're right. I'll go see how things are progressing," he said. He found a good stopping point, placed his pen down, and stood up.

"Enjoy your time out, Sire."

When Jade arrived at the destroyed sector, workers were removing piles of rubble as others brought in construction materials. Lumber and building stones lay all over. Being as powerful as they were, the dragonkin were most actively carrying in all of the new materials.

Ever since the Nation of the Dragon King was formed, countless kingdoms sent their soldiers to invade and gain control of the nation, but none of them had damaged the castle like this. It was safe to assume that not even the First Dragon King, Weidt, would have ever guessed that a Beloved would cause this much destruction.

However, although Sector One had never been damaged to this degree before, every time the dragonkin had one of their booze-happy "dinner parties," they would go on a never-ending drunken rampage that would trash parts of the castle. The reason that reconstruction was going so smoothly now was because fixing the castle had become a regular post-party practice.

Because of the restoration, a number of people who normally wouldn't be allowed access were coming through Sector One. Jade employed so many for the job because he wanted repairs done as quickly as possible. However, in order to prevent infiltrators like the fake Reapers from raiding the castle again, they checked all of the entry routes in detail, renovating any weak spots in the castle's defense and setting up magic traps in any location that seemed like a possible way in. Such a thorough investigation took time and resources, so construction was proceeding much slower than expected.

Jade couldn't rush them since this was all to ensure Ruri's safety, but he was growing impatient, nonetheless. He wanted to see Ruri now. He tried to use his work to distract him from that nearly irresistible urge, but each day it grew stronger than the last.

Once Ruri left, so did his comfort cat. It went without saying, since Ruri *was* the cat in question, but the loss hit him twice as hard as a result. In his spare moments during work, his hand would naturally travel toward his lap only to pet thin air, reminding him that she was indeed gone. He noticed his subconscious habit and smiled self-deprecatingly at how utterly hopeless he had become.

Jade was burying himself in work not only to get his mind off of things but to assure nothing would stop him from leaving the castle once repairs were done. Waiting for Ruri to return on her own accord was simply out of the question. He intended on going to the Nation of the Beast King to pick her up himself. That was why reconstruction was paramount. Everyone, dragonkin included, was working hard, but Jade could feel his want-to-see-Ruri-itis flaring up. No, in fact, it had long since flared and was in full blaze.

Jade asked the dragonkin acting as foreman, "How are things progressing?"

"Progressing well, Sire. However, we're also employing all the countermeasures at the same time, so it will still take a while before we're done."

"I see."

Jade thought of hiring more people in order to speed things up, but he worried about carelessly adding more people to the mix. There were already people in this sector who were normally not allowed, but those people were only involved with the reconstruction efforts, not laying the anti-infiltrator traps and other such countermeasures. For those, Jade only employed people he could trust. However, those very countermeasures were taking up the most time.

"Should I assign more workers?" Jade asked.

"No, I don't believe that will be necessary, Sire. We already have the anti-infiltrator traps set in place. It'd be best if as few people as possible knew of their specifics, for security reasons. We can't let the number and location of those slip else the Beloved might be assaulted again. As they say, quality over quantity. I believe it's better to keep things focused to a trustworthy few."

"You have a point. Hmm, so it'll still take more time…"

Essentially, Jade would have to wait a while longer in order to see Ruri again. He let out a disappointed sigh, which the dragonkin foreman accurately picked up on and smirked.

"I assume you must be quite lonely without Lady Beloved around, Sire."

"Yes," Jade said, honestly confirming the foreman's assumption.

The dragonkin grinned from ear to ear. "I've also heard that you finally gave Lady Beloved your dragonheart."

Perhaps it was because he was excited about the news himself, but his booming voice traveled through the air, naturally catching the attention of the men around them. They all listened with great interest as they continued to work. Before she left, Ruri was prominently wearing a scale she'd received from Jade around her neck, so the news had already circulated around the castle.

"Seeing you gain a mate, after all this time refusing to marry, is a joyous occasion beyond compare, Your Majesty. And since it's Lady Beloved as well, everyone is positively thrilled."

"…I only gave it to her. Ruri herself doesn't know that it's a dragonheart, which is why she's not my mate yet."

"Heavens! Whatever do you mean? You've given her your one and only dragonheart without her knowing?"

"Yes, because I couldn't go along with her."

The dragonkin nodded his head. "Yes, yes. I understand. I understand indeed. We dragonkin can be quite jealous. And no man alive would ever try to approach a woman with a dragonheart around her neck."

Being in possession of a dragonheart was essentially telling people that you were a dragonkin's mate. Very few were reckless enough to try to court the mate of a dragonkin, the top of the natural hierarchy, and earn their ire. And if there were, they were either a fool or someone with a death wish.

"With that in mind, tell the others not to raise a fuss when Ruri comes back," Jade said.

He remembered how happy Ruri had been when she received the scale. She took it believing it was a simple good luck charm, and Jade found himself slightly disappointed she didn't realize the significance. However, he was also a tad relieved. Just as the dragonkin before him stated, he handed over his one-of-a-kind dragonheart in a snap decision to ward off the advances of any strange men she encountered in the Nation of the Beast King.

He had no regrets about what he did. He was confident he would never meet another girl he would want to give his dragonheart to more than Ruri. If Ruri wouldn't accept it, then he had no need for it in the first place. The fact he met someone that made him think that way was a miracle in itself. But that and Ruri's answer were two separate issues. Even though he wanted her to accept it, if she'd known it was a dragonheart when he handed it to her, then she would've probably been too conflicted to answer.

For whatever reason, Ruri was under the incorrect assumption that he viewed her as a pet and nothing else. He was getting impatient with how dense she was even though he was giving her all the signs. Ruri was the *only* one who didn't know. Someone would surely tell her about dragonhearts as soon as she got to the Nation of the Beast King. That would give Ruri some time to consider her answer. Jade hoped it would be a good answer if at all possible, but he wanted to leave it be until Ruri gave a proper response.

That was Jade's line of thinking, but the foreman looked rather awkward when Jade asked him to keep quiet.

"That might be quite difficult, Sire."

"Why's that?"

"Err, well, the elder members, including Lord Agate, have been hustling and bustling, you see. Word of you finally deciding on a mate is traveling to everyone. That was how I myself came upon this information."

The picture of the elder vassals dancing in joy popped up in Jade's mind.

"The news has been spreading so rapidly that practically everyone in the castle knows. While I would love to keep the matter under wraps, I believe it would be wiser to issue a gag order upon the entire castle before Lady Beloved returns."

Jade felt a headache coming on.

"What are Agate and the others doing right now?"

"They are currently in the queen's room."

"The queen's room? For what reason?"

"Well, I would assume they're preparing it for when Lady Beloved returns. They have been giving very specific orders for everything from furnishings to sheets. As busy as we all are, they have been persistently annoyi—err, I mean, persistently eager to display their best efforts."

Next to the king's room that Jade occupied was a room with a connected bedroom—the room meant for the queen. It was unoccupied now, but Jade wished for Ruri to move into it sooner or later. Although, it seemed it was *sooner* rather than *later* as Agate and the elder vassals were in the middle of some major renovations to the room.

Since Ruri now wore the dragonheart, the elders hastily assumed she was now Jade's mate. In their elation, they were preparing the room for her return—conveniently while everyone else was busy reconstructing the damaged castle, no less. Honestly speaking, "annoying" described the situation perfectly.

"Sorry for the hassle," said Jade. "I'll personally see to Agate and the others."

"Oh, worry not. I can't say I don't understand how they feel," the dragonkin said with an awkward smile.

Jade then parted ways with him and headed to the queen's room. There, just as the dragonkin said, Agate and the others were giving orders left and right, remodeling everything.

"What are you all doing?"

"Ooh, Your Majesty! Look at this and tell us your impressions."

"These colors should please Ruri. Although, perhaps the curtains should be this color instead? What are your thoughts, Sire?"

A couple of the elders asked Jade for his opinion as they happily redecorated the room. Jade simply grimaced. The sentiment was appreciated, but seeing as Ruri hadn't given an answer yet, they were simply being a nuisance at the moment.

"I asked you all what you were doing," Jade repeated.

"As you can see, we are readying the queen's room," said one elder.

"We cannot have your new mate in a separate room forever, after all. We must make sure to tidy it up before she makes her return," said another.

"Oh, yes. When shall the marriage ceremony be? This is matrimony between Dragon King and Beloved. We must make it simply extravagant," said yet another.

Jade heaved a very exhausted-sounding sigh. "I'm not getting married yet. Nor am I using this room," he proclaimed.

"Egads! Whatever do you mean, Sire?!"

"You have given her your dragonheart. Is marriage not a given?!" stated an elder as the others stared on in shock.

"I simply gave her my dragonheart. She still hasn't given me her answer. That's why Ruri and I aren't mates. All of you are jumping to conclusions."

"Egads!"

"All of our jubilation for naught?!"

"How could this matter become so muddled?!"

The elders yelled and complained, but still nothing was finalized.

"At any rate, you needn't prepare anything yet. You are interrupting the people that are rebuilding the castle."

"But Sire…"

The elders slumped, crestfallen. It seemed the rejection hit them hard—perhaps even more intense than their happiness that the king had found his mate.

However, among the disheartened elders, Agate remained firm. "We mustn't concede just yet, comrades. If they have not solidified their status, then we must act as the mediators for their relationship and set the mood for romance," Agate said, his bold words stirring his elder fellows.

"Ooh, that is an option!"

"Hmm, what sort of mood do ladies like, I wonder."

The elders all clamored among each other, regaining their motivation all at once.

Jade panicked, saying, "Stop, stop. You needn't do *anything*." He didn't want them to interfere and make matters worse, but none of them were listening to what he was saying. They were all too psyched up.

"Right, time to question some girls and think up some romantic situations!"

"We shall make it come to fruition!"

"We shall not perish till we hold the Sire's child in our arms!"

"Yeah!" yelled the elderly men as they pumped their fists in unison and rushed out of the room.

Jade was left standing alone, clutching his head. He worried they would get involved where they shouldn't. This only made the nail-biting terror of waiting for Ruri's response even worse. Never had the elders' overzealous actions actually benefited him. How would they answer if those same actions were the reason Ruri turned him down?

"Please, don't do anything to muck this up..." Jade said to himself. He wanted to stop the stampede of silver-haired snoops, but he was powerless to do so. He could only hope they wouldn't cause any issues.

"I wonder how Ruri has taken to the news."

Jade was curious about how she reacted to learning that what she held was a dragonheart. He was equal parts excited and terrified of her potential answer. The one thing he knew was that he couldn't even *dream* of having a mate other than Ruri.

Hence, Jade silently prayed and waited for the moment of truth.

Side Story: First Love

The Nation of the Beast King, one of the four great nations, was home to many demi-humans. Several homogeneous settlements were scattered about within its confines, where inhabitants honored the traditions and customs of the days of old. One of those settlements belonged to the bird demi-humans. Even out of the many races of demi-humans, they had the most pride and devotion toward the spirits.

One day, a single baby girl was born to the house of their chief—a future successor to the mantle. The entire village celebrated the monumental event, but they soon noticed something strange. Spirits started to gather around the newborn child as if to bless her birth. This was by no means normal. There had been other babies born in the village that same year, but neither those children nor the ones who came before them ever garnered a reaction like this.

"This can't be…"

"She's a Beloved…"

The quiet murmurs of the crowd spread from person to person, astonishing all who heard. However, astonishment gradually evolved into cheers and elation. A Beloved was born in this village, a village more spirit-religious than any other.

Being bestowed with a Beloved was something that called for celebration. A never-ending line of people clasped their hands together and shed happy tears over the newborn girl. This joyous event prompted the village to hold a banquet in honor of the newborn Beloved's birth that lasted for three days and three nights.

However, when the festivities were over and the glee of the people had subsided, they were faced with a big dilemma. If a Beloved was born, it was their duty to report it to the kingdom. Yet there was currently a problem in the Nation of the Beast King which made them hesitant to do so.

The Andal, the Beast King, had suddenly announced that he was abdicating the throne and subsequently went missing. Since he hadn't declared a successor before stepping down, a battle for the crown erupted. At the moment, the nation was wrapped in a fierce war between the princes over who would next sit on the throne, inciting mayhem.

The Beast King wasn't crowned by seniority but by strength. Because of that, each of the princes' relatives schemed to crown their own prince as king, intensifying the conflict. And in the midst of this strife, a Beloved was born—one that would clearly be used as a tool for this war.

After days of discussion among all of the tribe, the decision was made to hide the news of the infant from the kingdom and raise it in the village. They chose the happiness of the child over their loyalty to the nation. The Beloved was both loved by the spirits and loved by the villagers. No one wanted to embroil their tribe's precious child into the nation's turmoil. As such, the Beloved named "Celestine" would be secretly yet tenderly raised in a bird demi-human village.

Celestine was raised under the care of her tribe and the spirits. Her father, the leader, looked at his child with the kindest and most gentle of gazes. He knew he would have to relinquish her one day and it tore him up inside. But Celestine was a Beloved. She wasn't meant to stay within the small confines of his village.

Her father also heard that Prince Arman had won the years-long fight for the throne. Although the scars of the conflict still remained on the nation, it would start to show signs of stability soon. When it did, they would need to do what they had put off—report Celestine's existence to the nation. That meant Celestine would likely be going to the royal capital. There, she would undoubtedly be treated with the utmost care and live in extravagance beyond what their meager village could offer—a noble lifestyle befitting a Beloved.

He knew it was probably the better choice for Celestine as well, but he couldn't contain his lament for giving up his child. Nevertheless, it was a matter for the future. Even though the battle for the throne was settled, there were still rumors of a bested prince lying in wait for their chance to steal it behind the scenes. He couldn't send his precious daughter somewhere that was potentially dangerous. Not until King Arman's reign was proven stable, at least. Everyone in the village thought that, in fact, but...

"Father, I am going to the royal capital."

One day, Celestine uttered those very words. She was still a mere child, but she was beautiful and had been raised to be wiser than the other children her age. Or perhaps that was just favoritism influencing her father's thought. Regardless, his eyes widened at her unbelievable statement.

"What are you saying, Celestine?"

"I am a Beloved. Beloveds must be reported to the kingdom, do they not?"

"The capital is dangerous. The Beast King's reign isn't fully stable yet. We have to wait a little while longer, okay?"

He said this nice and slow, as if instructing a small child—an actual small child, in this case. However, Celestine was wiser than her father gave her credit for.

"Father, I've heard that the war has left the capital in shambles. In which case, I believe I should go there since I am a Beloved. Any place with a Beloved prospers, correct? My power can help the lives of many. I can share the blessings of the spirits with so many more. That is my duty as someone born a Beloved."

"Celestine..." her father started, his refusal stuck on the very tip of his tongue, but he swallowed it back as he peered into his daughter's determined eyes.

For all her life, he had taught her that spirits were sacred and that Beloveds existed to link man and spirit. Celestine was attempting to faithfully uphold those teachings. If this was just childish play talk, then Celestine's father would've been able to turn her down, but he decided to show Celestine the respect a Beloved deserved.

After everyone in the tribe saw them off, Celestine and her father left for the capital. They traveled the whole way by horse-drawn carriage. Since Celestine normally had an entourage of spirits around her, she rode inside to avoid detection. After a few days of this, they reached the capital.

The carriage proceeded to the castle, and when they arrived, the occupants declared they sought an audience with the king. However, there was no way the gatekeeper was letting a random civilian off the streets inside the gate. This prompted an argument back and forth between the gatekeeper and Celestine's father.

Hearing their bickering, Celestine poked her head out of the carriage. "Father," she said, as she took his hand to descend.

The gatekeeper's eyes widened. Spirits floated around the young girl as if protecting her. It was an abnormal sight to anyone who saw it.

257

"Please let me see His Majesty," Celestine said to the gatekeeper nervously yet firmly.

The gatekeeper stared in awe before snapping back to his senses. He quickly dashed inside of the castle.

It was almost as if someone had poked a beehive. An uproar ensued. A rush of people, who seemed to be of high ranking, filed in front of Celestine, kneeling.

Celestine was respected in her village, but she had never been treated in such a bombastic way before. She was frightened by their conduct and hid herself behind her father. Slowly peeking from behind him, she could see they were apparently welcoming her with joy, albeit in an overwhelming display.

Celestine's father held her in his arms as they were shown to the throne room. A man with yellow hair and yellow eyes sat atop a regal throne set high above the floor. He was the man who, a few years ago, bested all of his brothers to be crowned the new king—Arman, the Beast King.

With an air of intimidation akin to an apex predator, Arman looked down upon Celestine. The young girl felt his mighty presence and froze, like a frog caught in the deadly leer of a snake.

"Eek!"

Her father immediately took a knee, and Celestine was about to follow his example and do the same, but Arman stood up from his throne and stopped her.

"That won't be necessary. You are a Beloved. There is no being who stands above a Beloved, so you needn't bow to me."

As Arman slowly descended the throne, Celestine could feel herself getting more nervous and tense.

"Your name?" he asked.

"U-Um…" Celestine stammered, too nervous to form sentences correctly. The more flustered she grew, the harder it was to speak.

Celestine battled her nerves as Arman reached his large hand over to her. She instinctively shut her eyes and ducked down, cowering in fear. However, all she felt was a few gentle pats on the head. She looked up at him, dumbfounded by the unexpected turn of events, to see that Arman was smiling at her as gently as could be.

Arman then suddenly picked her up and held her in his arms, naturally putting her at eye-level with him. "Your name?" he asked once more.

"Um, Celestine, Sire."

"I see. Such a pretty name for a pretty little girl," he said, messily rustling her hair with his hand—a large hand packed with warmth. The fear she felt not two seconds ago melted away.

"My name is Arman. Pleasure to meet you, Celestine."

That was the story of how Celestine and Arman met.

And so Celestine began living in the royal castle. Her father, the chief of her tribe, couldn't abandon his people, so he left Celestine in Arman's care and returned to the village. This saddened Celestine, but she was the one who proposed going to the castle in the first place, so she kept it to herself and patiently watched as her father walked off, out of sight.

Still, Celestine was only just a child, so she couldn't fully contain her sadness and disappointment. Noticing that, Arman once again rustled her hair. The consoling gesture lifted Celestine's spirit ever so slightly.

"If you're feeling down, I'll play with you," Arman said, acting extremely kind despite his intimidating appearance.

Knowing that Celestine was still just a child separated from her parents, Arman would frequently check on her and give her lots of attention even though he was busy with his kingly duties. Thanks to that, Celestine was able to live in the castle without difficulty. She couldn't help but feel some degree of sadness, but she had the spirits and the occasional correspondence from her parents. She spent her days in contentment, without wishing to go back to the village.

Her life in the castle was altogether different from the village. Celestine was raised with tenderness and care, but the castle was on a whole other level. Servants attended to her every need, worshiping her, respecting her, and heeding her every beck and call. This seemed bound to spoil her, but in spite of her new lifestyle, she kept to her family's teachings, never growing arrogant, and maintained her dignity as a Beloved.

Celestine's attitude earned her the favor of the castle's workers and garnered her popularity. However, the one who was a little disappointed was actually Arman.

"Hey, you know, you're getting more popular than me. Even my aides are telling me to learn by your example."

"Master Arman, I think that's because your principles toward women are so lacking. Just how many queens do you intend to have? You've only been king for a few years and the number is already in the double digits. It's quite unsettling."

"Oh, well, look at that. Someone's lips have gotten a lot more limber, haven't they? When I first met you, you looked like you were about to wet yourself," Arman stated.

"Th-That isn't true!" Celestine contested.

Some time had passed since she first came to the castle, and the two had opened up to one another quite a lot. Nowadays, they were friendly enough to crack jokes.

"Oh, right. We'll be having visitors from the Nation of the Dragon King."

"Nation of the Dragon King? A dragonkin?"

"Yes, the Dragon King and company. You've never met a dragonkin before, have you?"

"Never."

"You're in for a surprise. They're all lookers. Jade, the Dragon King, is especially handsome. Try not to fall in love, now."

"I am not you, Master Arman. I don't fall in love so easily. But dragonkin are a race who keep faithful to one wife, yes? I respect them for that. Unlike a certain *someone*..."

"Hey, now," Arman replied, his temple twitching.

Since they lived in the castle together, it was better that she was this way than constantly scared, but Arman had a feeling she was getting more and more ruthless as the days rolled on. A Beloved was equal to a king—no, beyond a king. That was why no one rebuked her no matter what biting remark she gave. Granted, Arman personally wouldn't seriously reprimand her since she was still a child. On the contrary, his exchanges with Celestine were a relaxing distraction from his daily stress.

Arman had been all smiles up until that point, but his face suddenly tightened and he looked at Celestine with a more stern gaze.

"You know of the fight for the throne from a few years ago, right, Celestine?"

"You're referring to the battling you did with your brothers over the mantle of king, yes?"

"The one and the same. Most of my brothers were purged along with their retainers and the nobles who fought alongside them. But there's one who made an escape. And I've heard he's been making moves in the shadows as of late. He is after you," Arman explained.

Despite being wise beyond her years, Celestine didn't seem to understand what he meant.

"A Beloved is a precious entity in many nations. Especially here, in a nation so spirit-religious. If they were able to exploit your powers, and if he were to make you say he's more suited to be king, the people would want him in power instead. In power as a king watching over a Beloved. That is what he's after."

"I wouldn't know who is more suited to be king, though."

"Right. Probably too difficult of a decision for you since you're still a child. But they're after you exactly *because* you wouldn't know any better, to get some sort of vote of confidence that works in their favor. Still, you can rest easy. I've put more security detail on you," Arman said, gently stroking Celestine's head as an apology for frightening her. His hand was as big, as warm, and as kind as always.

Celestine stared straight at Arman. "I'm glad that you're king, Master Arman," she said without a hint of cynicism.

Arman was taken back, as if he'd just heard a lie, but the truth set in and a tender smile appeared on his face.

Although the added security did make her feel constrained, Celestine continued to live in tranquility. With nothing much happening, everyone began to drop their guards. That was when Arman's fears came to fruition.

"Lady Beloved, run!" sounded a shriek around dinnertime. A flood of armed soldiers stormed the room and took it over in the blink of an eye.

It was a mystery as to what happened. There was supposed to be additional security outside of the tower where the Beloved stayed, annexed from the main tower Arman occupied. However, that mystery dispersed once Celestine saw a man take her caretaker hostage and point a sword at her.

"Lady Beloved, will you come with us?"

"And if I said no?"

"We cannot harm you since the spirits attend you, of course. Which means…"

"Eeeeecek!"

The man stabbed his sword into the woman. She hit the floor with a thud as globs of blood came spilling from her and she ceased to move any longer.

"Eep!" Celestine shrieked, her face pale.

The man then dragged out another woman. This one was also one of Celestine's caretakers. "Now then, will you be coming with us?"

Celestine hesitated, and the man wasted no time in cutting down the second caretaker as well.

"If you don't hurry…"

"I-I'll go! Just please, don't hurt anyone!"

Celestine could have easily subdued them if she asked the spirits. However, she was taught that she should never thoughtlessly ask the spirits for favors since they were such sacred beings, so the idea of simply asking them for assistance never crossed her mind.

"Well then, step this way. Please tell the spirits not to follow you."

"B-But…"

"Shall I kill someone else, then?"

Celestine was still a child. Seeing her caretakers mercilessly slain before her had completely terrified her. Her usual boldness to refute others had wilted and she complied with his instructions. The thought of asking the spirits for help still didn't occur to her.

"Everyone, please don't follow me."

The concerned-looking spirits around her protested in response, but Celestine continued to warn them to stay away. Reluctantly, they followed her orders and dispersed elsewhere.

"Well then, right this way."

Celestine barely managed to move her trembling legs as they brought her to the hall in the tower. There, a door that she had never seen was standing open. She *did* remember there being a big painting there, however.

"This annex has an escape route for Beloveds in case of emergency. Though, it seems the king didn't know about its existence."

"A secret path…" Celestine whispered. They'd used this to get inside, going undetected by the guards outside the tower.

"That is correct. Now, let us depart to our master."

Celestine had neither spirits nor guards. Fear occupied her entire being. She wondered if Arman had noticed she was gone and if he would come rescue her.

The secret route was connected to an old shed outside the capital. She anxiously exited the shed and was forced to walk a little while longer. When she reached their destination, she saw more armed soldiers and a well-dressed man under the moonlight.

The man kneeled before Celestine in an overly hammy manner and said, "Ooh, greetings and salutations, Lady Beloved. I am so glad to have saved you from that usurper, Arman."

Celestine couldn't hide her fear or her confusion. "Usurper? Save? What do you mean?"

"Aah, so, you are not aware. Arman is a usurper who stole the throne from me. You see, considering I am the first prince, I should've been crowned king. But he snatched it away from me! That place is not safe for you. After all, who *knows* what kind of treachery he might use you for, Lady Beloved. That is exactly why I've come to rescue you from him."

Celestine had no idea what he was talking about. Arman won the throne by his own merits, and he wasn't using her for any treachery.

Just as she was about to refute him, the man interrupted her. "But all is fine now. For I shall protect you. Let us take back the throne together."

Arman's words ran past her mind. He said he had a brother that lost in the battle for the throne and escaped. He was targeting Celestine in hopes to gain custody of a Beloved so he could become king. That was most likely who this man and his soldiers were.

"Please return me back to the castle," Celestine urged with a shaky voice.

Despite her plea, he wasn't going to just let her go back. "Why, whatever do you mean? After finally rescuing you, you wish to go back to that den of evil? Aah, I'm guessing he told you a mixture of truth and lies. My, how dreadful. However, everything he told you is false. For, you see, *I* am just."

"Please, return me."

"As soon as you recognize me as king and I take the throne, we shall go back to the castle together. So, please, worry not."

How was she supposed to *not* worry? There was no getting through to him at all. Celestine was gradually growing more *angry* than afraid.

"Enough! Take me back to the castle! You aren't fit to be a ruler. Master Arman is far more suited! I will *never* recognize you as king!" she firmly declared.

And just like that, the man's warm, sweet smile turned cold and bitter. His eyes squinted into an icy glare that made Celestine flinch.

"It would seem he has corrupted you to the very core. I will ask you once more. Will you recognize me as king?"

"I-I will not! Master Arman is king!"

"I see. Then, you no longer have use for me. Kill her."

All of the soldiers pointed their swords at Celestine. The color drained from her face.

"What are you...? I am a Beloved. The spirits will not sit idly by as harm befalls a Beloved."

Harming a Beloved in a nation so devout toward spirits was sheer madness. Not even Celestine herself ever imagined anyone from this nation would hurt her. She had been feeling a tinge of worry, but she hadn't felt her life was in jeopardy. However, now things were different. Her gut warned her of the danger.

"And *where* are those spirits now?" the man asked.

Celestine then realized—she had told the spirits not to follow her per *their* instructions.

Slowly but surely, the soldiers drew closer to the girl. Their eyes showed serious intent to kill a Beloved without an ounce of hesitation. Celestine's body trembled. This was the first time she'd ever felt scared for her life.

"No... S-Someone..." Celestine stammered before turning on her heels and running.

"After her! Don't let her escape!" said the man as the gang of soldiers followed after her.

Celestine screamed as she desperately fled. "Someone! Master Arman! Help me!"

However, she was a mere child running from adults. They had far larger strides and far more stamina. She started panting. Her smaller, weaker body had reached its limit. A soldier caught up with her and snagged her hair, sending a jolt of pain through her scalp.

"Oww!"

The soldier swung his sword, the tip glinting in the moonlight. Celestine shut her eyes, thinking she was done for, but that was when a fierce wind blew past. She heard several thuds from around her and realized the grip on her hair was no longer there.

"Who are you?!" asked a soldier.

She slowly opened her eyes to find a group of unfamiliar faces opposing the soldiers.

"No, who are *you* for pointing your sword at a small child?" asked one of the men.

"It's none of your damn business! Hand over the kid!" replied the soldier.

"Only a fool would comply with that," retorted the man.

The soldiers looked at one another and then decided to carry out their master's orders, charging at the group of uninvited guests with designs to eliminate them.

Who were these people? She couldn't discern if they were friend or foe. As she debated staying or fleeing, they unceremoniously beat the soldiers to a pulp. She was astonished by what she saw.

One of the new men came over to her and kneeled down to her eye level. "Are you hurt?" he asked.

"No. Thank you very much...?" Celestine replied, sounding slightly uncertain. She had no idea if the people in front of her were here to save her or not.

"What shall we do with them, Your Majesty?"

"We can't leave these criminals unpunished for attempting to kill a child. Bind them to trees for the time being. We can tell Arman and he can send his men to collect them later."

Arman? The familiar name made Celestine pounce on the man before her. "Master Arman! The Beast King! You know of him?!"

"Yes, we're on our way to the castle now."

"Please, you must take me with you!"

"That is fine, but do you belong to the castle? Arman has no children to my recollection."

"I am a Beloved, sir."

Celestine's words caused not only the man to stare at her in shock but also the others who were tying the soldiers to trees.

"A Beloved? Well, I heard of a Beloved appearing in the Nation of the Beast King, but where are your spirits?" the man asked, looking around her. It was to no avail, however, as Celestine had ordered them not to follow.

"I left my spirits behind because those people told me to."

"What were you thinking?! The spirits shield and protect a Beloved. You're practically asking for harm to befall you," the man shouted, scolding her for her supposed carelessness.

Celestine figured that out firsthand, but she had no other option. "They took my caretakers hostage, so I..." She saw people killed before her eyes. The mere memory made her body shiver and her heart sink.

The man placed his hand upon her head and gently stroked her hair. The relieving gesture prompted streams of tears to flow from her cheeks.

"I don't know what happened exactly, but let's return to the castle. I'm sure Arman has been searching, worried sick," he said.

"Yes, sir."

The man then told Celestine to step back a bit. The next thing she knew, he'd transformed into a gigantic dragon. She gazed in awe at his majestic form. One by one, the other men started to transform into dragons as well.

"That reminds me, Master Arman said that the Dragon King would be here. Are you him, by any chance?"

"*Yes. I am Jade, the Dragon King. Step up on my foot. I will take you back to the castle,*" said the jet-black dragon who had been a man not even a moment ago.

His scales sparkled in the moonlight with a beautiful luster, entrancing Celestine. As she admired his form, they arrived back at the castle in no time flat.

Quite some time had passed since Celestine was taken away. The castle was normally silent this late at night, but lamps glowed all around and people frantically rushing back and forth.

Once the dragonkin party descended to the castle with Celestine in tow, everyone ran to meet them.

"Lady Beloved!" yelled one soldier.

"Oh, thank heavens! She's safe!" yelled another.

After a short while, Arman came frantically dashing up. "Celestine! You're safe!"

"Master Arman!" Celestine cried as she ran into Arman's outstretched arms.

The spirits she left at the castle also crowded around.

The honest relief of finally being back at the castle set over her. However, her ordeal wasn't quite over.

269

"You fool! What were you thinking casting the spirits to the side?! Your safety is of utmost importance. No matter how many people may die, think of your safety above all. That is your duty as a Beloved," Arman said, bringing down his wrath.

Celestine had an excuse, however. "But I never thought that anyone would actually try to harm a Beloved. I thought I would be safe even without them. But when he ordered them to kill me, I…"

Celestine trailed off. She had been taught that spirits were sacred, so she couldn't wrap her head around it. Harming a Beloved was tantamount to rebelling against the spirits.

Seeing the tears forming in Celestine's eyes, Arman took a breath to regain his composure and said, "There are people in this world who value their own desires more than anything else—Beloved or not. People who couldn't give a damn about faith in the spirits. That is why I assigned so much security. I take responsibility for not being able to protect you this time. But something of this nature may happen again. So, you must *never* separate from the spirits."

"Okay."

Celestine was then escorted to her room. Since the annex for the Beloved was compromised with that secret route around, Arman had a room closer to his own prepared for her. She made sure to relay who had kidnapped her. Arman would probably deal with him later.

"That reminds me, I haven't said my thanks," Celestine said, remembering the party of dragonkin that saved her—especially the Dragon King, Jade. She didn't get a good look at his face, but the beautiful glistening of his scaly, jet-black form was imprinted on her memory. He had also constantly and courteously asked if Celestine was all right during their trip back. His kind voice echoed through her mind.

The following day, the commotion from the previous night still hadn't died down, and the soldiers in the castle bustled about. Celestine dashed through the crowd and headed toward the room where Arman and another man were having breakfast.

"Oh, Celestine. What's wrong?" Arman asked, pausing his meal.

"Um, I need to say thanks to the Dragon King. And I heard that this is where he was," she replied.

"Oh, yes. Jade is right here."

She met eyes with the man sitting across from Arman. His face was more beautiful than any she had seen before. She couldn't take her eyes off of him.

"What are you doing? C'mere and sit down," Arman said.

She walked toward them, but the closer she got to Jade, the harder her heart beat.

"U-Um, thank you very much for yesterday. I am sincerely grateful."

"I just so happened to find a child being assaulted on my way to the castle. I never would have dreamed it was a Beloved, but I'm glad you seem to be safe," Jade said with a gentle smile.

Celestine's heart fluttered and she avoided eye contact with him.

Celestine listened in on Arman and Jade's general banter as they enjoyed their meal, sneaking peeks at Jade's face all the while. They avoided talking about what happened last night out of consideration for Celestine, but Celestine was so transfixed on Jade that she never noticed.

"Oh, yeah, So, have you finally found yourself a mate yet?"

A bitter expression settled on Jade's face. "Quit talking like you're one of those old codgers. I already get enough of that back at the kingdom. I *don't want* to hear it here as well."

"Ha ha ha, well, I'm sure you'll find one sooner or later."

"I would hope, but I haven't found anyone suitable at the moment."

A mate for Jade. Once Celestine heard that, she felt a bevy of emotions swell inside her. She *hated* the prospect of someone else being by his side. By the time she realized it, the words had already come from her mouth.

"In that case, please take me as your mate, Dragon King!"

Arman and Jade both stared at Celestine, speechless. However, Jade responded to her by saying, "...No, I'm sorry."

"But why?!" Celestine asked, shocked from being turned down so quickly.

"Well, because it's not feasible, now is it?" Arman interjected. "You're the Beloved of the Nation of the Beast King and Jade is the Dragon King."

"Plus, a child can't be the object of my affection," Jade said, obviously avoiding the advances of a child like Celestine. If he were to agree to make her his mate, he would likely be branded a pedophile.

"Well, dragonkin live long lives, so I'm sure it wouldn't be an issue once she gets older. I'd be in her corner if she weren't a Beloved."

"I'd rather not form rifts in our nation's cordial relations."

Arman and Jade seemed opposed due to the massive problems it would cause. Be that as it may, Celestine couldn't sit with that.

"I will *not* concede!" she declared.

From that moment on, Celestine launched her aggressive approach.

"I love you, Master Jade! Please make your mate!"

"Who is that woman?!"

Every time she met Jade, she would convey her feelings. And if there were any women smitten with Jade, she would hear of it from all the way in the Nation of the Beast King and dedicate herself to eliminating them. Not even Celestine, who tried to be a proper Beloved, could contain her temper when she saw another woman coiled around Jade.

Through all of this, Arman remained confounded, not knowing that Celestine had this sort of side to her.

Celestine knew that Jade was growing weary of this and that she was using the fact he couldn't strongly refuse her to her advantage, but things weren't going according to plan. She really wanted to be by Jade's side forever, but she, a Beloved of the Nation of the Beast King, couldn't afford to leave the nation for very long. The nation's senior vassals staunchly disapproved. Having a sense of responsibility, Celestine couldn't just disregard their opinions either. She lamented that she could rush off to Jade's side unfettered. If only another Beloved were around to take her place.

However, one day, there was news a Beloved showed up in the Nation of the Dragon King. Celestine was elated, thinking she had found a possible replacement. But Jade showed an extraordinary attachment to this new Beloved and strongly opposed the idea of Celestine swapping places with her. She had never seen Jade display such affinity before, and it troubled her heart.

She finally asked if the Beloved was his mate, and Jade didn't refute it—which left her stunned. When in the world could this have happened? She couldn't contain her shock. Although she tried to gather info about this Beloved, all she managed to find out was that she was enjoying quite the happy, intimate relationship with Jade.

The fact that Jade held her so near and dear was the biggest shock to Celestine. Women had approached Jade in the past, but he showed no interest in them. He would always keep them at arm's length. The only woman Jade ever treated with any form of intimacy was her. That attention developed into a superiority complex. However, now she didn't even have *that* to hold on to.

"I *must* find out what kind of woman she is."

And if she found out that she *wasn't* worthy of Jade, then...

Feeling something ominous, she convinced Arman and Jade to let her visit. Despite their refusal, they reluctantly agreed and she made her way to the Nation of the Dragon King.

 # Side Story: Sightseeing

The case with the Church of God's Light was concluded and the half-destroyed castle was repaired. Jade had come to the Nation of the Beast King to pick Ruri up and they planned to return tomorrow.

Ruri was getting her luggage in order, but she was suddenly interrupted by someone opening the door and making a lot of noise.

"Let's go, brat!" Heat said, barging into Ruri's room without knocking.

Ruri stopped what she was doing and glared at him. "Heat-sama, *at least* knock before you come into a lady's room."

"Hurry yourself up."

"No one filled me in. *Where* are we going in the first place?"

Celestine, who had entered the room after Heat, answered, "Since the issues with the Church of God's Light are resolved, I've gained permission to go into town. Since you'll be going back tomorrow, I thought it'd be a good chance to show you and the others around, Lady Ruri."

"Wow, really? Let's go, let's go!"

"Then be quick about it, brat."

"Okey dokey!" Ruri replied. She quickly squared away her belongings, shoved them into her pocket space, and ran up to Celestine. "Can Kotaro and the others come as well?"

"Yes, but of course. I'm sure the townspeople will shed tears at the good fortune of meeting spirits with physical bodies," Celestine explained.

"So, that will be okay?" Ruri asked. The people of the Nation of the Beast King worshiped spirits as a religion, so Ruri worried about the massive panic that would ensue from a couple of Beloveds and a pack of supreme-level spirits walking around town.

"The people of the Nation of the Beast King are very aware of where they stand. They would never stir up trouble for a Beloved or spirit." If Celestine was willing to insist it was safe, then it must've been.

Randomly, Ruri realized something was off about Celestine's hair. After a pause, she realized what it was.

"Did you cut your hair?"

"Yes, a little off the ends," Celestine said with a tiny chuckle. "Women truly do have an acute sense for these matters. I went to see Master Arman and Master Jade a moment ago, but *neither* of them noticed. Men can be so thickheaded."

Good point. Neither of those two seemed like the type to care. With long hair herself, Ruri was bound to notice Celestine's shoulder-length cut.

With that, Ruri and her group sallied forth to the city. Of course, they weren't without an entourage. The two girls were in the center of a formation of soldiers packed so tight not even a cat could squeeze through. Ruri knew there was no way they wouldn't assign guards to a couple of Beloveds walking in a crowded town, but she felt it was too overboard and sort of ruining half the fun. At the same time, she also understood why it was necessary to begin with.

"Aah, it's Lady Beloved!" shouted a man.

"Lady Beloved!" yelled someone else.

A woman shrieked, "Eeek! She just looked at me!"

All over, the cheers rang out for Celestine—with more passion than when Ruri walked through town in the Nation of the Dragon King, in fact. Although, that was probably inevitable. Celestine had been protecting this nation for several years as a Beloved, and Ruri practically showed up yesterday. Celestine had gained far more popularity and trust among the people as a Beloved.

The townspeople were passionate for sure, but they were well-mannered just as Celestine said. They all kept a certain distance as if there were an invisible wall between Ruri's group and them. They simply cheered and screeched from afar. In order to avoid an event that would harm a Beloved by getting too close, they naturally assumed that position without even being ordered to. People in this nation worshiped Beloveds and spirits to an extraordinary degree. If anyone were to ever lay a hand on one, they would probably rue their existence and take their own life.

As the people watched from a distance, Celestine showed Ruri her favorite establishments around the capital.

The first shop they went to was for clothing and apparel. It was apparently the shop that specially made all of Celestine's clothes, from casual wear to festival garments. They were visiting in order to pick up the new clothes she'd ordered for Heat since his old ones were reduced to ash in the eruption. The shop had already made his clothes super express, and they were fresh out of the metaphorical oven. While delivery was always an option, they were already in the city anyway, so no harm, no foul.

After receiving the outfit, Heat went to the back room to change. He returned in a few moments, redressed and looking satisfied. Apparently, the tailoring was to his liking as he struck a variety of poses in vain admiration before the full-length mirror.

"Hm, yes, not too shabby."

"It looks wonderful on you, sir," the female clerk said, flattering him.

"Heh heh heh quite naturally," Heat replied, pleased as punch by her compliment.

The shop was filled with the native garb Celestine always wore. The beautiful selection caught Ruri's eyes. She couldn't help her womanly impulses. She was interested in the apparel, and now that she was sightseeing, she had a desire to wear this nation's native garb for reasons she couldn't explain. While she still found the skimpiness embarrassing and only wore the clothes she brought with her from the Nation of the Dragon King, that didn't mean she had no interest in the clothes here at all. This shop had more reserved outfits in stock as well. She laid her hands on an outfit that caught her eye, one that seemed wearable, and tested the texture with her fingers.

"That is a brand-new design that just arrived the other day. You have quite the keen eye, as one would expect," the clerk said, flattering Ruri.

"Will you be taking that, Lady Ruri?" asked Celestine.

"Oh, no, I was just looking," Ruri said, slightly embarrassed that it must've looked like she wanted the clothes.

Celestine suggested, "Why don't you try on some things while you're here? You won't get this chance very often, I believe. Put them on and let us see the sights around town."

After some slight indecision, Ruri happily nodded in agreement.

Once she changed into her new outfit, Heat saw her and commented, "Hmm, I suppose *anyone* can look good in the right clothes."

"God, can't you just say it looks good on me? Even as a *lie*?" Ruri had grown pretty accustomed to his particular brand of speech, but it still irked her nonetheless.

Wearing her new clothes, she continued sightseeing. Much like any good tourist location, the town was bustling with scores of lively-looking people. Stares came from all around them, and they had to look past a wall of guards, but experiencing the town without the threat of the Church of God's Light was a pleasant change of pace.

That being said, the sheer amount of "Beloved goods" was still concerning. Celestine knew many of the shops in the capital, which meant she must've frequented them before the incident with the Church of God's Light. She had her own go-to shops and engaged in friendly banter with the clerks.

As they looked at a variety of different stores, Ruri stumbled upon Amarna, the woman from the Nation of the Dragon King. She was waving at Ruri, so Ruri waved back.

"Lady Ruri, good day to you."

"Good afternoon. How is business?"

"The Nation of the Beast King is indeed a nation that embraces their Beloved. I've seen so many goods and have learned much. And among those goods, I've found something that would likely fetch a high price!" She was extremely excited and holding a pair of scissors for some reason. "Lady Ruri, your hair has gotten quite long. Would you care for a haircut?"

"Huh? Now? I can just cut it on my own when I get back."

"Oh, fret not. You needn't be shy."

"Uh, why are you so eager to cut my hair?"

Amarna shuffled up to Ruri with an ear-to-ear grin. It set off warning bells in Ruri's mind.

"*Oh, Ruri, look at that,*" Rin said, pointing over to a stall that people were gathered around. It was selling…Beloved hair.

Ruri was taken aback and turned to Celestine. "Celestine-san, what is that?! By 'Beloved hair,' do they mean *your* hair?!" she asked, remembering that Celestine just got her hair cut.

"Oh, that? Apparently, parts of a Beloved seem to bring good fortune, so they're sold at high prices. When I cut my hair, it ends up being sold in town before I realize it."

"Who has been selling off your hair on the side? I think you should say something. Don't you find it creepy?"

A bunch of strangers walking around with your own hair? What were these people even *thinking* wanting something like that? She couldn't wrap her head around their logic.

"This is part of a Beloved's duty. So long as it can help contribute to the nation." It was an admirable comment, but Celestine looked like she agreed with Ruri. It seemed it creeped her out just a little bit.

"The Nation of the Beast King's Beloved is magnificent. She will stop at no lengths to support the people of her nation. So, Ruri, to what *lengths* shall I cut your hair? I believe it will sell nicely."

"Forget it!"

"I'll give you a *cut* of the profits~"

"I said *forget it*. Nothing you say will get me to cut my hair, so quit showing off your clippers!"

Amarna disappointedly put down her scissors. However, her eyes remained glued to Ruri's hair.

This was not good. Ruri felt like this girl was likely to sneak a clip of her hair at this point, so she quickly said her goodbyes and left the area. By no means was Ruri willing to do *anything* for the nation to the same degree as Celestine.

"The Nation of the Beast King is not a place to be trifled with— in more ways than one," Ruri said to herself. The people here would sell anything and everything pertaining to a Beloved. She couldn't tell if it was because they worshiped Beloveds that much or if they were just that shrewd of business people.

"Is there anywhere else you'd like to go, Lady Ruri?" Celestine asked.

Ruri answered without a moment's hesitation. The hot springs. When she got back to the Nation of the Dragon King, she was going to build herself one of her own. There were so many hot springs in the castle, but she wanted to see a public bath in order to instill the culture of hot springs into the Nation of the Dragon King.

Once Ruri explained that to Celestine, she happily escorted her to one. Since she had only come to scout and not to bathe, Heat begrudgingly moaned for her to hurry up, but the receptionist was a pretty lady, so he began to occupy his time with hitting on her. While she felt sorry for the poor lady, Ruri needed her to keep him company for a little while longer.

It was an informative experience. The public bath had parts she expected and some she didn't. She jotted down the things that interested her. They would serve as reference when she built one in the Nation of the Dragon King.

After some good reconnaissance, Ruri returned to the castle with a satisfied smile. As soon as she saw Jade, she headed straight for him.

"Jade-sama, what do you think? It's an outfit of the Nation of the Beast King." She twirled around, showing off the outfit she bought in town.

Jade tenderly smiled and said, "Yes, it looks quite nice on you."

"I went to a hot spring in town as well. Perfect preliminary research. I'm going to build hot springs in the Nation of the Dragon King, so I'd suggest you take a dip when they're done."

"So I see. Well, I look forward to it."

It would only be a little longer before Ruri's wishes were granted.

VI

VOL. 6
ON SALE NOW!

Tearmoon Empire

Nozomu Mochitsuki
Illustrator: Gilse

Jessica Bannister
Author: Janet Farell
Cover Art: ttl
Available from All Major Ebook Stores!
Ghosts. Mysteries. Deadlines.
Which is the scariest of them all?

J-Novel Club Lineup

Latest Ebook Releases Series List

Altina the Sword Princess
Animeta!**
The Apothecary Diaries
An Archdemon's Dilemma: How to Love Your Elf Bride*
Are You Okay With a Slightly Older Girlfriend?
Arifureta: From Commonplace to World's Strongest
Arifureta Zero
Ascendance of a Bookworm*
Bibliophile Princess*
Black Summoner*
By the Grace of the Gods
Campfire Cooking in Another World with My Absurd Skill*
Can Someone Please Explain What's Going On?!
Chillin' in Another World with Level 2 Super Cheat Powers
Cooking with Wild Game*
Culinary Chronicles of the Court Flower
Dahlia in Bloom: Crafting a Fresh Start with Magical Tools
Deathbound Duke's Daughter
Demon Lord, Retry!*
Der Werwolf: The Annals of Veight*
Dragon Daddy Diaries: A Girl Grows to Greatness
Dungeon Busters
The Emperor's Lady-in-Waiting Is Wanted as a Bride*
Endo and Kobayashi Live! The Latest on Tsundere Villainess Lieselotte
Fantasy Inbound
The Faraway Paladin*
Forget Being the Villainess, I Want to Be an Adventurer!
Full Metal Panic!
Full Clearing Another World under a Goddess with Zero Believers*
Fushi no Kami: Rebuilding Civilization Starts With a Village*
Goodbye Otherworld, See You Tomorrow
The Great Cleric
The Greatest Magicmaster's Retirement Plan
Girls Kingdom
Grimgar of Fantasy and Ash

Hell Mode
Her Majesty's Swarm
Holmes of Kyoto
Housekeeping Mage from Another World: Making Your Adventures Feel Like Home!
How a Realist Hero Rebuilt the Kingdom*
How NOT to Summon a Demon Lord
I Shall Survive Using Potions!*
I'll Never Set Foot in That House Again!
The Ideal Sponger Life
In Another World With My Smartphone
Infinite Dendrogram*
Invaders of the Rokujouma!?
Jessica Bannister
JK Haru is a Sex Worker in Another World
John Sinclair: Demon Hunter
A Late-Start Tamer's Laid-Back Life
Lazy Dungeon Master
A Lily Blooms in Another World
Maddrax
The Magic in this Other World is Too Far Behind!*
Magic Knight of the Old Ways
The Magician Who Rose From Failure
Mapping: The Trash-Tier Skill That Got Me Into a Top-Tier Party*
Marginal Operation**
The Master of Ragnarok & Blesser of Einherjar*
Min-Maxing My TRPG Build in Another World
Monster Tamer
My Daughter Left the Nest and Returned an S-Rank Adventurer
My Friend's Little Sister Has It In for Me!
My Quiet Blacksmith Life in Another World
My Stepmom's Daughter Is My Ex
My Instant Death Ability is So Overpowered, No One in This Other World Stands a Chance Against Me!*
My Next Life as a Villainess: All Routes Lead to Doom!

Otherside Picnic
Perry Rhodan NEO
Prison Life is Easy for a Villainess
Private Tutor to the Duke's Daughter
Reborn to Master the Blade: From Hero-King to Extraordinary Squire ♀*
Record of Wortenia War*
Reincarnated as the Piggy Duke: This Time I'm Gonna Tell Her How I Feel!
The Reincarnated Princess Spends Another Day Skipping Story Routes
Seirei Gensouki: Spirit Chronicles
Sexiled: My Sexist Party Leader Kicked Me Out, So I Teamed With a Mythical Sorceress!
She's the Cutest... But We're Just Friends!
The Sidekick Never Gets the Girl, Let Alone the Protag's Sister!
Slayers
The Sorcerer's Receptionist
Sorcerous Stabber Orphen*
Sweet Reincarnation**
The Tales of Marielle Clarac*
Tearmoon Empire
To Another World... with Land Mines!
The Unwanted Undead Adventurer*
Villainess: Reloaded! Blowing Away Bad Ends with Modern Weapons*
Welcome to Japan, Ms. Elf!*
When Supernatural Battles Became Commonplace
The White Cat's Revenge as Plotted from the Dragon King's Lap
The World's Least Interesting Master Swordsman

...and more!
* Novel and Manga Editions
** Manga Only
Keep an eye out at j-novel.club for further new title announcements!